NEW TESTAMENT GREEK
FOR BEGINNERS

New Testament Greek For Beginners

By

J. Gresham Machen, D.D.

Assistant Professor of New Testament
Literature and Exegesis
in
Princeton Theological Seminary

Ithaca Classics

Originally Published March, 1923. Retyped and printed by Ithaca Classics 2024.

TO MY MOTHER

PREFACE

This textbook is intended primarily for students who are beginning the study of the Greek Testament either without any previous acquaintance with the Greek language or with an acquaintance so imperfect that a renewed course of elementary instruction is needed. Owing to the exigencies of the present educational situation, many who desire to use the Greek Testament are unable to approach the subject through a study of classical Attic prose. The situation is undoubtedly to be regretted, but its existence should not be ignored. It is unfortunate that so many students of the New Testament have no acquaintance with classical Greek, but it would be still more unfortunate if such students, on account of their lack of acquaintance with classical Greek, should be discouraged from making themselves acquainted at least with the easier language of the New Testament.

The New Testament usage will here be presented without any reference to Attic prose. But a previous acquaintance with Attic prose, even though it be only a smattering, will prove to be an immense assistance in the mastery of the course. By students who possess such acquaintance the lessons can be covered much more rapidly than by mere beginners.

The book is an instruction book, and not a descriptive grammar. Since it is an instruction book, everything in it is made subservient to the imparting of a reading acquaintance with the language. In a descriptive grammar, for example, the rules may be formulated with a lapidary succinctness which would here be out of place. The effort is made here to enter upon those explanations which the fifteen years' experience of the author in teaching New Testament Greek has shown to be essential. In a descriptive grammar, moreover, the illustrations would have to be limited to what can actually be found in the New Testament, but in the present book they are reduced so far as possible to an ideally simple form, which does not always appear in the New Testament books. In this way the vocabulary at every point can be confined to what the student has actually studied, and confusing footnotes can be avoided. It is highly important that only one grammatical point should be considered at a time. An introduction of illustrations taken from the New Testament would often so overlay the explanation with new words and with subsidiary usages unfamiliar to the student that the specific grammatical point under discussion would be altogether obscured. Of course, however, the effort has been made not to introduce into the illustrations any usages except those which are common in the New Testament idiom.

The character of the book as an instruction book has also determined the choice and order of the material. The treatment has been limited to a few essential points, and no attempt has been made to exhibit the real richness and flexibility of the New Testament language, which can be discovered only through reading. This limitation may in places give rise to criticism, as for example in connection with the treatment of participles. The author is well aware of the fundamentally non-temporal character of the tenses in the participle, and also of the great variety in the shades of thought which the participle can express. But after all it is highly important for the beginner to understand clearly the distinction between the present and the aorist participle, and that distinction can be made clear at the beginning only through the proper use of our temporal mode of thought. Only when what is simple and usual has been firmly impressed upon the student's mind by patient repetition can the finer and more difficult points be safely touched. The treatment of the participle, moreover, has been thrust as far forward as possible in the book, in order that ample time may be allowed for practising the usages which it involves. Experience shows that in learning to read New Testament Greek, the participle is almost the crux of the whole matter.

Special attention has been given to the exercises. Until the very last few lessons (and then only in the GreekEnglish exercises) the sentences have not for the most part been taken from the New Testament, since the book is intended as an instruction book in Greek and not as a stimulus to memory of the English Bible. At a later stage in the study of New Testament Greek, the student's memory of the English Bible is not an unmixed evil, for repeated reading of already familiar passages will often fix the meaning of a word in the mind far

ii

better than it could ever be fixed by the mere learning of a vocabulary. But in the early stages, such assistance will do far more harm than good. In the exercises, the effort has been made to exhibit definitely the forms and grammatical usages which have just been discussed in the same lesson, and also to keep constantly before the mind, in ever new relationships, the most important usages that have been discussed before.

The vocabularies have been limited to words which are very common in the New Testament or which require special explanation. Everywhere the effort has been made to introduce the words in the illustrations and exercises. The learning of lists of words, unless the words so learned are actually used, is a waste of time.

The author desires to express appreciation of the pioneer work which has been done in this country by Professor John Homer Huddilston, Ph.D., in his Essentials of New Testament Greek, First Edition, 1895, and also of the larger English book of Rev. H. P. V. Nunn, M.A., entitled TheElements of New Testament Greek, First Edition, 1913. The two books by John Williams White, The Beginner's Greek Book, 1895, and The First Greek Book; 1896, have also been consulted with profit, especially as regards the form of presentation. Among reference works, the new grammar of J. H. Moulton, A Grammar of New Testament Greek, edited by Wilbert Francis Howard, especially Part ii of Vol. II, on Accidence, 1920, and the work by E. D. Burton on Moods and Tenses in New Testament Greek, 1906, have been found particularly useful. Acknowledgment is also to be made to Blass-Debrunner, Grammatik des neutestamentlichen Griechisch, 1913, and to the convenient summary of classical usage in Goodwin's Greek Grammar. And both the Greek-English Lexicon of the New Testament of Grimm-Thayer and Moulton and Geden's Concordance to the Greek Testament have been found absolutely indispensable throughout. The advanced student will find much useful material in the large work of A. T. Robertson, A Grammar of the Greek New Testament in the Light of Historical Research, 1914.

The author is deeply grateful to Professor Edward Capps, Ph.D., LL.D., of Princeton University, who, in the most gracious possible way, has examined the proof of the book throughout, and (of course without becoming at all responsible for any faults or errors) has rendered invaluable assistance at many points. Much encouragment and help have also been received from the wise counsel and unfailing kindness of the Rev. Professor William Park Armstrong, D.D., of Princeton Theological Seminary.

TABLE OF CONTENTS

vi

Introduction

During the classical period, the Greek language was divided into a number of dialects, of which there were three great families—the Doric, the Aeolic, and the Ionic. In the fifth century before Christ, one branch of the Ionic family, the Attic, attained the supremacy, especially as the language of prose literature. The Attic dialect was the language of Athens in her glory—the language of Thucydides, of Plato, of Demosthenes, and of most of the other great prose writers of Greece.

Various causes contributed to make the Attic dialect dominant in the Greek-speaking world. First and foremost must be put the genius of the Athenian writers. But the political and commercial importance of Athens was also not without its effect. Hosts of strangers came into contact with Athens through government, war and trade, and the Athenian colonies also extended the influence of the mother city. The Athenian Empire, indeed, soon fell to pieces. Athens was conquered first by Sparta in the Peloponnesian war, and then, in the middle of the fourth century before Christ, along with the other Greek cities, came under the domination of the king of Macedonia, Philip. But the influence of the Attic dialect survived the loss of political power; the language of Athens became also the language of her conquerors.

Macedonia was not originally a Greek kingdom, but it adopted the dominant civilization of the day, which was the civilization of Athens. The tutor of Philip's son, Alexander the Great, was Aristotle, the Greek philosopher; and that fact is only one indication of the conditions of the time. With astonishing rapidity Alexander made himself master of the whole eastern world, and the triumphs of the Macedonian arms were also triumphs of the Greek language in its Attic form. The empire of Alexander, indeed, at once fell to pieces after his death in 323 B.C.; but the kingdoms into which it was divided were, at least so far as the court and the governing classes were concerned, Greek kingdoms. Thus the Macedonian conquest meant nothing less than the Hellenization of the East, or at any rate it meant an enormous acceleration of the Hellenizing process which had already begun.

When the Romans, in the last two centuries before Christ, conquered the eastern part of the Mediterranean world, they made no attempt to suppress the Greek language. On the contrary, the

1

conquerors to a very considerable extent were conquered by those whom they conquered. Rome herself had already come under Greek influence, and now she made use of the Greek language in administering at least the eastern part of her vast empire. The language of the Roman Empire was not so much Latin as it was Greek.

Thus in the first century after Christ Greek had become a world language. The ancient languages of the various countries did indeed continue to exist, and many districts were bilingual—the original local languages existing side by side with the Greek. But at least in the great cities throughout the Empire—certainly in the East—the Greek language was everywhere understood. Even in Rome itself there was a large Greek-speaking population. It is not surprising that Paul's letter to the Roman Church is written not in Latin but in Greek.

But the Greek language had to pay a price for this enormous extension of its influence. In its career of conquest, it experienced important changes. The ancient Greek dialects other than Attic, although they disappeared almost completely before the beginning of the Christian era, may have exerted considerable influence upon the Greek of the new unified world. Less important, no doubt, than the influence of the Greek dialects, and far less important than might have been expected, was the influence of foreign languages. But influences of a more subtle and less tangible kind were mightily at work. Language is a reflection of the intellectual and spiritual habits of the people who use it. Attic prose, for example, reflects the spiritual life of a small city-state, which was unified by an intense patriotism and a glorious literary tradition. But after the time of Alexander, the Attic speech was no longer the language of a small group of citizens living in the closest spiritual association; on the contrary it had become the medium of exchange for peoples of the most diverse character. It is not surprising, then, that the language of the new cosmopolitan age was very different from the original Attic dialect upon which it was founded.

This new world language which prevailed after Alexander has been called not inappropriately "the Koiné." The word "Koiné" means "common"; it is not a bad designation, therefore, for a language which was a common medium of exchange for diverse peoples. The Koiné, then, is the Greek world language that prevailed from about 300 B.C.

2

to the close of ancient history at about A.D. 500. The New Testament was written within this Koiné period. Linguistically considered, it is united in a very close way with the Greek translation of the Old Testament called the "Septuagint," which was made at Alexandria in the centuries just preceding the Christian era, and with certain Christian writings of the early part of the second century after Christ, which are ordinarily associated under the name "Apostolic Fathers." Within this triple group, it is true, the language of the New Testament is easily supreme. But so far as the bare instrument of expression is concerned the writings of the group belong together. Where, then, within the development of the Koiné is this whole group to be placed?

It has always been observed that the language of the New Testament differs strikingly from the great Attic prose writers such as Thucydides or Plato or Demosthenes. That fact is not surprising. It can easily be explained by the lapse of centuries and by the important changes which the creation of the new cosmopolitanism involved. But another fact is more surprising. It is discovered, namely, that the language of the New Testament differs not merely from that of the Attic prose writers of four centuries before, but also from that of the Greek writers of the very period within which the New Testament was written. The Greek of the New Testament is very different, for example, from the Greek of Plutarch.

This difference used sometimes to be explained by the hypothesis that the New Testament was written in a Jewish-Greek dialect—a form of Greek very strongly influenced by the Semitic languages, Hebrew and Aramaic. But in recent years another explanation has been coming increasingly into vogue. This other explanation has been given an important impetus by the discovery, in Egypt, of the "non-literary papyri." For the most part the Koiné had until recently been known to scholars almost exclusively through literature. But within the past twenty or thirty years there have been discovered in Egypt, where the dry air has preserved even the fragile writing-material of antiquity, great numbers of documents such as wills, receipts, petitions and private letters. These documents are not "literature." Many of them were intended merely to be read once and then thrown away. They exhibit, therefore, not the polished language of books but the actual spoken language of everyday life. And on account of their important divergence from the language of such writers as Plutarch they have revealed with new clearness the interesting fact that in the Koiné period there was a wide gap between the language of literature and the language of every day. The literary men of the period imitated the great Attic models with more or less exactitude; they maintained an artificial literary tradition. The obscure writers of the non-literary papyri, on the other hand, imitated nothing, but simply expressed themselves, without affectation, in the language of the street.

But it is discovered that the language of the New Testament, at various points where it differs from the literature even of the Koiné period, agrees with the non-literary papyri. That discovery has suggested a new hypothesis to account for the apparent peculiarity of the language of the New Testament. It is now supposed that the impression of peculiarity which has been made upon the minds of modern readers by New Testament Greek is due merely to the fact that until recently our knowledge of the spoken as distinguished from the literary language of the Koiné period has been so limited. In reality, it is said, the New Testament is written simply in the popular form of the Koiné which was spoken in the cities throughout the whole of the Greek-speaking world.

This hypothesis undoubtedly contains a large element of truth. Undoubtedly the language of the New Testament is no artificial language of books, and no Jewish-Greek jargon, but the natural, living language of the period. But the Semitic influence should not be underestimated. The New Testament writers were nearly all Jews, and all of them were strongly influenced by the Old Testament. In particular, they were influenced, so far as language is concerned, by the Septuagint, and the Septuagint was influenced, as most ancient translations were, by the language of the original. The Septuagint had gone far toward producing a Greek vocabulary to express the deepest things of the religion of Israel. And this vocabulary was profoundly influential in the New Testament. Moreover, the originality of the New Testament writers should not be ignored. They had come under the influence of new convictions of a transforming kind, and those new convictions had their effect in the sphere of language. Common words had to be given new and loftier meanings, and common men were lifted to a higher realm by a new and glorious experience. It is not surprising, then, that despite linguistic similarities in detail the New Testament books, even in form, are vastly different from the letters that have been discovered in Egypt. The New Testament writers have used the common, living language of the day. But they have used it in the expression of uncommon thoughts, and the language itself, in the process, has been to some extent transformed. The Epistle to the Hebrews shows that even conscious art could be made the instrument of profound sincerity, and the letters of Paul, even the shortest and simplest of them, are no mere private jottings intended to be thrown away, like the letters that have been discovered upon the rubbish heaps of Egypt, but letters addressed by an apostle to the Church of God. The cosmopolitan popular language of the Graeco-Roman world served its purpose in history well. It broke down racial and linguistic barriers. And at one point in its life it became sublime.

NEW TESTAMENT GREEK

LESSON I

The Alphabet

1. The Greek alphabet is as follows:

Capital Letters	Small Letters	Name	Pronunciation
A	α	alpha	a as in *father*
B	β	beta	b
Γ	γ	gamma	as in *got*[1]
Δ	δ	delta	d
E	ε	epsilon	e as in *get*
Z	ζ	zeta	z
H	η	eta	a as in *late*
Θ	θ	theta	th
I	ι	iota	i as in *pit*, ee as in *feet*
K	κ	kappa	k
Λ	λ	lambda	l
M	μ	mu	m
N	ν	nu	n
Ξ	ξ	xi	x
O	ο	omicron	o as in *obey*
Π	π	pi	p
P	ϱ[2]	rho	r
Σ	σ(ς)[3]	sigma	s
T	τ	tau	t
Υ	υ	upsilon	French u
Φ	φ	phi	ph
X	χ	chi	German ch as *ach*
Ψ	ψ	psi	ps
Ω	ω	omega	o as in *note*

---

[1] Before another γ or κ or χ, γ is pronounced like ng.
[2] At the beginning of a word ϱ is written ῥ, rh.
[3] ς is written at the end of a word, elsewhere σ.

6

2. The student is advised to learn the small letters thoroughly, in connection with the first lesson, leaving the capital letters to be picked up later, as they occur. It should be observed that sentences are begun with small letters, not with capitals. Before the formation of the letters is practised, guidance should be obtained from the teacher, since it is impracticable to copy exactly the printed form of the letters, and since bad habits of penmanship ought by all means to be avoided. For example, and p should be formed without lifting the pen and by beginning at the bottom. In these matters the help of a teacher is indispensable.

3. The Greek vowels are as follows:

Short	Long
α	α
ε	η
ο	ω
ι	ι
υ	υ

It will be noted that α, ι, and υ can be either long or short. The long α and υ are pronounced very much like the corresponding short letters, except that the sound is held longer; the short ι is pronounced like i in *pit* and the long ι like ee in *feet*. ε is always short, and η is the long of it; o is always short, and ω is the long of it. This clear distinction in appearance between the long and short ε and o makes the matter of *quantity* very much easier in Greek than it is in Latin

ι and υ are called *close* vowels; and the others open vowels.

4. A *diphthong* is a combination of two vowels in a single syllable. The second letter of a diphthong is always a close vowel. The first letter is always an open vowel except in the case of υι. The common diphthongs are as follows:

αι, pronounced like ai in *aisle*

ει, pronounced like a in *fate* (thus ει and η are pronounced alike)

οι, pronounced like oi in *oil*

αυ, pronounced like ow in *cow*

ευ, pronounced like eu in *feud*

ου, pronounced like oo in *food*

υι, pronounced like ee in *queen*

The diphthongs ηυ and ωυ (pronounced by drawing the sounds of each letter closely together) are rare. When ι unites with long α, η or ω to form one sound, the ι is written under the other letter instead of after it, and is called *iota subscript*. Thus ᾳ, ῃ, ῳ. This iota subscript has no effect whatever upon the pronunciation; ᾳ being pronounced like long a, ῃ like η, ῳ like ω.

5. A vowel or diphthong at the beginning of a word always has a *breathing*. The breathing stands over a vowel; and in the case of a diphthong it stands over the second of the two component vowels.

The *rough* breathing (῾) indicates that an h-sound is to be pronounced before the initial vowel or diphthong; the *smooth* breathing (᾿) indicates that no such h-sound is to be pronounced. Thus ἐν is to be pronounced *en*, and ἑν is to be pronounced *hen*; οὐ is to be pronounced *oo*, and οὑ is to be pronounced *hoo*.

6. There are three *accents*, the *acute* (´), the *circumflex* (˜), and the *grave* (`). These accents, like the breathings, stand over a vowel, and, in the case of a diphthong, over the second of the two component vowels. When a breathing and an accent stand over the same vowel, the breathing comes first, except in the case of the circumflex accent, which stands over the breathing. Thus οἴκου, οἶκος. The use of the accents will be studied in Lesson II. Here it should simply be observed that the stress in pronunciation is to be placed on the syllable that has any one of the accents.

7. Punctuation

There are four marks of punctuation: the comma (,) and the period (.), both written on the line and corresponding to the comma and the period in English; the colon, which is a dot above the line (·), and takes the place of the English colon and semicolon; and the question mark (;) which looks like an English semicolon.

8. Exercise

After learning to write the small letters of the alphabet and give the names of the letters in order, the student should practise pronouncing Greek words and sentences found anywhere in the book. Throughout the entire study, great care should be devoted to pronunciation, and the Greek sentences should always be read aloud both in the preparation of the lessons and in the work of the classroom. In this way the language will be learned not only by the eye, but also by the ear, and will be fixed much more firmly in the memory. The student should try to read the Greek sentences with expression, thinking of the meaning as he reads.

Lesson II

Accent

9. The Greek accents indicated in ancient times not stress (what we call accent), but musical pitch. But since it is impossible for us to reproduce the original pronunciation, the best we can do is to place the stress of the voice upon the syllable where the accent occurs, and give up any distinction in pronunciation between the acute, the circumflex and the grave. Having adopted this method of pronunciation, we should adhere to it rigidly; for unless some one method is adhered to, the language can never be fixed in the memory. It is also important to learn to write the accents correctly, since the accents serve to distinguish various forms from one another and are therefore a great help and not a hindrance in the learning of the language.

10. Preliminary Definitions

The last syllable of a word is called the *ultima*; the one before that, the *penult*; and the one before that, the *antepenult*.

Thus, in the word λαμβάνομεν, the ultima is -μεν, the penult is -νο-, and the antepenult is -βα.

Syllables containing a long vowel or a diphthong are long. But final αι and οι (that is, αι and οι coming at the very end of a word) are considered short so far as accent is concerned.

Thus the last syllable of ἀνθρώπους is long because it contains the diphthong ου; the last syllable of ἄνθρωποι is short because the οι is here final οι; the last syllable of ἀνθρώποις is long because here the οι has a letter after it and so, not being final οι, is long like any other diphthong.

It will be remembered that ε and ο are always short, and η and ω always long. The quantity (long or short) of α, ι, and υ, must be learned by observation in the individual cases.

11. General Rules of Accent

1. The acute (´) can stand only on one of the last three syllables of a word; the circumflex (˜) only on one of the last two; and the grave (`) only on the last.

Examples: This rule would be violated by ἀποστολος, for here the accent would stand on the fourth syllable from the end. It would also be violated by πιστεύομεν, for here the circumflex would stand on the third syllable from the end.

2. The circumflex accent cannot stand on a short syllable.

3. If the ultima is long,

(a) the antepenult cannot be accented,

(b) the penult, if it is accented at all, must have the acute.

Examples: Rule 3a would be violated by ἀπόστολῳ or ἀπόστολου, because in these cases the ultima is long; but it is not violated by ἀπόστολε or ἀπόστολοι, because here the ultima is short. Rule 3b would be violated by δοῦλου or δοῦλων, but is not violated by δοῦλος or δοῦλοι.

4. If the ultima is short, a long penult, if it is accented at all, must have the circumflex.

Examples: This rule would be violated by δούλε or δούλοι; but it is not violated by δούλου, because here the ultima is not short, or by υἱός, because here, although a long penult comes before a short ultima, the penult is not accented at all. The rule does not say that a long penult before a short ultima must have the circumflex, but only that if it is accented at all it must have the circumflex rather than some other kind of accent.

5. A long ultima can have either the acute or the circumflex.

Examples: ἀδελφοῦ and ἀδελφού both conform to the general rules of accent. Further observation, based on other considerations, is necessary in order to tell which is right.

6. An acute accent on the last syllable of a word is changed to the grave when followed, without intervening mark of punctuation, by other words in a sentence.

Examples: ἀδελφός is right where ἀδελφός stands alone; but ἀδελφός ἀποστόλου violates the rule—it should be ἀδελφὸς ἀποστόλου.

12. It should be observed that these general rules of accent do not tell what the accenting of any individual word is to be; they only tell what it cannot be. In other words, they merely fix certain limits within which the accenting of Greek words must remain. What the accent actually is, within these limits, can be determined in part by the special rules which follow, but in very many cases must be learned by observation of the individual words. Thus if we have a form λυομενου to accent, the general rules would permit λυομενού or λουμενοῦ or λυομένου; any other way of accenting would violate the general rules. But which of the three possibilities is actually to be chosen is a matter for further observation. Or if we have a form προσωπον to accent, the general rules would permit πρόσωπον, προσῶπον or προσωπόν.

There are two special rules which help to fix the accent of many words more closely than it is fixed by the general rules. They are as follows:

13. Rule of Verb Accent

Verbs have recessive accent.

Explanation: The rule means that, in verbs, the accent goes back as far as the general rules of accent will permit. This rule definitely fixes the accent of any verb form; it is not necessary to know what verb the form is derived from or to have any other information whatever. Knowing that it is a verb form, one needs only to look at the ultima. If the ultima is short, an acute must be placed on the antepenult (supposing the word to have as many as three syllables); if the ultima is long, an acute must be placed on the penult.

Examples: Suppose a verb form εγινωσκου is to be accented. In accordance with the rule of verb accent, the accent is trying to get as far back as the general rules of accent will permit. But ἔγινωσκου would violate Rule 1; and, since the ultima is long, ἐγίνωσκου would violate Rule 3a. Therefore the penult must be accented. But ἐγινῶσκου would violate Rule 3b. Therefore ἐγινώσκου is correct. On the other hand, if a verb form εγινωσκε is to be accented, although ἔγινωσκε is forbidden by Rule 1, ἐγίνωσκε is permitted; and since verbs have recessive accent, that accenting, ἐγίνωσκε, is correct, and ἐγινῶσκε or ἐγινωσκέ would be wrong. If the verb has only two syllables, Rule 4 often comes into play. Thus if the verb form σωζε is to be accented, the rule of recessive verb accent decrees that the former of the two syllables shall be accented. But Rule 4 decrees that the accent shall be not σώζε but σῶζε.

14. Rule of Noun Accent

In nouns, the accent remains on the same syllable as in the nominative singular, so nearly as the general rules of accent will permit.

Explanation: This rule differs from the rule of verb accent in that it does not of itself fix the accent of noun forms. The accent on the nominative singular (the form given in the vocabularies) must be learned by observation for every noun separately, just as the spelling of the word must be learned. So much is merely a part of the learning of the vocabularies. But when once the accent on the nominative singular has been given, the accent on the other forms of the noun is fixed by the rule.

Examples:

(1) If there be a noun λογος, neither the general rules of accent in §11 nor the rule of noun accent will determine whether the accent is λόγος or λογός. But once it has been determined that the accent is λόγος, then the accent on the other forms of the noun can be determined. The other forms, without the accent, are λογου, λογω, λογον, λογε, λογοι, λογων, λογοις, λογους. On every one of these forms the acute will stand on the penult; since (a) the rule of noun accent decrees that the accent remains there if the general rules of accent permit, and since (b) the general rules of accent never forbid the accent to be placed on a penult, and since (c) Rule 2 decrees that only an acute accent can stand on a short syllable.

(2) In the case of a noun οἶκος, its various forms being after the analogy of λόγος above, (a) and (b) of the considerations mentioned above with regard to λόγος still hold. But (c) does not hold, since here the penult is not short but long. In this case, Rules 3b and 4 will determine when the accent is acute and when it is circumflex; when the ultima is long, the accent (on the penult) will be acute, and when the ultima is short, the accent (on the penult) will be circumflex. Thus οἶκος, οἴκου, οἴκῳ, οἶκον, οἶκε, οἶκοι, οἴκων, οἴκοις, οἴκους.

(3) In the case of a noun ἄνθρωπος the accent is trying in every other form to get back to the antepenult, in accordance with the rule of noun accent, since it is the antepenult which is accented in the nominative singular. But where the ultima is long, the accent cannot

get back to the antepenult, since that would violate Rule 3a. The nearest syllable to the antepenult which it can reach in these cases is the penult. The rule of noun accent decrees that the nearest syllable is the one upon which the accent must stand. But since the ultima is long in these cases, Rule 3b decrees that the accent (upon the penult) shall be an acute not a circumflex. Thus ἄνθρωπος, ἀνθρώπου, ἀνθρώπῳ, ἄνθρωπον, ἄνθρωπε, ἄνθρωποι, ἀνθρώπων, ἀνθρώποις, ἀνθρώπους.

(4) In the case of a noun ὁδός the accent will stand in every form upon the ultima, since the general rules of accent never prevent the accent from standing on an ultima. If the ultima is short the accent must of course be acute. But if the ultima is long, the accent, so far as the general rules are concerned, can be either acute or circumflex. In these cases, therefore, the rules so far given will not determine which accent is to be used. Thus ὁδός, ὁδόν, ὁδέ, ὁδοί. But whether ὁδού, ὁδῴ, ὁδών, ὁδοίς, ὁδούς, or ὁδοῦ, ὁδῷ, ὁδῶν, ὁδοῖς, ὁδοῦς are correct must be left for future determination. The decision is part of the learning of the declension of this particular class of nouns.

15. Exercises

(In all written exercises, the breathings and accents should be put in immediately after each word has been written just as the i's are dotted and the t's crossed in English. It is just as wrong to wait until the end of a whole paradigm or a whole sentence to add the breathings and accents as it would be to wait similarly in English before one crosses the t's.)

I. Write the following verb forms with the accent, and then pronounce them:

1. ἐλυομεν, ἐλυομην, ἐλυσω. 2. ἐλυου, ἐλυε, ἐλυσαμην. 3. διδασκε, διδασκονται, διδασκομεθα (the final α is short). 4. λυε (the υ here, as in all these forms beginning with λυ, is long), λυου, λυουσι (the final ι is short). 5. λυσαι, λυσω, λυετε.

II. Accent the following forms of the nouns whose nominative singular is (1) ἀπόστολος, (2) κώμη, (3) πλοῖον: 1. ἀποστολοις, ἀποστολους, ἀποστολου, ἀποστολοι, ἀποστολω. 2. κωμαις, κωμαι, κωμας (α long), κωμη. 3. πλοια (final α short), πλοιων, πλοιοις, πλοιου, πλοιω, πλοιον.

III. Are the following words accented correctly, so far as the general rules of accent are concerned? If not, tell in each case what rule (or rules) has been violated. Then accent each of the words in all the ways which the general rules of accent would permit.

1. ἐδίδομεν, ὦραι, προφήταις. 2. δόξῃ, ἐρῆμου, οὐρανον. 3. ἔρημος, βουλαί, λὺε.

[Note. The student should apply the principles of accent in the study of all subsequent lessons, observing how the rules are followed, and never passing by the accenting of any word in the paradigms or exercises until it is thoroughly understood. In this way, correct accenting will soon become second nature, and the various logical steps by which it is arrived at will no longer need to be consciously formulated]

Lesson III

Present Active Indicative

16. Vocabulary

(The vocabularies should be learned after the paradigms and explanatory parts of the lessons, but before the exercises.)

βλέπω, *I see*	λαμβάνω, *I take*
γινώσκω, *I know*	λέγω, *I say*
γράφω, *I write*	λύω, *I loose, I destroy*
διδάσκω, *I teach*	ἔχω, *I have*

17. The Greek verb has *tense, voice,* and *mood,* like the verb in other languages. The *present* tense (in the indicative) refers to present time; the *active* voice represents the subject as acting instead of being acted upon; the *indicative* mood makes an assertion, in distinction, for example, from a command or a wish.

18. The present active indicative of the verb λύω, I loose, is as follows:

	Sing.			Plur.	
1.	λύω	*I loose* or *I am loosing*	1.	λύομεν	*we loose* or *we are loosing*
2.	λύεις	*thou loosest* or *thou art loosing*	2.	λύετε	*ye loose* or *ye are loosing*
3.	λύει	*he looses* or *he is loosing*	3.	λύουσι	*they loose* or *they are loosing*

19. It will be observed that the distinctions between *first person* (person speaking), *second person* (person spoken to), *third person* (person spoken of), and between *singular* and *plural numbers,* which in English are indicated for the most part by subject-pronouns, are indicated in Greek by the endings. Thus no pronoun is necessary to translate *we loose* into Greek; the we is sufficiently indicated by the ending -ομεν.

20. The part of the verb which remains constant throughout the conjugation and has the various endings added to it is called the *stem.*

16

Thus the present stem of λύω is λυ-. The present stem of a verb can be obtained by removing the final ω from the form given in the vocabulary. Thus the present stem of λέγω, I say, is λεγ-. The conjugation of the present active indicative of any verb in the vocabulary can be obtained by substituting the present stem of that verb for λυ- and then adding the endings -ω, -εις, -ει, -ομεν, -ετε, -ουσι, as they are given above.

The *primary* personal endings, which would naturally stand in the tenses called *primary tenses*[4], were, it seems, originally as follows:

	Sing.		Plur.
1.	-μι	1.	-μεν
2.	-σι	2.	-τε
3.	-τι	3.	-ντι

Between the stem and these personal endings was placed a variable vowel which before μ and ν was o and before other letters ε. But in the present active, at least in the singular, this scheme is not carried out, and the beginner is advised for the present simply to regard -ω, -εις, -ει, -ομεν, -ετε, -ουσι as the endings which by their addition to the stem indicate the various persons and numbers.

21. In the present tense there is in Greek no distinction between *I loose*, which simply represents the action as taking place in present time, and *I am loosing*, which calls attention to the continuance of the action. Both of these ideas, therefore, should be connected with the Greek form λύω. The distinction between the two will become exceedingly important when we pass over to past time; for there Greek makes the distinction even more sharply than English.

22. The second person, *you loose* or *you are loosing*, in English may of course be either singular or plural, and may be translated by the student either by λύεις or by λύετε except where the context makes plain which is meant. Where it is desired, in the exercises, to indicate whether singular or plural is meant, the archaic forms *thou loosest*, etc., and *ye loose*, etc., will be used.

---

[4] The primary tenses are the present, the future, and the perfect; the *secondary* tenses are the imperfect, the aorist, and the pluperfect.

23. Exercises

(All English-Greek exercises should be written.)

I. 1. βλέπεις, γινώσκεις, λαμβάνεις. 2. γράφει, ἔχει, λέγει. 3. λύει, διδάσκει, βλέπει. 4. λαμβάνομεν, ἔχομεν, γινώσκομεν. 5. βλέπετε, λέγετε, γράφετε. 6. διδάσκουσι, λαμβάνουσι, λύουσι. 7. γινώσκετε, γινώσκεις, γινώσκομεν. 8. βλέπομεν, διδάσκουσι, λέγει. 9. ἔχεις, βλέπουσι, λαμβάνομεν.

II. 1. We are knowing, we see, we are seeing. 2. They are loosing, they loose, he looses. 3. He is loosing, ye have, thou knowest. 4. I am taking, we know, they say. 5. He has, we are writing, they see.

[The teacher should continue such drill orally, until the student can recognize the Greek words rapidly both by sight and by sound, and translate the English sentences rapidly into Greek.]

Lesson IV

The Second Declension. Order of Words. Movable v.

24. Vocabulary

ἀδελφός, ὁ, *a brother*

ἄνθρωπος, ὁ, *a man*

ἀπόστολος, ὁ, *an apostle*

δοῦλος, ὁ, *a servant*

δῶρον, τό, *a gift*

θάνατος, ὁ, *a death*

ἱερόν, τό, *a temple*

καί, conj., *and*

λόγος, ὁ, *a word*

νόμος, ὁ, *a law*

οἶκος, ὁ, *a house*

υἱός, ὁ, *a son*

25. There are three *declensions* in Greek. The second declension is given before the first for purposes of convenience, since it is easier, and has a larger number of common nouns.

26. There is no indefinite article in Greek, and so ἀδελφός means either *brother* or *a brother* (usually the latter). Greek has, however, a definite article, and where the Greek article does not appear, the definite article should not be inserted in the English translation, Thus ἀδελφός does not mean *the brother*. In the plural, English, like Greek, has no indefinite article. ἄνθρωποι, therefore, means simply *men*. But it does not mean *the men*.

27. The noun in Greek has *gender, number,* and *case.*

28. There are three genders: *masculine, feminine,* and *neuter.* The gender of nouns must often be learned by observation of the individual nouns. But nearly all nouns of the second declension ending in -ος are masculine; and all nouns of the second declension in -ον are neuter. The gender is indicated in the vocabulary by the article placed after the noun. The masculine article, ὁ, indicates masculine gender; the feminine article, ἡ , feminine gender; and the neuter article, τό, neuter gender.

29. There are two numbers, *singular* and *plural.* Verbs agree with their subject in number.

30. There are five cases; *nominative, genitive, dative, accusative,* and *vocative.*

19

31. The declension of ἄνθρωπος, ὁ, *a man*, is as follows:

	Singular		Plural
Nom.	ἄνθρωπος *a man*	N.V.	ἄνθρωποι *men*
Gen.	ἀνθρώπου *of a man*	G.	ἀνθρώπων *of men*
Dat.	ἀνθρώπῳ *to or for a man*	D.	ἀνθρώποις *to or for men*
Acc.	ἄνθρωπον *a man*	A.	ἀνθρώπους *men*
Voc.	ἄνθρωπε *man*		

32. The student should observe carefully how the principles of accent apply to this noun and all the others. In oral practice and recitations the stress in pronunciation should be placed carefully on the syllables where the accent appears.

33. The stem of a noun is that part of the noun which remains constant when the various endings are added. The stem of ἄνθρωπος is ἀνθρωπο-, and all other second-declension nouns, like ἄνθρωπος, have stems ending in o. The second declension, therefore, is sometimes called the o-declension. But this final o of the stem becomes so much disguised when the endings enter into combination with it, that it is more convenient to regard ἀνθρωπ- as the stem and -ος, -ου, etc., as the endings. It should at any rate be observed, however, that o (with the long of it, ω) is the characteristic vowel in the last syllable of second-declension nouns.

34. The subject of a sentence is put in the nominative case. Thus ἀπόστολος γινώσκει means *an apostle knows*.

The object of a transitive verb is placed in the accusative case. Thus βλέπω λόγον means *I see a word*.

35. The *genitive* case expresses possession. Thus λόγοι ἀποστόλων means *words of apostles* or *apostles' words*. But the genitive has many other important uses, which must be learned by observation. The functions of the Latin ablative are divided, in Greek, between the genitive and the dative.

36. The *dative* case is the case of the indirect object. Thus λέγω λόγον ἀποστόλοις means *I say a word to apostles*. But the dative has many other important uses which must be learned by observation.

37. The *vocative* case is the case of direct address. Thus ἀδελφέ, βλέπομεν means *brother, we see*. In the plural the vocative case in words of all declensions is in form like the nominative. The vocative plural may therefore be omitted in repeating paradigms.

38. Learn the declension of λόγος, ὁ, *a word*, and of δοῦλος, ὁ, *a servant*, in §557. These nouns differ from ἄνθρωπος only in that the accent is different in the nominative singular and therefore the application of the general rules of accent works out differently.

39. The declension of υἱός, ὁ, *a son*, is as follows:

	Sing.	Plur.
N.	υἱός	υἱοί
G.	υἱοῦ	υἱῶν
D.	υἱῷ	υἱοῖς
A.	υἱόν	υἱούς
V.	υἱέ	υἱοί

40. Here the rule of noun accent decrees that the accent must be on the ultima in all cases, because it was there in the nominative singular. But which accent shall it be? The general rules of accent answer this question where the ultima is short; for of course only an acute, not a circumflex, can stand on a short syllable. But where the ultima is long, the general rules of accent will permit either an acute or a circumflex. A special rule is therefore necessary. It is as follows:

In the second declension, when the ultima is accented at all, it has the circumflex in the genitive and dative of both numbers, elsewhere the acute.

Explanation: The "elsewhere" really refers only to the accusative plural, because in the nominative and vocative singular and plural and in the accusative singular the general rules of accent would forbid the circumflex, the ultima being short in these cases.

41. The declension of δῶρον, τό, a gift, is as follows:

	Sing.	Plur.
N.V.	δῶρον	δῶρα
G.	δώρου	δώρων
D.	δώρῳ	δώροις
A.	δῶρον	δῶρα

42. It will be observed that δῶρον is a neuter noun. In all neuter nouns, of all declensions, the vocative and accusative of both numbers are like the nominative, and the nominative, vocative and accusative plural always end in short α.

43. Order of Words

The normal order of the sentence in Greek is like that in English— subject, verb, object. There is no special tendency, as in Latin, to put the verb at the end. But Greek can vary the order for purposes of emphasis or euphony much more freely than English. Thus the sentence, *an apostle says a word*, is in Greek normally ἀπόστολος λέγει λόγον. But λέγει ἀπόστολος λόγον and λόγον λέγει ἀπόστολος are both perfectly possible. The English translation must be determined by observing the *endings*, not by observing the order.

44. Movable ν

When the -ουσι of the third person plural of the verb comes either before a vowel or at the end of a sentence, a ν, called *movable ν*, is added to it. Thus βλέπουσιν ἀποστόλους. Sometimes the movable ν is added even before a word that begins with a consonant. Thus either λύουσι δούλους or λύουσιν δούλους is correct. It must not be supposed that this movable ν occurs at the end of every verb form ending in a vowel when the next word begins with a vowel. On the contrary, it occurs only in a very few forms, which must be learned as they appear.

45. Exercises

I.   1. ἀδελφὸς βλέπει ἄνθρωπον. 2. δοῦλος γράφει λόγους. 3. ἀπόστολοι διδάσκουσιν ἄνθρωπον. 4. ἀπόστολοι λύουσι δούλους. 5. δοῦλος λαμβάνει δῶρα. 6. λαμβάνουσιν υἱοὶ οἴκους. 7. δούλους καὶ οἴκους λαμβάνουσιν ἀδελφοί. 8. βλέπομεν ἱερὰ καὶ ἀποστόλους. 9. δούλους βλέπετε καὶ ἀδελφούς. 10. γράφεις λόγον ἀποστόλῳ. 11. διδάσκει ἄνθρωπον. 12. ἀδελφὸς λέγει λόγον ἀποστόλῳ. 13. ἀδελφὸς ἀποστόλων γινώσκει νόμον. 14. δοῦλοι γινώσκουσι νόμον καὶ λαμβάνουσι δῶρα. 15. γινώσκουσιν ἄνθρωποι θάνατον. 16. λαμβάνομεν δῶρα καὶ ἔχομεν ἀδελφούς. 17. ἀποστόλοις καὶ δούλοις λέγομεν λόγους θανάτου. 18. ἀδελφοὶ καὶ δοῦλοι γινώσκουσιν καὶ βλέπουσιν ἱερὰ καὶ δῶρα. 19. γράφει ἀπόστολος νόμον καὶ λέγει λόγους υἱοῖς δούλου. 20. υἱοὶ ἀποστόλων λέγουσι λόγους καὶ λύουσι δούλους.

II. 1. A servant is writing a law. 2. A son sees words. 3. Brothers are loosing servants. 4. Sons take gifts. 5. An apostle sees a servant and a gift. 6. Servants and sons are saying a word to a brother. 7. We see gifts and servants. 8. Men see words and gifts of a brother and houses of apostles and sons. 9. Words and laws we write to brethren; a word of death we say to a servant. 10. A son is seeing temples and houses. 11. Ye know death. 12. Thou takest an apostle's gift (= a gift of an apostle). 13. Thou art writing a brother's word to a servant. 14. I loose servants and say words to sons and brothers. 15. A son sees death. 16. They know laws and teach servants of an apostle.

Lesson V

The First Declension

46. Vocabulary

ἀλήθεια, ἡ, *truth*
βασιλεία, ἡ, *a kingdom*
γραφή, ἡ, *a writing, a Scripture*
δόξα, ἡ, *glory*
εἰρήνη, ἡ, *peace*
ἐκκλησία, ἡ, *a church*
ἐντολή, ἡ, *a commandment*

ζωή, ἡ, *life*
ἡμέρα, ἡ, *a day*
καρδία, ἡ, *a heart*
παραβολή, ἡ, *a parable*
φωνή, ἡ, *a voice*
ψυχή, ἡ, *a soul, a life*
ὥρα, ἡ, *an hour*

47. All nouns of the first declension ending in α or η are feminine.

48. The declension of ὥρα, ἡ, *an hour*, is as follows:

	Sing.	Plur.
N.V.	ὥρα	ὥραι
G.	ὥρας	ὡρῶν
D.	ὥρᾳ	ὥραις
A.	ὥραν	ὥρας

49. The stem of ὥρα is ὡρα-, and the first declension is sometimes called the α- declension, because its stems end in α. Since, however, the final vowel of the stem enters into various combinations with the endings it is more convenient for the beginner to regard ὡρ- as the stem and -α, -ας, etc., as the endings. It should be noticed that α is characteristic of this declension as ο is of the second declension.

50. It should be observed that the α in the nominative, genitive, and accusative singular, and in the accusative plural is long.

51. The genitive plural shows an exception to the rule of noun accent. The rule of noun accent would require the accent to remain on the same syllable as in the nominative singular. But nouns of the first declension have a circumflex on the ultima in the genitive plural no matter where the accent was in the nominative singular.

52. The declension of βασιλεία, ἡ, *a kingdom*, is exactly like that of ὥρα, since here also there is a long accented penult in the nominative singular followed by a long α in the ultima.

53. The declension of ἀλήθεια, ἡ, *truth*, is as follows:

	Sing.	Plur.
N.V.	ἀλήθεια	ἀλήθειαι
G.	ἀληθείας	ἀληθειῶν
D.	ἀληθείᾳ	ἀληθείαις
A.	ἀλήθειαν	ἀληθείας

This noun has a short α in the ultima in the nominative singular, and when in the first declension the α is short in the nominative singular it is also short in the accusative singular. In the accusative plural the α is long in all first-declension nouns. The accent follows the noun rule everywhere except in the genitive plural (see §51).

54. The declension of δόξα, ἡ, *glory*, is as follows:

	Sing.	Plur.
N.V.	δόξα	δόξαι
G.	δόξης	δοξῶν
D.	δόξῃ	δόξαις
A.	δόξαν	δόξας

55. The α in the nominative singular of first-declension nouns is changed to η in the genitive and dative singular except after ε, ι, or ρ.

56. The declension of γραφή, ἡ, *a writing*, a Scripture, is as follows:

	Sing.	Plur.
N.V.	γραφή	γραφαί
G.	γραφῆς	γραφῶν
D.	γραφῇ	γραφαῖς
A.	γραφήν	γραφάς

57. When a first-declension noun ends in η in the nominative singular, the η is retained throughout the singular. But the plurals of all first-declension nouns are alike.

58. In the first declension (exactly as in the second, see §40), when the ultima is accented at all, it has the circumflex in the genitives and datives of both numbers, elsewhere the acute.

59. Exercises

I. 1. ψυχὴ βλέπει ζωήν. 2. βασιλεία γινώσκει ἀλήθειαν. 3. ἄνθρωπος γράφει ἐντολὰς καὶ νόμους. 4. ἀπόστολοι λαμβάνουσι δούλους καὶ δῶρα καὶ ἐκκλησίας. 5. ἀπόστολοι καὶ ἐκκλησίαι βλέπουσι ζωὴν καὶ θάνατον. 6. υἱὸς δούλου λέγει παραβολὴν ἐκκλησίᾳ. 7. παραβολὴν λέγομεν καὶ ἐντολὴν καὶ νόμον. 8. βασιλείας γινώσκετε καὶ ἐκκλησίας. 9. ἐκκλησίαν διδάσκει ἀπόστολος καὶ βασιλείαν δοῦλος. 10. νόμον καὶ παραβολὴν γράφει ἄνθρωπος ἐκκλησίᾳ. 11. καρδίαι ἀνθρώπων ἔχουσι ζωὴν καὶ εἰρήνην. 12. φωνὴ ἀποστόλων διδάσκει ψυχὰς δούλων. 13. ὥρα ἔχει δόξαν. 14. φωναὶ ἐκκλησιῶν διδάσκουσι βασιλείας καὶ ἀνθρώπους. 15. βλέπεις δῶρα καὶ δόξαν. 16. γράφει ἐκκλησίᾳ λόγον ζωῆς. 17. λέγει καρδίαις ἀνθρώπων παραβολὴν καὶ νόμον. 18. γράφει ἐκκλησίᾳ υἱὸς ἀποστόλου.

II. 1. A kingdom takes glory. 2. Churches are saying parables to hearts of men. 3. A heart of a man is teaching an apostle, and a voice of an apostle is teaching a servant. 4. We have writings of apostles. 5. Churches have peace and glory. 6. A day sees life and death. 7. Apostles take temples and kingdoms. 8. We see houses and temples and churches. 9. A servant says a parable to hearts of men. 10. We know voices of churches and words of truth. 11. A voice of an apostle says a parable to souls of men.

Lesson VI

The Article. Adjectives of the First and Second Declension. Agreement. Use of the Article. Attributive and Predicate Positions of Adjectives. Substantive Use of Adjectives.

60. Vocabulary

ἀγαθός, ή, όν, adj., *good*

ἄλλος, η, ο, adj., *other*

δίκαιος, α, ον, adj., *righteous*

ἐγείρω, *I raise up*

ἔρημος, ἡ, *a desert*

ἔσχατος, η, ον, adj., *last*

κακός, ή, όν, adj., *bad*

καλός,ή,όν,adj.,*good, beautiful*

κύριος, ό, a lord, *the Lord*

μικρός, ά, όν, adj., *small, little*

νεκρός, ά, όν, adj., *dead*

ό, ἡ, τό, art., *the*

ὁδός, ἡ, *a way*

πιστός, ή, όν, adj., *faithful*

πρῶτος, η, ον, adj., *first*

It will be observed that ἔρημος and ὁδός are feminine, though nearly all nouns of the second declension ending in -ος are masculine.

61. The declension of the adjective ἀγαθός, *good*, is as follows:

	Sing.				Plur.		
	Masc.	Fem.	Neut.		Masc.	Fem.	Neut.
N.	ἀγαθός	ἀγαθή	ἀγαθόν	N.V.	ἀγαθοί	ἀγαθαί	ἀγαθά
G.	ἀγαθοῦ	ἀγαθῆς	ἀγαθοῦ	G.	ἀγαθῶν	ἀγαθῶν	ἀγαθῶν
D.	ἀγαθῷ	ἀγαθῇ	ἀγαθῷ	D.	ἀγαθοῖς	ἀγαθαῖς	ἀγαθοῖς
A.	ἀγαθόν	ἀγαθήν	ἀγαθόν	A.	ἀγαθούς	ἀγαθάς	ἀγαθά
V.	ἀγαθέ	ἀγαθή	ἀγαθόν				

This declension, like all declensions of adjectives, and of the article, etc., is to be learned across and not in vertical columns—that is, the nominative singular is to be given in all three genders before the genitive is given, and the genitive singular is to be given in all three genders before the dative is given, and so on.

It will be observed that the masculine of the adjective ἀγαθός is declined exactly like a masculine noun of the second declension, the feminine exactly like a feminine noun in η of the first declension, and the neuter exactly like a neuter noun of the second declension.

62. Learn the declension of μικρός, *small*, and of δίκαιος, *righteous* (in §569, §570). Note that long α not η stands in the feminine of these adjectives when the preceding letter is ϱ or a vowel (compare §55). The accent in the genitive plural feminine of all adjectives of the second and first declension follows the regular noun rule and not the special rule for nouns of the first declension (§51).

63. The declension of the article is as follows:

	Sing.				Plur.		
	Masc.	Fem.	Neut.		Masc.	Fem.	Neut.
N.	ὁ	ἡ	τό	N.	οἱ	αἱ	τά
G.	τοῦ	τῆς	τοῦ	G.	τῶν	τῶν	τῶν
D.	τῷ	τῇ	τῷ	D.	τοῖς	ταῖς	τοῖς
A.	τόν	τήν	τό	A.	τούς	τάς	τά

64. The forms ὁ, ἡ, οἱ, αἱ are *proclitics*. A proclitic is a word that goes so closely with the following word as to have no accent of its own.

65. Note that except for (1) these irregular proclitic forms, (2) the form τό in the nominative and accusative singular (instead of τόν), and (3) the absence of the vocative, the article is declined like the adjective ἀγαθός.

66. Agreement

Adjectives, including the article, agree with the nouns that they modify, in gender, number, and case.

Examples: (1) ὁ λόγος, τοῦ λόγου, τῷ λόγῳ, βλέπω τὸν λόγον, οἱ λόγοι, τῶν λόγων, τοῖς λόγοις, βλέπω τοὺς λόγους. (2) τὸ δῶρον, τοῦ δώρου, etc. (3) ἡ ὥρα, τῆς ὥρας, τῇ ὥρᾳ, βλέπω τὴν ὥραν, αἱ ὧραι, etc. (4) ἡ ὁδός (see §60), τῆς ὁδοῦ, τῇ ὁδῷ, βλέπω τὴν ὁδόν, αἱ ὁδοί, τῶν ὁδῶν, ταῖς ὁδοῖς, βλέπω τὰς ὁδούς. (5) καλὸς λόγος, etc., καλὴ ὥρα, καλὴ ὁδός, etc.

67. Use of the Article

The use of the article in Greek corresponds roughly to the use of the definite article in English. Thus λόγος means a word; ὁ λόγος means *the word*; λόγοι means *words*; οἱ λόγοι means *the words*. The differences between the Greek and the English use of the article must be learned by observation, as they occur. For the present, the presence or absence of the Greek article should always be carefully indicated in the English translation.

Attributive And Predicate Use Of Adjectives

68. Adjectives are used in two distinct ways: (1) attributively, (2) predicatively.

In the phrase *the good word*, the adjective *good* is an attributive adjective; it tells what word we are mentioning. We are not mentioning all words or any word, but only the *good* word.

In the sentence, *the word is good*, the adjective *good* is a predicate adjective; with the verb is it makes an assertion about the subject, *the word*.

69. In Greek, the distinction between the attributive and the predicate adjective is of vastly more importance than in English; indeed, as will be observed later, some of the most important and characteristic parts of Greek grammar are based upon this distinction.

70. *The good word* can be expressed in two common ways in Greek— either by ὁ ἀγαθὸς λόγος or by ὁ λόγος ὁ ἀγαθός. It will be observed that what is characteristic about this *attributive position* of the Greek adjective is that the adjective comes immediately after the article. The former of the two alternatives, ὁ ἀγαθὸς λόγος, is just like English; it has the order (1) article, (2) attributive adjective, (3) noun, and is a literal translation of *the good word*. The latter of the two alternatives, ὁ λόγος ὁ ἀγαθός, means literally *the word— namely the good one*. But it is of course vastly commoner than this cumbersome usage is in English, and like ὁ ἀγαθὸς λόγος should be translated simply *the good word*.

71. *The word is good* can be expressed in two ways in Greek— either by ὁ λόγος ἀγαθός or by ἀγαθὸς ὁ λόγος (the simple copula, meaning is, can be omitted). What is characteristic about this *predicate position* of the adjective in Greek is that the adjective does not come immediately after the article.

72. The matter can be summarized as follows:

Attributive Positions of the Adjective	ὁ ἀγαθὸς λόγος or ὁ λόγος ὁ ἀγαθός	= the good word.
Predicate Position of the Adjective	ὁ λόγος ἀγαθός or ἀγαθὸς ὁ λόγος	= the word is good.

73. The student should fix this distinction in his mind by thoughtful reading aloud of the above and similar phrases, until ἀγαθὸς ὁ λόγος, for example, comes to mean to him, even without conscious translation, *good (is) the word*, and comes to be dissociated entirely from the idea *the good word*. If this advice be heeded, a solid foundation will have been laid for the mastery of a large part of Greek syntax.

74. It should be observed that the distinction between the attributive and the predicate position of the adjective can be made in Greek only when the noun has the article. ἀγαθὸς λόγος or λόγος ἀγαθός (the noun here not having the article) may mean either *a good word* (attributive) *or a word is good* (predicate).

75. Substantive Use of the Adjectives

The adjective may be used as a noun, especially with the article.

Examples: (1) ἀγαθός may mean *a good man*; ἀγαθή, *a good woman*; ἀγαθόν, *a good thing*; ἀγαθοί, *good men*; ἀγαθαί, *good women*; ἀγαθά, *good things*. (2) ὁ ἀγαθός means *the good man*; ἡ ἀγαθή, *the good woman*; τὸ ἀγαθόν, *the good thing*; οἱ ἀγαθοί, *the good men*; αἱ ἀγαθαί, *the good women*; τὰ ἀγαθά, *the good things*.

Sometimes, in the plural masculine, the English language, like Greek, can use the adjective as a noun without adding the word men. Thus οἱ ἀγαθοί may be translated the good meaning the good men or *the good people*; οἱ νεκροί, *the dead,* meaning *the dead people,* etc.

76. Exercises

I 1. ἀγαθὴ ἡ ἐκκλησία καὶ ἡ βασιλεία κακή. 2. ἡ κακὴ καρδία τῶν ἀνθρώπων γινώσκει θάνατον. 3. οἱ ἀπόστολοι βλέπουσι τοὺς μικροὺς οἴκους καὶ τὰς κακὰς ὁδούς. 4. οἱ δοῦλοι οἱ κακοὶ λύουσι[1] τὸν οἶκον τοῦ ἀποστόλου. 5. οἱ κακοὶ λύουσι τὸ ἱερόν. 6. ὁ κύριος τῆς ζωῆς[2] ἐγείρει τοὺς νεκρούς. 7. οἱ λόγοι τῆς ἀληθείας διδάσκουσι τοὺς ἄλλους ἀποστόλους. 8. οἱ δίκαιοι λαμβάνουσι τὰ δῶρα τοῦ κυρίου τὰ καλά. 9. ὁ κακὸς βλέπει τὴν ἔρημον καὶ τοὺς ἐσχάτους οἴκους. 10. πρῶτοι οἱ δοῦλοι· ἔσχατοι οἱ κύριοι. 11. τῇ ἐκκλησίᾳ τῇ μικρᾷ γράφει ὁ κύριος λόγον ἀγαθόν. 12. τοὺς πιστοὺς βλέπει ὁ πιστός. 13. ἔσχατοι οἱ δοῦλοι οἱ κακοί· πρῶτοι οἱ υἱοὶ οἱ ἀγαθοί. 14. ὁ υἱὸς τοῦ ἐσχάτου ἀδελφοῦ βλέπει τὰς καλὰς ἐκκλησίας τοῦ κυρίου. 15. ἄλλην παραβολὴν λέγομεν τῇ κακῇ βασιλείᾳ. 16. πρώτη ἡ ἐκκλησία· ἐσχάτη ἡ ἄλλη βασιλεία. 17. ταῖς πισταῖς λέγει ὁ κύριος παραβολὴν καλὴν καὶ τοῖς πιστοῖς. 18. ὁ ἀγαθὸς γράφει ἀγαθά· ὁ κακὸς κακά. 19. ἀγαθὸς ὁ δοῦλος καὶ λέγει καλά. 20. ἡ ἀλήθεια πιστὴ καὶ ἡ ὥρα κακή.

II 1. To the first church the Lord writes the first parable. 2. The good woman sees the ways of the desert. 3. The good things are first and the bad things last. 4. Death is bad and life is good. 5. The Lord of the kingdom raises up the faithful men and the faithful women. 6. The good know the bad, and the bad the good. 7. The good words we say to the Church, and the bad words we write to the brethren. 8. Thou seest the good days of the Lord of life. 9. The roads are good and the men bad. 10. The first gift is last and the last (gift) first. 11. The good servants know the truth and the glory of the Lord. 12. The last day takes the bad servants. 13. The men are destroying the beautiful temples and the small houses. 14. The righteous have another house.

---

[1] λύω sometimes means I destroy
[2] Abstract nouns, and nouns such as ζωή, often have the article where it is omitted in English.

31

15. The church is taking the other house. 16. I know the other ways. 17. The Lord is saying the other parable to the first church.

Lesson VII

Masculine Nouns of the First Declension. Prepositions.

77. Vocabulary

ἄγγελος, ὁ, *an angel, a messenger*

ἄγω, *I lead*

ἀπό, prep. with gen., *from*

βάλλω, *I throw, I cast, I put*

διά, prep. with gen., *through*; with acc., *on account of*

εἰς, prep. with acc., *into*

ἐκ (ἐξ before vowels), prep. with gen., *out of*

ἐν, prep. with dat., *in*

θεός, ὁ, *a god, God* (When it means *God*, θεός may have the article)

κόσμος, ὁ, *a world*

λίθος, ὁ, *a stone*

μαθητής, ὁ, *a disciple*

μένω, *I remain*

μετά, prep. with gen., *with*; with acc., *after*

οὐρανός, ὁ, *heaven*

πέμπω, *I send*

πρός, prep. with acc., *to*

προφήτης, ὁ, *a prophet*

τέκνον, τό, *a child*

τόπος, ὁ, *a place*

φέρω, *I bear, I bring*

78. Nouns of the first declension ending in -ης are masculine.

79. The declension of προφήτης, ὁ, a prophet, is as follows:

	Sing.		Plur.
N.	προφήτης	N.V.	προφῆται
G.	προφήτου	G.	προφητῶν
D.	προφήτῃ	D.	προφήταις
A.	προφήτην	A.	προφήτας
V.	προφῆτα		

It will be observed that although προφήτης is masculine it is a true first-declension noun, being just like a feminine noun of the first declension except in the nominative, genitive, and vocative singular.

μαθητής is declined like προφήτης, except for the accent, see §556.

33

Prepositions

80. Prepositions express relationship. Thus in the sentence, *the book is in the desk*, the preposition in expresses a certain relationship between the book and the desk. In the sentence, *the book is on the desk*, a different relationship is expressed (by the preposition on). In English, nouns standing after prepositions are always in the same case (the "objective" case). But in Greek different prepositions take different cases.

81. The preposition ἐν, meaning *in*, always takes the dative case. Thus *in the house* is expressed by ἐν τῷ οἴκῳ; *in the truth* by ἐν τῇ ἀληθείᾳ, etc. The preposition εἰς, meaning *into*, on the other hand, always takes the accusative. Thus *into the house* is expressed by εἰς τὸν οἶκον. Finally, the preposition ἀπό always takes the genitive. Thus *from the house* is expressed by ἀπὸ τοῦ οἴκου.

82. These three prepositions illustrate the general principle that the genitive is the case of *separation*, the dative the case of *rest* in a place, and the accusative the case of *motion toward* a place. Prepositions expressing separation naturally take the genitive, prepositions expressing rest in a place naturally take the dative, and prepositions expressing motion toward a place naturally take the accusative.

83. But a very great number of usages of prepositions cannot be reduced to any such general rule. Thus many prepositions that do not express any idea of separation take the genitive.

84. It should be observed that ἐν, εἰς, and ἐκ are all proclitics (see §64).

85. ἐν, εἰς, ἐκ, and ἀπό each take only one case, and πρός is not commonly used with any case except the accusative. But many other prepositions take several cases. Those that take several cases often have quite a different meaning when used with one case from their meaning when used with another case. Thus διά with the genitive means *through*; διά with accusative, *on account of*: μετά with the genitive means *with*; μετά with the accusative, *after*.

86. In studying the vocabularies it is quite insufficient to learn how the prepositions are to be translated, but it is also necessary to learn with what case they are construed in any particular meaning. Thus it is quite insufficient to say that ἐν means *in*. What should rather be said is that "ἐν-with-the-dative" means in. The phrase "ἐν-with-the-dative" should form in the student's mind one absolutely indivisible idea; ἐν should never be thought of apart from its case. In the same way, but still more obviously, it is insufficient to say that μετά means *with* or *after*. What should rather be said is that "μετά-with-the-genilive" means *with*, and that "μετά-with-the-accusative" means *after*. This same method of study should be applied to all prepositions.

87. A further important principle is that of *precision* in learning the meanings of prepositions. It is true that no one English word or phrase is capable of translating in all instances a single Greek preposition. Sometimes, for example, ἐν with the dative cannot be translated by in in English. But the proper method is to learn first the usual meaning before proceeding to the unusual. A reversal of this method will lead to hopeless confusion. Let the student, therefore, so far as prepositions are concerned, adhere for the present rigidly to the translations given in the vocabularies. In that way a feeling for the really fundamental meaning of the prepositions will be formed, and further on the derived meanings can be studied without confusion.

88. Finally, the importance of this subject should be noticed. Few things are more necessary for a correct understanding of the New Testament than a precise acquaintance with the common prepositions. The prepositions therefore should always be singled out from the vocabularies for special attention, and when new prepositions are learned the old ones should be reviewed.

89. Exercises

I 1. οἱ μαθηταὶ τῶν προφητῶν μένουσιν ἐν τῷ κόσμῳ. 2. οἱ κακοὶ βάλλουσιν λίθους εἰς τὸν οἶκον τῶν μαθητῶν. 3. ὁ θεὸς πέμπει τοὺς ἀγγέλους εἰς τὸν κόσμον. 4. ὁ προφήτης πέμπει τοὺς μαθητὰς τοῦ κυρίου ἐκ τῶν οἴκων εἰς τὴν ἐκκλησίαν. 5. ὁ θεὸς ἐγείρει τοὺς νεκροὺς ἐκ θανάτου. 6. λαμβάνετε τὰ καλὰ δῶρα ἀπὸ τῶν τέκνων. 7. ἄγομεν τὰ τέκνα ἐκ τῶν οἴκων. 8. μετὰ τοὺς ἀγγέλους πέμπει ὁ θεὸς τὸν υἱόν. 9. μετὰ τῶν ἀγγέλων ἄγει ὁ κύριος τοὺς δικαίους εἰς τὸν οὐρανόν. 10. διὰ τῶν ὁδῶν τῆς ἐρήμου φέρουσιν οἱ δοῦλοι τὰ δῶρα εἰς ἄλλον τόπον. 11. διὰ τῶν γραφῶν τῶν προφητῶν γινώσκομεν τὸν κύριον. 12. διὰ τὴν δόξαν τοῦ θεοῦ ἐγείρει ὁ κύριος τοὺς νεκρούς. 13. φέρουσιν τοὺς νεκροὺς εἰς τὴν ἔρημον. 14. οἱ μαθηταὶ διδάσκουσι τὰ ἀγαθὰ τέκνα ἐν τῇ ἐκκλησίᾳ. 15. ὁ κύριος λέγει παραβολὴν τοῖς μαθηταῖς ἐν τῷ ἱερῷ. 16. διὰ τὴν ἀλήθειαν βλέπουσιν οἱ προφῆται τὸν θάνατον. 17. ἀπὸ τῆς ἐρήμου ἄγουσιν οἱ μαθηταὶ τοὺς ἀγαθοὺς δούλους καὶ τοὺς υἱοὺς τῶν προφητῶν πρὸς τοὺς μικροὺς οἴκους τῶν μαθητῶν. 18. διὰ τὴν βασιλείαν τοῦ θεοῦ φέρομεν τὰ κακά. 19. διὰ τὰς ψυχὰς τῶν ἀδελφῶν βλέπει κακά. 20. καλὸς ὁ οὐρανός· κακὸς ὁ κόσμος.

II 1. In the world we have death, and in the Church life. 2. The prophets lead the righteous disciples of the Lord into the way of the desert. 3. The child is throwing a stone into the little house. 4. The man is saying a good word to the disciples and is leading the disciples to the Lord.[1] 5. The disciples are remaining in the church and are saying a parable to the other prophets. 6. Through the voice of the prophet the Lord is teaching the disciples. 7. On account of the Church the disciples and the apostles write good words to the brethren. 8. On account of the children the prophet is sending the evil men into the desert. 9. After the Lord the apostle sees the disciple. 10. The prophets are teaching the disciples with the children. 11. They are bringing the disciples to the Lord. 12. The Lord is remaining with the prophet in another place. 13. The righteous are leading the disciples through the desert to the Lord. 14. We see the days of the Son of God in the evil world. 15. Evil are the days; good are the churches. 16. Through the word of the Lord God raises the dead.

---

[1] Care should be taken to distinguish the two ways in which the English word to is used in this sentence.

Lesson VIII

Enclitics. Personal Pronouns. Present Indicative of εἰμί.

90. Vocabulary

αὐτός, ή, ό, pron., *he*

δέ, conj., *but, and*

ἐγώ, pron., *I*

εἰμί, *I am*

σύ, pron., *thou*

91. The conjunction δέ is *postpositive*—that is, it cannot stand first in its clause. Ordinarily it stands second.

Example: ὁ δοῦλος γινώσκει τὸν ἀπόστολον, ὁ δὲ ἀπόστολος βλέπει τὸν κύριον, *the servant knows the apostle and the apostle sees the Lord.*

Enclitics

92. An enclitic is a word that goes so closely with the preceding word as to have normally no accent of its own.

Enclitics are thus to be distinguished from *proclitics*, which go so closely with the *following* words as to have no accent of their own (see §64). Proclitics give rise to no special rules of accent; they simply have no accent and produce no changes in the accenting of preceding or following words. But the case is very different with enclitics, which give rise to the following rules:

I. Accenting of the word before an enclitic

(1) The word before an enclitic does not change an acute on the last syllable to a grave.

Example: ἀδελφὸς μου is incorrect; ἀδελφός μου is correct.

(2) If the word before an enclitic has an acute on the antepenult, or a circumflex on the penult, it takes an additional accent (an acute) on the ultima.

Examples: ἄνθρωπός μου, δῶρόν σου, ἄνθρωπός ἐστιν, δῶρόν ἐστιν.

(3) If the word before an enclitic is itself a proclitic or an enclitic it has an acute on the ultima.

Examples: εἴς με, ἄνθρωπός μού ἐστιν.

II. Cases in which an enclitic has an accent of its own:

(1) An enclitic of two syllables retains its own accent when it follows a word that has an acute on the penult.

Example: ὥρα ἐστίν is correct because ἐστίν is an enclitic of two syllables, ὥρα μου, on the other hand, is correct because μου is an enclitic of only one syllable.

(2) An enclitic retains its accent when there is emphasis on the enclitic or when the enclitic begins a clause.

93. It may help to fix these rules in the memory, if the enclitic in every case be regarded as forming one word with the word that precedes it and then the general rules of accent be applied. These enclitic rules may then be regarded as attempts to avoid violations of the general rules. Thus if ἄνθρωποσεστιν or ἄνθρωποσμου or ἄνθρωποσμε be regarded as one word the accenting of that word violates the general rule that the accent cannot get further back than the antepenult; and δῶρονμου violates the general rule that the circumflex cannot get further back than the penult. Something, therefore, needs to be done. And what is actually done is to put in an additional accent to break up the long series of unaccented syllables. Following out a similar principle, the accent of ὥραεστιν would become ὥράεστιν. But two acutes were not desired in immediate juxtaposition in a single word. Therefore in this case an alternative way out of the difficulty was adopted, and the enclitic was made to retain its own accent.

It should be observed, however, that this way of considering the matter will not quite work out in all cases; for ὥραμου, for example, would violate the general rule that the accent cannot stand on the antepenult if the ultima is long.

Personal Pronouns

94. The declension of the personal pronoun of the first person is as follows:

	Sing.		Plur.
N.	ἐγώ *I*	N.	ἡμεῖς *we*
G.	ἐμοῦ or μου *of me*	G.	ἡμῶν *of us*
D.	ἐμοί or μοι *to* or *for me*	D.	ἡμῖν *to* or *for us*
A.	ἐμέ or με *me*	A.	ἡμᾶς *us*

The forms ἐμοῦ, ἐμοί, ἐμέ are the forms used when emphasis is desired. The unemphatic forms, μου, μοι, με, are enclitic.

95. The declension of the personal pronoun of the second person is as follows:

	Sing.		Plur.
N.	σύ *thou*	N.	ὑμεῖς *ye*
G.	σοῦ *of thee*	G.	ὑμῶν *of you*
D.	σοί *to* or *for thee*	D.	ὑμῖν *to* or *for you*
A.	σέ *thee*	A.	ὑμᾶς *you*

The forms σοῦ, σοί, and σέ are enclitic except when they are emphatic. When they are emphatic, they have the accents given in the paradigm.

96. The declension of the personal pronoun of the third person is as follows:

	Masc.	Fem.	Neut.
		Sing.	
N.	αὐτός *he*	αὐτή *she*	αὐτό *it*
G.	αὐτοῦ *of him*	αὐτῆς *of her*	αὐτοῦ *of it*
D.	αὐτῷ *to* or *for him*	αὐτῇ *to* or *for her*	αὐτῷ *to* or *for it*
A.	αὐτόν *him*	αὐτήν *her*	αὐτό *it*

	Masc.	Fem.	Neut.
		Plur.	
N.	αὐτοί *they*	αὐταί *they*	αὐτά *they*
G.	αὐτῶν *of them*	αὐτῶν *of them*	αὐτῶν *of them*
D.	αὐτοῖς *to* or *for them*	αὐταῖς *to* or *for them*	αὐτοῖς *to* or *for them*
A.	αὐτούς *them*	αὐτάς *them*	αὐτά *them*

It will be observed that the declension of αὐτός is like that of ἀγαθός (omitting the vocative), except for the form αὐτό in the nominative and accusative singular neuter.

97. The Use of Pronouns

(1) A pronoun is a word that stands instead of a noun.

Example: The sentence, *I see the disciple and teach him*, means the same thing as *I see the disciple and teach the disciple*. The pronoun *him* stands instead of the second occurrence of the noun *disciple*.

(2) The noun for which a pronoun stands is called its antecedent. Thus in the sentence, *I see the disciple and teach him*, the antecedent of *him* is *disciple*.

(3) A pronoun agrees with its antecedent in gender and number.

Examples:

(a) βλέπω τὸν μαθητὴν καὶ διδάσκω αὐτόν, *I see the disciple and teach him*. Here μαθητήν is the antecedent of αὐτόν, and since μαθητήν is of masculine gender and singular number αὐτόν also is masculine singular.

(b) μένω ἐν τῷ οἴκῳ καὶ γινώσκω αὐτόν, *I remain in the house and know it*. Here οἴκῳ is the antecedent of αὐτόν, and since οἴκῳ is of masculine gender and singular number αὐτόν also is masculine singular. In English the neuter pronoun *it* is used, because the noun *house*, like all nouns denoting inanimate objects, is neuter in English. But in Greek the word for house is masculine, and therefore the masculine pronoun is used in referring to it. Hence the translations, *he, she*, etc., given in the paradigm above for the masculine and feminine of the Greek pronoun of the third person are correct only when the antecedents are nouns denoting persons. In other cases, the pronouns will be neuter in English even when they are masculine or feminine in Greek. It will be observed, further, that the pronoun does not agree with its antecedent in case, but only in gender and number. In the sentence just given the antecedent οἴκῳ is dative after the preposition ἐν, whereas αὐτόν has its own construction, being the object of the verb γινώσκω.

(c) ἡ ἐκκλησία διδάσκει ἐμέ, καὶ ἐγὼ διδάσκω αὐτήν, *the Church teaches me and I teach it*.

(d) βλέπω τοὺς μαθητὰς καὶ διδάσκω αὐτούς, *I see the disciples and teach them*.

(e) βλέπω τὰ τέκνα καὶ διδάσκω αὐτά, *I see the children and teach them*. It will be observed that in English in the plural the personal

40

pronoun is the same in form for all three genders, whereas in Greek it varies.

(4) The personal pronouns are not used in the nominative case unless there is emphasis upon them.

(a) The reason for this rule is that the ending of the verb indicates sufficiently whether the subject is first, second, or third person. Thus λέγω means I say. The ἐγώ, therefore, is not put in unless there is emphasis upon it.

(b) Emphasis is usually caused by contrast. Thus in the sentence ἐγώ λέγω, σὺ δὲ γράφεις, I say, but you write, ἐγώ and σὺ are emphatic because they are contrasted with each other. And in the sentence ἐγώ λέγω, "I say," the natural inference is that some one else does *not* say. The insertion of the emphatic ἐγώ naturally suggests an implied (though here not an expressed) contrast.

(c) αὐτός is almost never used as a personal pronoun in the nominative case. The place of it, in the nominative, is taken usually by certain other words, and it itself has in the nominative case a use distinct from its use as a personal pronoun. These matters will be reserved for future study.

(5) To express possession the unemphatic forms of the personal pronouns should be used, and the English phrases my word and the like should be turned around into the form, the word of me, before they are translated into Greek.

Examples: *My word*, ὁ λόγος μου; *thy word*, ὁ λόγος σου; *his word*, ὁ λόγος αὐτοῦ; *her word*, ὁ λόγος αὐτῆς; *its word*, ὁ λόγος αὐτοῦ; *their word*, ὁ λόγος αὐτῶν.

If it is desired to emphasize the possessive idea— e. g., "*my* word" — a possessive adjective, which will be learned later, is ordinarily used instead of the genitive of the personal pronoun.

(6) After prepositions, the emphatic forms of the personal pronouns are ordinarily used.

Examples: ἐξ ἐμοῦ, not ἔκ μου; ἀπ' ἐμοῦ[1], not ἀπό μου; δι' ἐμοῦ, not διά μου; ἐν ἐμοί, not ἔν μοι. But πρός με is common.

---

[1] The final vowel of prepositions is frequently elided before words that begin with a vowel. The elision is marked by an apostrophe

Present Indicative Of Εἰμί

98. The present indicative of the verb εἰμί, *I am*, is as follows:

Sing.		Plur.	
1.	εἰμί *I am*	1.	ἐσμέν *we are*
2.	εἶ *thou art*	2.	ἐστέ *ye are*
3.	ἐστί(ν) *he is*	3.	εἰσί(ν) *they are*

All these forms except εἶ are enclitic. The accents given in the paradigm occur only when required by the rules given above in §92. ἐστί(ν) and εἰσί(ν) have the movable ν (see §44).

99. The verb εἰμί takes a predicate nominative, not an accusative, to complete its meaning.

Examples: ὁ ἀπόστολος ἄνθρωπός ἐστιν, *the apostle is a man*; ὁ ἀπόστολός ἐστιν ἀγαθός, *the apostle is good*. In the sentence, *the apostle says the word*, it is asserted that the apostle does something to the word; *the word* is therefore the object of the action denoted by the verb, and stands in the accusative case. But in the sentence, *the apostle is a man*, it is not asserted that the apostle does anything to a man. *A man*, therefore, stands here not in the accusative case but in the predicate nominative.

100. Exercises

I 1. οἱ μαθηταί σου γινώσκουσι τὴν Βασιλείαν καὶ ἄγουσι τοὺς ἀδελφοὺς αὐτῶν εἰς αὐτήν. 2. διδάσκω τοὺς ἀδελφούς μου καὶ λέγω αὐτοῖς παραβολήν. 3. ἄγει με ὁ κύριος πρὸς τοὺς μαθητὰς αὐτοῦ. 4. δι᾽ ἐμὲ βλέπεις σὺ τὸν θάνατον, σοὶ δὲ ἐγὼ λέγω λόγους κακούς. 5. διὰ σοῦ ἄγει ὁ θεὸς τοὺς πιστοὺς εἰς τὴν βασιλείαν αὐτοῦ καὶ δι᾽ αὐτῶν τοὺς ἄλλους. 6. δι᾽ ἡμᾶς μένει ὁ κύριος ἐν τῷ κόσμῳ. 7. ἐγώ εἰμι δοῦλος, σὺ δὲ ἀπόστολος. 8. ἀγαθός ἐστιν ὁ κύριος καὶ ἀγαθοί ἐστε ὑμεῖς. 9. μαθηταί ἐστε τοῦ κυρίου καὶ ἀδελφοὶ τῶν ἀποστόλων αὐτοῦ. 10. ὁ ἀπόστολος πιστός ἐστιν, οἱ δὲ δοῦλοι αὐτοῦ κακοί. 11. ἡ ἐκκλησία πιστή ἐστιν, ἡμεῖς δὲ βλέπομεν αὐτήν. 12. βλέπομέν σε καὶ λέγομέν σοι παραβολήν. 13. δοῦλοι ἐσμέν, δούλους δὲ διδάσκομεν. 14. οἱ δοῦλοι ἡμῶν βλέπουσιν ἡμᾶς, ἡμεῖς δὲ διδάσκομεν αὐτούς. 15. ἀφ' ὑμῶν[1] λαμβάνει ὁ ἀδελφός μου δῶρα καλά, καὶ πέμπει αὐτὰ πρός με διὰ τῶν δούλων αὐτοῦ. 16. γινώσκομεν τὴν ὁδόν, καὶ δι' αὐτῆς ἄγομέν σε εἰς τὸν οἶκον ἡμῶν. 17. μετὰ τῶν ἀδελφῶν ἡμῶν βλέπομεν τοὺς μαθητὰς τοῦ κυρίου ἡμῶν. 18. μετὰ τὰς ἡμέρας τὰς κακὰς βλέπομεν τὴν βασιλείαν τοῦ κυρίου ἡμῶν. 19. μεθ' ἡμῶν[2] βλέπεις αὐτόν. 20. μεθ' ὑμῶν ἐσμεν ἐν τοῖς οἴκοις ὑμῶν.

II 1. Your servants are in the house of the Lord. 2. My house is in the desert. 3. The prophet knows his disciples and brings them into his houses. 4. Through my word ye have glory. 5. On account of our children ye see evil days. 6. In our days the world is evil. 7. God knows our souls and brings them out of death. 8. Ye are our sons and we are your disciples. 9. We are in the kingdom of God with Thy faithful disciples. 10. We say a parable to thee, but thou sayest another word to us. 11. The way is bad, but we lead the children in it. 12. My brother takes gifts from you, but ye write an evil word to him. 13. My house is bad, but your disciples bring the children out of it. 14. My disciples are leading their brethren to me. 15. I see and know my sons and lead them to my Lord. 16. God knows his Church and leads it out of death into his kingdom. 17. Thy commandments are good and righteous, and lead us into life. 18. Our Lord is sending His apostles to me. 19. We are sending our servants into your house, but ye are taking our gifts from us. 20. Ye are good, but your disciples are evil.

---

[1] Before the rough breathing, the π of ἀπ' becomes φ
[2] Before the rough breathing, τ of μετ' becomes θ.

Lesson IX

Demonstrative Pronouns. Further Uses of αὐτός.

101. Vocabulary

ἀγάπη, ἡ, *love*	κρίνω, *I judge*
ἁμαρτία, ἡ, *a sin, sin*	νῦν, adv., *now*
βαπτίζω, *I baptize*	οὗτος, pron., *this*
διδάσκαλος, ὁ, *a teacher*	οὕτως, adv., *thus, so*
ἐκεῖνος, η, ο, pron., *that*	πονηρός, ά, όν, adj., *evil*
ἐπαγγελία, ἡ, *a promise*	πρόσωπον, τό, *a face*
εὐαγγέλιον, τό, *a gospel*	χαρά, ἡ, *joy*

102. The declension of οὗτος, *this*, is as follows:

	Sing.				Plur.		
	Masc.	Fem.	Neut.		Masc.	Fem.	Neut.
N.	οὗτος	αὕτη	τοῦτο	N.V.	οὗτοι	αὗται	ταῦτα
G.	τούτου	ταύτης	τούτου	G.	τούτων	τούτων	τούτων
D.	τούτῳ	ταύτῃ	τούτῳ	D.	τούτοις	ταύταις	τούτοις
A.	τοῦτον	ταύτην	τοῦτο	A.	τούτους	ταύτας	ταῦτα

The puzzling variations between ου and αυ in the first syllable of this word may be fixed in the memory if it be observed that an ο-vowel (in the diphthong ου) stands in the first syllable where an ο-vowel (ο or the long of it, ω) stands in the second syllable, and an α-vowel (in the diphthong αυ) stands in the first syllable where an α-vowel (α or the closely related vowel η) stands in the second syllable.

103. The declension of ἐκεῖνος, *that*, is like the declension of adjectives in -ος, -η, -ον, except that ἐκεῖνο stands instead of ἐκεῖνον in the nominative and accusative singular neuter.

104. Use of οὗτος and ἐκεῖνος

1. οὗτος and ἐκεῖνος are frequently used with nouns. When they are so used, the noun with which they are used has the article, and they

themselves stand in the predicate, not in the attributive, position (see §68-§74).

Examples: *This word,* οὗτος ὁ λόγος or ὁ λόγος οὗτος; *that word,* ἐκεῖνος ὁ λόγος or ὁ λόγος ἐκεῖνος; *I see this church,* βλέπω ταύτην τὴν ἐκκλησίαν (or τὴν ἐκκλησίαν ταύτην); *these words,* οὗτοι οἱ λόγοι or οἱ λόγοι οὗτοι; *those words,* ἐκεῖνοι οἱ λόγοι or οἱ λόγοι ἐκεῖνοι; *this good word,* οὗτος ὁ καλὸς λόγος or ὁ καλὸς λόγος οὗτος.

2. οὗτος and ἐκεῖνος are frequently used by themselves, without nouns.

Examples: οὗτος, *this man* (or this person); αὕτη, *this woman;* τοῦτο, *this thing;* οὗτοι, *these men;* αὗται, *these women;* ταῦτα, *these things.*

105. Further Uses of αὐτός.

In addition to its use as a personal pronoun of the third person, αὐτός is also used as follows:

1. It has an intensive use with nouns. When so used it stands in the predicate position.

Examples: αὐτὸς ὁ ἀπόστολος or ὁ ἀπόστολος αὐτός, *the apostle himself;* αὐτὴ ἡ ἐκκλησία or ἡ ἐκκλησία αὐτή, *the church itself;* αὐτὸ τὸ δῶρον or τὸ δῶρον αὐτό, *the gift itself.*

2. It is often used with nouns to mean *same.* When so used it stands in the attributive position.

Examples: ὁ αὐτὸς ἀπόστολος or ὁ ἀπόστολος ὁ αὐτός, *the same apostle;* ἡ αὐτὴ ἐκκλησία or ἡ ἐκκλησία αὐτή, *the same church,* etc.

3. In its intensive use it often goes with pronouns or with the unexpressed subject of a verb.

Examples: αὐτὸς ἐγὼ λέγω or αὐτὸς λέγω, *I myself say,* αὐτὸς σὺ λέγεις or αὐτὸς λέγεις, *thou thyself sayest;* αὐτὸς λέγει, *he himself says;* αὐτὴ λέγει, *she herself says;* αὐτὸ λέγει, *it itself says;* αὐτοὶ ἡμεῖς λέγομεν or αὐτοὶ λέγομεν, *we ourselves say;* αὐτοὶ ὑμεῖς λέγετε or αὐτοὶ λέγετε, *ye yourselves say;* αὐτοὶ λέγουσιν, *they themselves say.*

106. The principal uses of adjectives and of the pronouns studied thus far may be reviewed as follows:

$$The\ good\ word = \begin{cases} ὁ\ καλὸς\ λόγος \\ or \\ ὁ\ λόγος\ ὁ\ καλός \end{cases}$$

$$The\ word\ is\ good = \begin{cases} καλὸς\ ὁ\ λόγος \\ or \\ ὁ\ λόγος\ καλός \end{cases}$$

$$This\ word = \begin{cases} οὗτος\ ὁ\ λόγος \\ or \\ ὁ\ λόγος\ οὗτος \end{cases}$$

$$That\ word = \begin{cases} ἐκεῖνος\ ὁ\ λόγος \\ or \\ ὁ\ λόγος\ ἐκεῖνος \end{cases}$$

$$The\ word\ itself = \begin{cases} αὐτὸς\ ὁ\ λόγος \\ or \\ ὁ\ λόγος\ αὐτός \end{cases}$$

$$The\ same\ word = \begin{cases} ὁ\ αὐτὸς\ λόγος \\ or \\ ὁ\ λόγος\ ὁ\ αὐτός \end{cases}$$

My word = ὁ λόγος μου
His word = ὁ λόγος αὐτοῦ
I see him = βλέπω αὐτόν
I see this man = βλέπω τοῦτον
I see these things = βλέπω ταῦτα

107. Exercises

I. 1. οὗτοι οἱ διδάσκαλοι κρίνουσιν αὐτὸν τὸν ἀπόστολον. 2. ὁ δὲ αὐτὸς διδάσκαλος ἔχει τὴν αὐτὴν χαρὰν ἐν τῇ καρδίᾳ αὐτοῦ. 3. νῦν λαμβάνω αὐτὸς τὸ αὐτὸ εὐαγγέλιον ἀπὸ τοῦ κυρίου μου. 4. οὗτος βλέπει ἐκεῖνον καὶ κρίνει αὐτόν. 5. μετὰ ταῦτα ἔχετε αὐτοὶ τὴν ἀγάπην τοῦ κυρίου ἐν ταῖς καρδίαις ὑμῶν. 6. οὗτοι ἔχουσι χαράν, ἐκεῖνοι δὲ ἔχουσιν ἁμαρτίαν. 7. αὕτη δὲ ἐστιν ἡ φωνὴ τοῦ κυρίου αὐτοῦ. 8. οὕτως γινώσκομεν τοῦτον καὶ βλέπομεν τὸ πρόσωπον αὐτοῦ. 9. λαμβάνομεν ταῦτα τὰ δῶρα ἀπὸ τοῦ αὐτοῦ καὶ βλέπομεν αὐτόν. 10. αὐτὸς βαπτίζεις ἐκεῖνον καὶ εἶ ἀδελφὸς αὐτοῦ. 11. εἰς τὴν αὐτὴν ἐκκλησίαν ἄγομεν τούτους τοὺς διδασκάλους ἡμῶν τοὺς ἀγαθούς. 12. αὐτὸς ἐγὼ ἔχω ταύτην τὴν ἐπαγγελίαν τοῦ κυρίου μου. 13. αὕτη βλέπει τὸ πρόσωπον τοῦ κυρίου αὐτῆς. 14. αὐτὴ γινώσκει αὐτὴν τὴν ἀλήθειαν. 15. ἀγαθή ἐστιν ἡ ἐπαγγελία σου καὶ ἀγαθὴ εἰ αὐτή. 16. ἐκεῖνοί εἰσιν μαθηταὶ τοῦ αὐτοῦ διδασκάλου. 17. οὗτός ἐστιν διδάσκαλος ἐκείνου, ἐκεῖνος δὲ τούτου. 18. οὗτος διδάσκει τοὺς ἀγαθοὺς καὶ αὐτός ἐστιν ἀγαθός. 19. μετὰ τὰς ἡμέρας ἐκαίνας διδάσκαλοί ἐσμεν τούτων τῶν δούλων. 20. μετὰ τῶν πιστῶν ἔχομεν ἐπαγγελίας ἀγαθάς, οἱ δὲ πονηροὶ βλέπουσιν ἡμέρας κακάς.

II 1. These churches know the Lord Himself. 2. The same disciples know Him and see His face. 3. Those teachers judge the same churches and lead them into the same joy. 4. We ourselves have this sin in our hearts. 5. This is the love of our God. 6. These are the faithful churches of our Lord. 7. The apostle himself baptizes his brothers and leads them to thee. 8. Through this gospel we have life. 9. On account of these teachers we see death. 10. He Himself knows us and from Him we receive this promise. 11. On account of the same gospel we ourselves send these apostles to you. 12. Into this world he sends the Lord Himself. 13. I see this man and the brethren see him. 14. Now we are baptizing those disciples of our Lord and are sending the same disciples into the desert. 15. My disciples know my voice and bring these things to me. 16. Through these things we bring the same gospel into the same world. 17. We are disciples of the Lord, but ye are disciples of the evil one. 18. This sin leads our children into death. 19. The sins of these churches are leading other men into the same sins. 20. His disciples have this sin in their hearts and are teaching men so. 21. I know the sins of the disciples and the disciples themselves.

Lesson X

Present Middle and Passive Indicative, ὑπό with the Genitive. The Dative of Means. Deponent Verbs. Compound Verbs. The Position of οὐ. Various Cases with Verbs.

108. Vocabulary

ἀλλά, conj., *but* (stronger adversative than δέ)

ἀκούω, *I hear* (may take the genitive, but also takes the accusative)

ἁμαρτωλός, ὁ, *a sinner*

ἀποκρίνομαι, dep., *I answer* (takes the dative)

ἄρχω, *I rule* (takes the genitive); middle, *I begin*

γίνομαι, dep., *I become* (takes a predicate nominative, not an accusative)

διέρχομαι, dep., *I go through*

εἰσέρχομαι, dep., *I go in, I enter*

ἐξέρχομαι, dep., *I go out*

ἔρχομαι, dep., *I come, I go*

ὅτι, conj., *that, because*

οὐ (οὐκ before vowels, οὐχ before the rough breathing), proclitic, *not*

πορεύομαι, dep., *I go*

σώζω, *I save*

ὑπό, prep. with gen., *by* (expressing agent); with accusative, *under*

109. There are three voices in Greek: *active, middle* and *passive*.

The *active* and the *passive* voices are used as in English.

The *middle* voice represents the subject as acting in some way that concerns itself, or as acting upon something that belongs to itself.

(1) Rarely the middle has the force which a verb followed by a reflexive pronoun in the objective case has in English. Thus λούω means *I wash*, and λούομαι means *I wash myself*. But usually the force of the middle is much more subtle. Sometimes, therefore, it is impossible to make any difference in an English translation between active and middle. In the case of some verbs, on the other hand, the difference in meaning is so great that in an English translation it is necessary to use one verb for the active and an entirely different verb for the middle. For example, ἄρχω means I rule, and ἄρχομαι (middle) means *I begin*.

48

(2) The middle of λύω does not occur in the New Testament. But it is very important to learn it, since it will enable the student to recognize the middle of other verbs. The translations given in the paradigms for the middle of λύω serve to indicate, in a rough sort of way, the fundamental meaning of the middle voice, rather than the actual meaning of the middle voice of this particular verb.

(3) In the present tense the middle and passive voices are exactly alike in form, though in certain other tenses they are entirely distinct. In the exercises in this lesson, the forms which might be either middle or passive should be regarded as passive.

110. The Present Middle Indicative of λύω is as follows:

	Sing.			Plur.	
1.	λύομαι	*I loose* (or *am loosing*) *for myself*	1.	λυόμεθα	*we loose* (or *are loosing*) *for ourselves*
2.	λύῃ	*thou loosest* (or *art loosing*) *for thyself*	2.	λύεσθε	*ye loose* (or *are loosing*) *for yourselves*
3.	λύεται	*he looses* (or *is loosing*) *for himself*	3.	λύονται	*they loose* (or *are loosing*) *for themselves*

111. The personal endings in the middle and passive of the so-called *primary tenses* are -μαι, -σαι, -ται, -μεθα, -σθε, -νται. Between the stem and the personal endings is placed, in the present tense, the *variable vowel* o/ε (o standing before μ and ν, ε before other letters). The second person singular, λύῃ is a shortened form instead of λύεσαι.[1]

---

[1] An alternative form for λύῃ is λύει. But the former seems to be preferred in the New Testament.

112. The Present Passive Indicative of λύω is as follows:

Sing.		Plur.	
1. λύομαι	*I am being loosed*	1. λυόμεθα	*we are being loosed*
2. λύῃ	*thou art being loosed*	2. λύεσθε	*ye are being loosed*
3. λύεται	*he is being loosed*	3. λύονται	*they are being loosed*

113. The present active indicative, λύω, it will be remembered, can be translated either *I loose* or *I am loosing*. The passive of *I loose*, in English, is *I am loosed*; the passive of *I am loosing* is *I am being loosed*. Both *I am loosed* and *I am being loosed* might, therefore, have been given in the translation of λύομαι (passive). But *I am loosed* is so ambiguous that the student is advised, at least in the earlier lessons, to adopt the alternative translation. *I am loosed* may mean *I am now in a loosed condition*, in which case it indicates a present state resultant upon a past action and would be translated, not by the present tense, but by the perfect tense in Greek.

Example: σώζομαι means *I am being saved*. It represents the action as taking place at the present time. It could also be translated *I am saved* in such a sentence as *every day I am saved from some new trouble*. Here *I am saved* is present because it indicates customary action. But in the majority of cases *I am saved* means *I am in a saved condition resultant upon an action that took place in the past*. And in these cases the English sentence *I am saved* would be translated by the perfect tense, not by the present tense, in Greek. It will be seen, therefore, that the translation *I am loosed* for λύομαι, though it is not wrong (since λύομαι may sometimes be translated in this way), would be misleading.

114. ὑπό with the Genitive

The preposition ὑπό with the genitive expresses the *agent* by which an action is performed. This usage occurs principally with the passive voice.

Example: ὁ ἀπόστολος λύει τὸν δοῦλον means *the apostle looses the servant*. If the same thought be expressed by the passive voice, the object of the active verb becomes the subject of the passive and the

50

subject of the active verb becomes ὑπό with the genitive. Thus ὁ δοῦλος λύεται ὑπὸ τοῦ ἀποστόλου means *the servant is being loosed by the apostle.*

115. The Dative of Means

The simple dative without any preposition sometimes expresses *means* or *instrument.*

Examples:

(1) ἐγείρονται τῷ λόγῳ τοῦ κυρίου, *they are being raised up by* (by means of) *the word of the Lord.* Compare ἐγείρονται ὑπὸ τοῦ κυρίου, *they are being raised up by the Lord.* The comparison will serve to distinguish ὑπό with the genitive (expressing the active personal agent) from the dative expressing means.

(2) ἄγομεν τοὺς δούλους μετὰ τῶν υἱῶν αὐτῶν λόγοις καλοῖς, *we are leading the servants with their sons with good words.* This example will serve to distinguish the dative expressing means from μετά with the genitive expressing accompaniment. The two ideas, though they are logically quite distinct, happen often to be expressed by the same preposition, *with*, in English. μετά *with* the genitive means with in the sense of *in company with*; the dative means *with* in the sense of *by means of.*

116. Deponent Verbs

Many verbs have no active forms, but only middle or passive forms with active meaning. These verbs are called *deponent.*

Example: πορεύομαι is passive in form, like λύομαι, but it is active in meaning, like λύω. It means simply *I go* or *I am going.*

117. Compound Verbs

Prepositions are frequently prefixed to verbs. The meaning of the verb is modified by the preposition in a way that is often easily understood from the common meaning of the preposition. Sometimes, however, the matter is not so simple; sometimes the meaning of the compound verb cannot easily be determined from the separate meanings of its two component parts.

Example: ἐκ means *out of,* and πορεύομαι means *I go.* Hence ἐκπορεύομαι means *I go out.* But the meaning of ἀποκρίνομαι, I answer, is not easily derived from the meanings of its component parts.

118. The Position of οὐ

The negative, οὐ, precedes the word which it negatives. And since in the great majority of cases the negative in a sentence negatives the verb, the normal place of οὐ is immediately before the verb.

Examples: οὐ λύω, *I do not loose*, or *I am not loosing*; οὐ λύομαι, *I am not being loosed*.

119. Various Cases With Verbs

Many verbs take the genitive case and many the dative case to complete their meaning, where the corresponding verbs in English take a direct object.

Examples: ἀκούω τῆς φωνῆς, *I hear the voice* (but ἀκούω may also take the accusative); ἀποκρίνομαι τῷ ἀποστόλῳ, *I answer the apostle*.

120. Exercises

I 1. λύονται οὗτοι οἱ δοῦλοι ὑπὸ τοῦ κυρίου. 2. τῷ λόγῳ τοῦ κυρίου ἀγόμεθα εἰς τὴν ἐκκλησίαν τοῦ θεοῦ. 3. οὐκ ἀκούετε τῆς φωνῆς τοῦ προφήτου, ἀλλ'[1] ἐξέρχεσθε ἐκ τοῦ οἴκου αὐτοῦ. 4. τῷ λόγῳ αὐτοῦ τοῦ κυρίου γίνεσθε μαθηταὶ αὐτοῦ. 5. ἐκεῖνοι οἱ ἀγαθοὶ διδάσκαλοι οὐκ εἰσέρχονται εἰς τοὺς οἴκους τῶν ἁμαρτωλῶν. 6. οὐ βαπτίζονται οἱ ἁμαρτωλοὶ ὑπὸ τῶν ἀποστόλων, ἀλλ' ἐξέρχονται ἐκ τούτων τῶν οἴκων πρὸς ἄλλους διδασκάλους. 7. λέγετε ἐκείνοις τοῖς ἁμαρτωλοῖς ὅτι σώζεσθε ὑπὸ τοῦ θεοῦ ἀπὸ τῶν ἁμαρτιῶν ὑμῶν. 8. ἄρχει αὐτὸς ὁ θεὸς τῆς βασιλείας αὐτοῦ. 9. εἰρήνην ἔχει ἡ ἐκκλησία, ὅτι σώζεται ὑπὸ τοῦ κυρίου αὐτῆς. 10. οὐκ ἀποκρινόμεθα τῷ ἀποστόλῳ ὅτι οὐ γινώσκομεν αὐτόν. 11. οὐχ ὑπὸ τῶν μαθητῶν σώζῃ ἀπὸ τῶν ἁμαρτιῶν σου, ἀλλ' ὑπ' αὐτοῦ τοῦ θεοῦ. 12. οὐ πορεύῃ ἐν τῇ ὁδῷ τῇ κακῇ, ἀλλὰ σώζῃ ἀπὸ τῶν ἁμαρτιῶν σου καὶ οἱ ἀδελφοί σου ἀκούουσι τῆς φωνῆς τοῦ κυρίου. 13. μετὰ τῶν ἀδελφῶν αὐτοῦ ἄγεται εἰς τὴν βασιλείαν τοῦ θεοῦ τῇ φωνῇ τῶν

---

[1] The final vowel of ἀλλά is often elided before a word that begins with a vowel. The elision is marked by an apostrophe.

ἀποστόλων. 14. οὐ γίνῃ μαθητὴς τοῦ κυρίου, ὅτι οὐκ εἰσέρχῃ εἰς τὴν ἐκκλησίαν αὐτοῦ.

II 1. These churches are being saved by God from death. 2. I am being saved by Him and am being taught by His word. 3. We are becoming disciples of the good apostle, but ye are not hearing his voice. 4. I am a sinner, but am being taught by the apostles of the Lord. 5. I am an evil servant, but thou art becoming a teacher of this church. 6. The evil men say to those churches that our brethren do not see the face of the Lord. 7. The world is being destroyed by the word of our God. 8. We know the Lord because we receive good gifts from Him and are being taught by Him in parables. 9. Thou art writing these things to thy brethren and art being saved from thy sin. 10. He is teaching others and is himself being taught by this apostle. 11. That disciple is not answering this prophet, because he does not know his words. 12. Thou art saying to this church that thou art a bad servant. 13. You are abiding in that temple, because you are not servants of the Lord. 14. We do not see the faces of our Lord's disciples[1], because we are not in their houses. 15. In our Lord's house are joy and peace. 16. God rules this world by His word. 17. These sinners are not entering into the Lord's house, but are going out into the desert. 18. These words are being written by God to His faithful churches.

---

[1] The phrase should be turned around into the form, the disciples of our Lord, before it is translated into Greek. A similar transposition should be made in other similar phrases.

Lesson XI

Imperfect Active Indicative. Imperfect Indicative of
εἰμί. Accent of ἔστι(ν).

121. Vocabulary

αἴρω, *I take up, I take away*

ἀναβαίνω, *I go up* (ἀνα-
means up)

ἀποθνήσκω, *I die*

ἀποκτείνω, *I kill*

ἀποστέλλω, *I send* (πέμπω is
the general word for *send*,
while ἀποστέλλω means *I
send with a commission*)

ἄρτος, *a piece of bread, a loaf,
bread*

βαίνω, *I go* (the simple verb
does not occur in the New
Testament, but the
compounds with various
prepositions are
exceedingly common)

ἐσθίω, *I eat*

κατά, prep. with gen., *against*;
with acc., *according to* (κατά,
of which the original
meaning was *down*, has

many meanings in the New
Testament)

καταβαίνω, *I go down*

μέν...δέ, *on the one hand. . .on
the other* (used in contrasts,
the μέν often being best left
untranslated and the δέ
being then best translated
by *but*)

οὐκέτι, adv., *no longer*

παρά, prep. with gen., *from*;
with dat., *beside, in the
presence of*; with acc.,
alongside of.

παραλαμβάνω, *I receive, I take
along*

σύν, prep. with dat., *with* (a
close synonym of μετά with
gen.)

συνάγω, *I gather together*

τότε, adv., *then*

122. In present time there is no special form of the verb in Greek to
indicate continued action - there is no distinction in Greek between *I
loose* and *I am loosing*. But in past time the distinction is made even
more sharply than in English.

The tense which in the indicative is used as the simple past tense is
called the aorist. It will be studied in Lesson XIV.

The tense which denotes continued action in past time is called the
imperfect.

54

The aorist active indicative of λύω means *I loosed*, etc., whereas the imperfect active indicative means *I was loosing*, etc. This distinction should be carefully observed.

123. The imperfect active indicative of λύω is as follows:

	Sing.			Plur.	
1.	ἔλυον	*I was loosing*	1.	ἐλύομεν	*we were loosing*
2.	ἔλυες	*thou wast loosing*	2.	ἐλύετε	*ye were loosing*
3.	ἔλυε(ν)	*he was loosing*	3.	ἔλυον	*they were loosing*

124. The imperfect indicative, like the indicative of the other *secondary* tenses (see §20 , footnote 4), places an *augment* at the beginning of the stem of the verb.

125. In verbs that begin with a consonant the augment consists in an ἐ- prefixed to the stem.

Examples: ἔλυον, *I was loosing*; ἐγίνωσκον, *I was knowing*.

126. In verbs that begin with a vowel, the augment consists in the lengthening of that vowel. But α lengthens not to long α but to η.

Examples: The imperfect of ἐγείρω is ἤγειρον ; of ἀκούω, ἤκουον ; of αἴρω, ἦρον.

127. The personal endings in the active of the *secondary tenses* are as follows:

	Sing.		Plur.
1.	-ν	1.	-μεν
2.	-ς	2.	-τε
3.	none	3.	-ν (or -σαν)

128. The variable vowel (placed between the stem and the personal endings) is, in the imperfect as in the present, ο before μ and ν and ε before other letters.

129. The third person singular, ἔλυε(ν), has the movable ν (under the conditions mentioned in §44).

130. It will be observed that the first person singular and the third person plural are alike in form. Only the context can determine whether ἔλυον means *I was loosing* or *they were loosing*.

Augment of Compound Verbs

131. In compound verbs (see §117), the augment comes after the preposition and before the stem. If the preposition ends with a vowel, that vowel is usually dropped both before a verb that begins with a vowel and before the augment.

Examples: The imperfect of ἐκβάλλω is ἐξέβαλλον; of ἀποκτείνω, ἀπέκτεινον; of ἀπάγω, ἀπῆγον

132. It should be observed that the accent does not go back of the augment. Thus ἀπῆγον is correct, not ἄπηγον.

133. Imperfect Indicative of εἰμί

The imperfect indicative of εἰμί is as follows:

	Sing.		Plur.
1.	ἤμην, *I was*	1.	ἦμεν, *we we*
2.	ἦς, *thou wast*	2.	ἦτε, *ye were*
3.	ἦν, *he was*	3.	ἦσαν, *they were*

134. Accent of ἔστι(ν)

After οὐκ and certain other words the third person singular present indicative of εἰμί is accented on the first syllable. This does not apply to the other forms of εἰμί. Thus οὐκ ἔστιν, but οὐκ ἐσμεν, etc.

135. Exercises

I 1. ἠκούομεν τῆς φωνῆς αὐτοῦ ἐν ἐκείναις ταῖς ἡμέραις, νῦν δὲ οὐκέτι ἀκούομεν αὐτῆς. 2. ὁ δὲ μαθητὴς τοῦ κυρίου ἔλεγε παραβολὴν τοῖς ἀδελφοῖς αὐτοῦ. 3. ἀπέκτεινον οἱ δοῦλοι τὰ τέκνα σὺν τοῖς μαθηταῖς. 4. τότε μὲν κατέβαινον εἰς τὸν οἶκον, νῦν δὲ οὐκέτι καταβαίνω. 5. παρελαμβάνετε τὸν ἄρτον παρὰ τῶν δούλων καὶ ἠσθίετε αὐτόν. 6. διὰ τὴν ἀλήθειαν ἀπέθνησκον οἱ μαθηταὶ ἐν ταῖς ἡμέραις ἐκείναις. 7. συνῆγεν οὗτος ὁ ἀπόστολος εἰς τὴν ἐκκλησίαν τοὺς μαθητὰς τοῦ κυρίου ἡμῶν. 8. νῦν μὲν διδασκόμεθα ὑπὸ τῶν ἀποστόλων, τότε δὲ ἐδιδάσκομεν ἡμεῖς τὴν ἐκκλησίαν. 9. ὁ κύριος ἡμῶν ἦρε τὰς ἁμαρτίας ἡμῶν. 10. τότε μὲν ἀνέβαινον εἰς τὸ ἱερόν, νῦν δὲ οὐκέτι. ἀναβαίνουσιν. 11. πονηροὶ ἦτε, ἀγαθοὶ δὲ ἐστέ. 12. ὑμεῖς μὲν ἐστε ἀγαθοί, ἡμεῖς δέ ἐσμεν πονηροί. 13. τότε ἤμην ἐν τῷ ἱερῷ καὶ ἐδίδασκέ με ὁ κύριος. 14. λέγομεν ὑμῖν ὅτι ἐν τῷ οἴκῳ ὑμῶν ἦμεν. 15. ἐξέβαλλες αὐτοὺς ἐκ τοῦ ἱεροῦ. 16. ἀπέστελλον οἱ ἄνθρωποι τοὺς δούλους αὐτῶν πρός με. 17. ὁ κύριος ἀπέστελλεν ἀγγέλους πρός ἡμᾶς. 18. ἐν τῷ κόσμῳ ἦν καὶ ὁ κόσμος οὐκ ἔβλεπεν αὐτόν. 19. δοῦλος ἦς τοῦ πονηροῦ, ἀλλὰ νῦν οὐκέτι εἶ δοῦλος. 20 . τοῦτό ἐστι τὸ δῶρον τοῦ ἀνθρώπου, καλὸν δὲ οὐκ ἔστιν.

II 1. The servant was saying these words against them. 2. According to the word of the apostle, they were going up into the temple. 3. The Lord was in His temple. 4. They were killing our children. 5. Ye were dying in those days on account of the kingdom of God. 6. Thou wast taking away the sins of Thy disciples. 7. The prophet was sending the same servants into the small house. 8. We are no longer sinners, because we are being saved by the Lord from the sin of our hearts. 9. I was receiving this bread from the apostle's servants. 10. Then he was writing these things to his brethren. 11. In that hour we were in the desert with the Lord. 12. They are good, but they were evil. 13. Thou wast good, but we were sinners. 14. Then I was a servant, but now I am a son. 15. The sons of the prophets were gathering these things together into the temple. 16. Now I am being sent by the Lord to the children of the disciples, but then I was sending the righteous men into the desert.

Lesson XII

Imperfect Middle and Passive Indicative. Singular Verb with Neuter Plural Subject. Uses of καί and οὐδέ.

136. Vocabulary

ἀπέρχομαι, dep., *I go away*
βιβλίον, τό, *a book*
δαιμόνιον, τό, *a demon*
δέχομαι, dep., *I receive*
ἐκπορεύομαι, dep., *I go out*
ἔργον, τό, *a work*
ἔτι, adv., *still, yet*
θάλασσα, ἡ, *a lake, a sea*
καί, conj., *and, also, even; καί . . . καί, both . . . and*
κατέρχομαι, dep., *I go down*

οὐδέ, conj., *and not, nor, not even;*
οὐδέ . . . οὐδέ, *neither . . . nor*
οὔπω, adv., *not yet*
περί, prep. with gen., *concerning, about; with acc., around*
πλοῖον, τό, *a boat*
συνέρχομαι, dep., *I come together*
ὑπέρ, prep. with gen., *in behalf of; with acc., above*

137. As in the present tense, so also in the imperfect, the middle and passive voices are alike in form.

138. The imperfect middle indicative of λύω is as follows:

	Sing.			Plur.	
1.	ἐλυόμην	*I was loosing for myself*	1.	ἐλυόμεθα	*we were loosing*
2.	ἐλύου	*thou wast loosing for thyself*	2.	ἐλύεσθε	*ye were loosing for yourselves*
3.	ἐλύετο	*he was loosing for himself*	3.	ἐλύοντο	*they were loosing for themselves*

58

139. The personal endings in the middle of the secondary tenses are as follows: Sing. Plur. 1 -μην -μεθα 2 -σο -σθε 3 -το -ντο

Sing.		Plur.	
1.	-μην	1.	-μεθα
2.	-σο	2.	-σθε
3.	-το	3.	-ντο

140. The variable vowel, as in the active of the imperfect, and in all three voices of the present, is o before μ and ν and ε before other letters.

141. In the second person singular, ἐλύου is a shortened form for an original ἐλύεσο.

142. Great care should be taken to pronounce clearly both the long vowel in the ultima of the form ἐλυόμην and the accent on the penult.

143. The imperfect passive indicative of λύω is as follows:

Sing.			Plur.		
1.	ἐλυόμην	I was being loosed	1.	ἐλυόμεθα	we were being loosed
2.	ἐλύου	thou wast being loosed	2.	ἐλύεσθε	ye were being loosed
3.	ἐλύετο	he was being loosed	3.	ἐλύοντο	They were being loosed

144. Verbs which are deponent in the present are also deponent in the imperfect.

Example: The imperfect indicative of ἔρχομαι, I come, is ἠρχόμην, I was coming.

145. The Neuter Plural Subject

A neuter plural subject may have its verb in the singular.

Examples: τὰ δαιμόνια ἐξέρχεται, the demons go out; ταῦτά ἐστι τὰ καλὰ δῶρα, these are the good gifts.

This strange idiom, however, is by no means invariable in New Testament Greek; the neuter plural subject often has its verb in the plural like any other plural verb.

Example: τὰ τέκνα σώζονται, the children are being saved.

Uses of καί and οὐδέ

146. The simple connective use of καί, where it means *and*, has already been studied. But καί has other uses. Frequently it means *also* or *even*. When it is thus used, it stands before the word with which it is logically connected. In the case of *also*, the English order is the reverse of the Greek order; in the case of *even*, it is the same as the Greek order.

Examples: τοῦτο δὲ καὶ ἐγὼ λέγω, *but this I also say;* γινώσκουσι καὶ τὰ τέκνα τὸν νόμον, *even the children know the law.*

147. οὐδέ, like καί, is often simply connective and means *and not* or *nor*. But like καί it has other uses. It often means *not even*.

Examples: τοῦτο δὲ οὐ λέγω ἐγὼ οὐδὲ λέγουσιν αὐτὸ οἱ ἄλλοι, *but this I do not say, nor do the others say it* (simple connective use of οὐδέ) ; τὴν δόξαν τοῦ θεοῦ βλέπουσιν οὐδὲ οἱ μαθηταί, *not even the disciples see the glory of God.*

148. Finally, καί . . . καί and οὐδέ . . . οὐδέ are used correlatively, and mean, respectively, *both . . . and,* and *neither . . . nor.*

Examples: (1) τοῦτο λέγουσιν καὶ οἱ ἀπόστολοι καὶ οἱ δοῦλοι, *both the apostles and the servants say this;* (2) τοῦτο λέγουσιν οὐδὲ οἱ ἀπόστολοι οὐδὲ οἱ δοῦλοι, *neither the apostles nor the servants say this.*

149. Exercises

I 1. ἐγράφοντο οὗτοι οἱ λόγοι ἐν βιβλίῳ. 2. ἐδιδασκόμην ὑπ᾽ αὐτοῦ ἐκ τῶν βιβλίων τῶν προφητῶν. 3. ἐν ἐκείναις ταῖς ἡμέραις καὶ ἐδιδασκόμεθα ὑπ᾽ αὐτοῦ καὶ ἐδιδάσκομεν τοὺς ἄλλους, ἀλλὰ νῦν οὐδὲ διδασκόμεθα οὐδὲ διδάσκομεν. 4. ἀπήρχοντο οἱ ἁμαρτωλοὶ πρὸς τὴν θάλασσαν. 5. ἐξεπορεύετο πρὸς αὐτὸν ἡ ἐκκλησία, ἀλλὰ νῦν οὐκέτι ἐκπορεύεται. 6. οὔπω βλέπομεν τὸν κύριον ἐν τῇ δόξῃ αὐτοῦ, ἀλλὰ ἐδιδασκόμεθα ὑπ᾽ αὐτοῦ καὶ ἐν ταῖς ἡμέραις ταῖς κακαῖς. 7. ἐλέγετο ἐν τῷ ἱερῷ καλὸς λόγος περὶ τούτου τοῦ ἀποστόλου. 8. περὶ αὐτὸν ἐβλέπετο ἡ δόξα αὐτοῦ. 9. ἐφέρετο τὰ δῶρα καὶ πρὸς τοὺς πονηρούς. 10. ἐδέχου τὰ βιβλία ἀπὸ τῶν προφητῶν. 11. συνήρχοντο οἱ μαθηταὶ πρὸς τοῦτον. 12. τὰ ἔργα τοῦ πονηροῦ πονηρά ἐστιν. 13. οὐδὲ αὐτὸς πονηρὸς οὐδὲ τὰ ἔργα πονηρά. 14. ὑπὲρ τῆς ἐκκλησίας αὐτοῦ ἀπέθνησκεν ὁ κύριος. 15. οὐκ ἔστιν μαθητὴς ὑπὲρ τὸν διδάσκαλον αὐτοῦ οὐδὲ δοῦλος ὑπὲρ τὸν κύριον αὐτοῦ. 16. ἐν τῷ πλοίῳ ἦγου πρὸς τὸν κύριον διὰ τῆς θαλάσσης. 17. ἐξήρχεσθε ἐκ τῶν οἴκων ὑμῶν. 18. ταῦτα τὰ δαιμόνια ἐξήρχετο διὰ τοῦ λόγου αὐτοῦ, 19. ἠκούοντο καὶ ἤκουον· ἀκούονται καὶ ἀκούουσιν. 20. ἠρχόμην πρὸς τὸν κύριον, ἦγον δὲ καὶ τοὺς ἄλλους.

II 1. Those words were being heard by the same apostle, but now they are no longer being heard. 2. These books were being written by him in behalf of his servants. 3. I was not yet being taught by this man, but I was leading the others to him. 4. Ye are not above me nor am I above you. 5. Thou wast sending others to him and wast being sent by him to others. 6. The demons were going out of the children. 7. Ye were coming in and going out in the church. 8. We were not yet going away to the sinners, but were still hearing the voice of the apostle and were being taught concerning the Lord out of the books of the prophets. 9. They were going down to the sea and were going through it in boats. 10. Neither the evil nor the good were answering the Lord. 11. We were both seeing and hearing these disciples. 12. Thou wast being saved by the word of the Lord. 13. Not by your works but by the Lord were ye being saved from your sins. 14. Not even the good are saved by works. 15. Through the word of the Lord we were becoming good disciples. 16. Thou wast not dying in behalf of him, but he was dying in behalf of thee.

Lesson XIII

Future Active and Middle Indicative.

150. Vocabulary

ἀναβλέπω, fut. ἀναβλέψω, I look up, I receive my sight

βήσομαι, I shall go, dep. fut. of βαίνω

γενήσομαι, I shall become, dep. fut. of γίνομαι

γνώσομαι, I shall know, dep. fut. of γινώσκω

διδάξω, I shall teach, fut. of διδάσκω

διώκω, fut. διώξω, I pursue, I persecute

δοξάζω, fut. δοξάσω, I glorify

ἐλεύσομαι, I shall come, I shall go, dep. fut. of ἔρχομαι

ἕξω, I shall have, fut. of ἔχω (note the breathing)

κηρύσσω, fut. κηρύξω, I proclaim, I preach

λήμψομαι, I shall take, dep. fut. of λαμβάνω

προσεύχομαι, dep., fut. προσεύξομαι, I pray

τυφλός, ὁ, a blind man

151. The present and imperfect tenses, in all three voices, are formed on the present stem, to which the personal endings, being joined to the stem by the variable vowel ο/ε, are added.

But the future active and middle are formed on the *future stem*, which is formed by adding the tense suffix σ to the stem of the verb. Thus, while λυ- is the stem of the verb (which in the case of λύω is also the present stem), λυσ- is the future stem.

152. The future, being a primary tense, has primary personal endings like the present tense. The variable vowel is also the same. Therefore the future active and middle indicative are conjugated exactly like the present active and middle, except that the future has λυσ- at the beginning instead of λυ-.

153. It will be remembered that in the present and imperfect tenses the middle and passive are alike in form. But in the future the passive is quite different from the middle and will be reserved for a subsequent lesson. λύσομαι, therefore, means *I shall loose for myself,* but it does not mean *I shall be loosed.*

154. The future active indicative of λύω is as follows:

Sing.		Plur.	
1.	λύσω, *I shall loose*	1.	λύσομεν, *we shall loose*
2.	λύσεις, *thou wilt loose*	2.	λύσετε, *ye will loose*
3.	λύσει, *he will loose*	3.	λύσουσι(ν), *they will loose*

155. The future middle indicative of λύω is as follows:

Sing.		Plur.	
1.	λύσομαι, *I shall loose for myself*	1.	λυσόμεθα, *we shall loose for ourselves*
2.	λύσῃ, *thou wilt loose for thyself*	2.	λύσεσθε, *ye will loose for yourselves*
3.	λύσεται, *he will loose for himself*	3.	λύσονται, *they will loose for themselves*

156. Future Active and Middle of Stems Ending in a Consonant

When the stem of a verb ends in a consonant, the addition of the tense suffix σ brings two consonants together. The following results then occur:

(1) π , β, φ (called *labial* mutes because they are pronounced by means of the lips) form with the following σ the double consonant ψ (ps).

Examples: The future of πέμπω is πέμψω, and of γράφω, γράψω.

(2) κ, γ, χ (called *palatal* mutes because they are pronounced by means of the palate) form with the following σ the double consonant ξ (ks).

Examples: The future of ἄγω is ἄξω, and of ἄρχω, ἄρξω.

(3) τ, δ, θ (called *lingual* mutes because they are formed by means of the tongue) drop out before the σ.

Example: The future of πείθω is πείσω.

Formation of the Future Stem and Other Tense Stems of Various Verbs

157. In the case of many verbs the verb stem is different from the present stem.

Examples: (1) The verb stem of κηρύσσω is not κηρυσσ- but κηρυκ-. From κηρυκ- the future κηρύξω is formed by the rule given in §156.

(2) The verb stem of βαπτίζω is not βαπτιζ- but βαπτιδ-, From βαπτιδ- the future βαπτίσω is formed by the rule given in §156.

158. In general, the future of a Greek verb cannot certainly be formed by any rules; it must be looked up in the lexicon for every individual verb, so numerous are the irregularities.

159. The Greek verb is for the most part exceedingly regular in deriving the individual forms indicating voice, mood, person and number from the basal tense stems. But the formation of those basal tense stems from the stem of the verb (and still more from the present stem) is often exceedingly irregular. The basal tense stems, from which all the rest of the verb is formed, are six in number. These six, given with the personal ending for the first person singular indicative, are called the principal parts. So far, only two of the six principal parts of λύω have been learned. From the first of the principal parts, λύω, all of the present and imperfect in all three voices is formed; from the second, λύσω, all of the future active and middle. The present and imperfect together form the *present system*; the future active and middle form the *future system*.

160. The regularity of the Greek verb in making the individual forms within each tense system from the first form of the tense system, and the great irregularity in making the first forms themselves, may be illustrated by the very irregular verb ἔρχομαι. The student would certainly never have expected that the future of ἔρχομαι would be ἐλεύσομαι; but once he has learned from the lexicon that ἐλεύσομαι is the first person singular of the future, the third plural, ἐλεύσονται, for example, can be derived from it exactly as λύσονται is derived from λύσομαι, which in turn is derived from λύσω.

161. From this point on, it will be assumed that the student will use the general vocabularies at the back of the book. The method of using them may be illustrated as follows:

(1) Suppose it is desired to translate *they will begin into Greek*. The first step is to look up the word *begin* in the English-Greek vocabulary.

It is there said that *begin* is expressed by the middle voice of ἄρχω. The next step is to look up the word ἄρχω in the Greek-English vocabulary. With it, in the Greek-English vocabulary, the principal parts are given. The second of the principal parts is the future ἄρξω. It is the future which is desired, because *they will begin* is future. But it is the middle voice of ἄρχω which means *begin*. Therefore we are looking for the future middle indicative (third person plural). That can be derived from ἄρξω after the analogy of λύω. If the paradigm of λύω be consulted, it will be discovered that the future middle indicative, third person plural, is formed from the second of the principal parts by retaining the λυσ- of λύσω and putting on -ονται instead of -ω. Treating ἄρξω in the same way, we keep ἀρξ- and add -ονται to it. Thus ἄρξονται is the form desired.

(2) If the form σώσει is found in the Greek-English exercises, the student will naturally guess that the second σ is the sign of the future just as the σ is in λύσει. He will therefore look up verbs beginning with σω-. Without difficulty σώζω will be found, and its future (the second of the principal parts) is discovered to be σώσω, of which, of course, σώσει is simply the third person singular.

(3) Similarly, if the student sees a form ἄξω he should at once surmise that the σ concealed in the double consonant ξ is the σ of the future. The present, therefore, will naturally be ἄκω or ἄγω or ἄχω. It may be necessary to try all three of these in the vocabulary until it be discovered that ἄγω is correct.

Of course these processes will soon become second nature and will be performed without thought of the individual steps.

162. The more difficult forms will be listed separately in the vocabularies, with references to the verbs from which they come.

163. But the forms of compound verbs will not be thus listed. For example, if the student sees ἀπελεύσεσθε in the exercises, he should observe that ἀπ- is evidently the preposition ἀπο with its final vowel elided. The simple verb form, then, with the preposition removed, is ἐλεύσεσθε. The first person singular would be ἐλεύσομαι. This form will be found in the Greek-English vocabulary and will be designated as the future of ἔρχομαι. Therefore, since ἐλεύσεσθε comes from ἔρχομαι, ἀπελεύσεσθε will come from ἀπέρχομαι, and that is the verb which the student must finally look up.

164. Deponent Future of Certain Verbs

Some verbs are deponent in one tense but not in another.

Examples: βαίνω has a future of the middle form, βήσομαι. It is thus deponent in the future but not in the present.

165. Exercises I

I. 1. ἄξει ὁ κύριος τοὺς μαθητὰς αὐτοῦ εἰς τὴν βασιλείαν. 2. γνωσόμεθα καὶ τοὺς ἀγαθοὺς καὶ τοὺς πονηρούς. 3. λήμψεσθε τὰ πλοῖα ἐκ τῆς θαλάσσης. 4. λύσεις τοὺς δούλους. 5. ἕξουσιν οἱ πονηροὶ οὐδὲ χαρὰν οὐδὲ εἰρήνην. 6. ἐν ἐκείνῃ τῇ ὥρᾳ ἐλεύσεται ὁ υἱὸς τοῦ ἀνθρώπου[1] σὺν τοῖς ἀγγέλοις αὐτοῦ. 7. ἁμαρτωλοὶ ἐστέ, γενήσεσθε δὲ μαθηταὶ τοῦ κυρίου. 8. διώκουσιν οἱ πονηροὶ τοὺς προφήτας, ἀλλ' ἐν ταῖς ἡμέραις τοῦ υἱοῦ τοῦ ἀνθρώπου οὐκέτι διώξουσιν αὐτούς. 9. προσεύξῃ τῷ θεῷ σου καὶ δοξάσεις αὐτόν. 10. τότε γνώσεσθε ὅτι αὐτός ἐστιν ὁ κύριος. 11. ταῦτα γνώσομαι οὐδὲ ἐγώ. 12. ἄλλους διδάξει ὁ δοῦλος, ἀλλ' ἐμὲ διδάξει ὁ διδάσκαλος ὁ πιστός. 13. ἐκεῖνα λήμψονται οἱ ἀπόστολοι, ταῦτα δὲ καὶ οἱ ἀδελφοί. 14. διὰ τοῦ λόγου τοῦ κυρίου ἀναβλέψουσιν οἱ τυφλοὶ οὗτοι. 15. ὁ προφήτης αὐτὸς γράψει ταῦτα ἐν ταῖς γραφαῖς. 16. ἐλεύσονται κακαὶ ἡμέραι. 17. ἀπελεύσῃ καὶ σὺ εἰς τὰς ὁδοὺς τῶν πονηρῶν καὶ διδάξεις οὕτως τοὺς ἀνθρώπους. 18. κηρύξουσιν καὶ αὐτοὶ τὸ εὐαγγέλιον ἐν τούτῳ τῷ κόσμῳ τῷ κακῷ. 19. ἐλεύσεται καὶ αὕτη πρὸς αὐτόν, καὶ αὐτὸς διδάξει αὐτήν. 20. ἐκηρύσσετο τὸ εὐαγγέλιον ἐν ταῖς ἡμέραις ταῖς κακαῖς, κηρύσσεται δὲ καὶ νῦν, ἀλλ' ἐν ἐκείνῃ τῇ ἡμέρᾳ ἐλεύσεται ὁ κύριος αὐτός.

II 1. The Church will send servants to me. 2. These women will become good. 3. These words I shall write in a book. 4. These things will come into the world in those days. 5. Now he is not yet teaching me, but in that hour he shall both teach me and know me. 6. They were pursuing these women in the evil days, and they will pursue them even into the other places. 7. Then will blind men pray to the Lord, but

---

[1] ὁ υἱὸς τοῦ ἀνθρώπου, the Son of Man. This is the form in which the phrase occurs in the gospels as a self-designation of Jesus.

evil men will not pray. 8. The gifts were being taken by us from the children, but we shall take them no longer. 9. We shall pray for (in behalf of) the same children in the Church. 10. In this world we have death, but in the kingdom of God we shall have both love and glory. 11. Then we were being taught by the apostles, but in that day we also shall teach. 12. In those days I was persecuting you, but now ye shall persecute me. 13. Thou wilt not go down to the sea, but wilt pursue these women with their children into the desert. 14. They were preaching this gospel, but now they will no longer preach it. 15. These things are evil, but you will have good things in that day. 16. The Lord will come to His Church in glory.

Lesson XIV

First Aorist Active and Middle Indicative.
Constructions with πιστεύω.

166. Vocabulary

ἀπολύω, ἀπολύσω, ἀπέλυσα,
  I release
ἐκήρυξα, I preached, I
  proclaimed, aor. of κηρύσσω
ἐπιστρέφω, ἐπιστρέψω,
  ἐπέστρεψα, I turn, I return
ἑτοιμάζω, ἑτοιμάσω,
  ἡτοίμασα, I prepare
ἤδη, adv., already

θαυμάζω, θαυμάσω,
  ἐθαύμασα, I wonder, I
  marvel, I wonder at
θεραπεύω, θεραπεύσω,
  ἐθεράπευσα, I heal
πείθω, πείσω, ἔπεισα, I
  persuade
πιστεύω, πιστεύσω,
  ἐπίστευσα, I believe
ὑποστρέφω, ὑποστρέψω,
  ὑπέστρεψα, I return

167. The *first aorist* is not a different tense from the *second aorist*, which will be studied in the next lesson, but first aorist and second aorist are merely two different ways of forming the same tense of a verb. Thus the English *I loved* is not a different tense from *I threw*, but the verb *love* and the verb *throw* form the "preterit" (simple past tense) in two different ways.

168. The aorist is like the imperfect in that it refers to past time. But the imperfect refers to continuous action in past time, while the aorist is the simple past tense. Thus the imperfect ἔλυον means *I was loosing*, while the aorist ἔλυσα means *I loosed*. It will be remembered that in present time this distinction between the simple assertion of the act and the assertion of continued (or repeated) action is not made in Greek (λύω, therefore, means either *I loose* or I am *loosing*). But in past time the distinction is very carefully made; the Greek language shows no tendency whatever to confuse the aorist with the imperfect.

169. It should be observed, however, that the aorist tense is often translated by the English perfect. ἔλυσα, therefore, may mean I have loosed as well as I loosed. The Greek perfect, which will be studied in

68

Lesson XXIX, though it is indeed often to be translated by *I have loosed*, has a very different range from that of this English tense. Where the English *I have loosed* merely asserts that the action has taken place in past time without any implications as to its present results, it is translated by the Greek aorist.

Examples: ἠκούσατε τὴν φωνήν μου, *ye have heard my voice*. This sentence merely asserts that the action has taken place at some unspecified *time* in the past. But if a *then* were added, and thus the interval between the past action and the present time when the assertion is being made were clearly marked, the English would have the simple preterit. Thus τότε ἠκούσατε τὴν φωνήν μου would be translated *then ye heard my voice*.

170. The context will usually determine quite clearly whether a Greek aorist is to be translated in English by the simple past tense (e.g. *I loosed*) or by the perfect tense (e.g. *I have loosed*). The former translation should be adopted in the exercises unless it is perfectly certain that the other is intended. What the student needs to understand first is that the aorist is the simple past tense.

171. The first aorist active indicative of λύω is as follows:

	Sing.		Plur.
1.	ἔλυσα, *I loosed*	1.	ἐλύσαμεν, *we loosed*
2.	ἔλυσας, *thou loosedst*	2.	ἐλύσατε, *ye loosed*
3.	ἔλυσε(ν), *he loosed*	3.	ἔλυσαν, *they loosed*

172. The aorist, being a secondary tense (like the imperfect), has the augment. The augment is the same for the aorist as it is for the imperfect (see §124-§126).

173. The aorist, like the imperfect, has the secondary endings. It will be remembered (see §127) that these, in the active voice, are as follows:

	Sing.		Plur.
1.	-ν	1.	-μεν
2.	-ς	2.	-τε
3.	none	3.	-ν (or –σαν)

174. It should be observed that in the first aorist the ν is dropped in the first person singular.

175. Before these personal endings, there stands, in the aorist, not a variable vowel, but the tense suffix, σα, which is added to the stem of the verb. Thus, where the future has σο/ε, the first aorist has σα.

176. In the third person singular this σα is changed to σε. ἔλυσε(ν) may have the movable ν, like the ἔλυε(ν) of the imperfect.

177. The form ἐλύσαμεν — to take it as an example — may be divided as follows: ἐ/λύ/σα/μεν. ἐ is the augment, λύ is the stem of the verb, σα is the sign of the first aorist, and μεν is the secondary personal ending in the first person plural active.

178. The first aorist middle indicative of λύω is as follows:

	Sing.			Plur.	
1.	ἐλυσάμην	*I loosed for myself*	1.	ἐλυσάμεθα	*we loosed for ourselves*
2.	ἐλύσω	*thou loosedst for thyself*	2.	ἐλύσασθε	*ye loosed for yourselves*
3.	ἐλύσατο	*he loosed for himself*	3.	ἐλύσαντο	*They loosed for themselves*

179. As in the future tense so in the aorist tense, the passive voice is entirely distinct in form from the middle. ἐλυσάμην, therefore, means I loosed for myself, but it does not mean I was loosed.

180. Like the aorist active, the aorist middle has the secondary personal endings. It will be remembered (see §139) that in the middle these secondary personal endings are as follows:

	Sing.		Plur.
1.	-μην	1.	-μεθα
2.	-σο	2.	-σθε
3.	-το	3.	-ντο

181. These are preceded, as in the active, by the tense suffix, σα. No changes occur except in the second person singular, where ἐλύσω is a shortened form for an original ἐλύσασο.

182. The form ἐλυσάμεθα — to take it as an example — is made up as follows: ἐ/λυ/σά/μεθα. ἐ is the augment, λυ is the stem of the verb, σά is the tense suffix, μεθα is the secondary personal ending in the first person plural middle.

183. The changes caused by the joining of the σα of the first aorist tense suffix to the stems of various verbs are like those caused by the σο/ε of the future. As in the case of the future, however, it cannot be predicted with certainty what the aorist of a Greek verb will be. Every verb must be looked up in the lexicon separately. For this purpose the student should use the general vocabulary at the end of the book in the manner described in §161-§163. Only, for the aorist active and middle, we shall be interested in the third of the principal parts, not in the second.

184. Constructions with πιστεύω

The verb πιστεύω takes the dative. Thus πιστεύω τῷ ἀνθρώπῳ means *I believe the man.*

The verb πιστεύω followed by εἰς with the accusative is to be translated by *I believe in* or *on.* Thus πιστεύω εἰς τὸν κύριον means *I believe in the Lord* or *I believe on the Lord.* It must not be supposed, however, that the preposition εἰς with the accusative here really means *in* like ἐν with the dative. Rather is it to be said that the Greek language merely looks at the act of believing in a different way from the English; Greek thinks of putting one's faith *into* some one.

185. Exercises

I. 1. ἀπέλυσεν ὁ κύριος τὸν δοῦλον αὐτοῦ, ὁ δὲ δοῦλος οὐκ ἀπέλυσε τὸν ἄλλον. 2. ἤδη ἐπέστρεψαν οὗτοι πρὸς τὸν κύριον, ἐκεῖνοι δὲ ἐπιστρέψουσιν ἐν ταῖς ἡμέραις ταῖς κακαῖς. 3. ἐπιστεύσαμεν εἰς τὸν κύριον καὶ σώσει ἡμᾶς. 4. καὶ ἐπίστευσας εἰς αὐτὸν καὶ πιστεύσεις. 5. ὑπέστρεψας πρὸς τὸν κύριον καὶ ἐδέξατό σε εἰς τὴν ἐκκλησίαν αὐτοῦ. 6. ἐν ἐκείναις ταῖς ἡμέραις ἐπορεύεσθε ἐν ταῖς ὁδοῖς ταῖς κακαῖς. 7. ἐπεστρέψατε πρὸς τὸν κύριον καὶ ἐθεράπευσεν ὑμᾶς. 8. ἐκεῖνοι πονηροί, ἀλλ᾽ ἡμεῖς ἐπείσαμεν αὐτούς. 9. ἡτοίμασα ὑμῖν τόπον ἐν τῷ οὐρανῷ. 10. ἐδεξάμην σε εἰς τὸν οἶκόν μου, ἀλλ᾽ οὗτοι οἱ πονηροὶ οὐκ ἐδέξαντο. 11. ἀνέβλεψαν οἱ τυφλοί. 12. ἔσωσα ὑμᾶς ἐγώ, ὑμεῖς δὲ ἐμὲ οὐκ ἐδέξασθε εἰς τοὺς οἴκους ὑμῶν. 13. πονηροὶ ἦσαν αὐτοί, πονηροὺς δὲ ἔπεμψαν εἰς τὴν ἐκκλησίαν. 14. ἐδίδαξάς με ἐν τῷ ἱερῷ. 15. τότε ἠκούσαμεν ταύτας τὰς ἐντολάς, ἄλλας δὲ ἀκούσομεν ἐν τῇ ἐκκλησίᾳ. 16. ἐν ἐκείνῃ τῇ ὥρᾳ ἐξελεύσονται ἐκ τοῦ κόσμου, τότε δὲ ἐδέξαντο ἡμᾶς. 17. ἤκουσαν αὐτοῦ καὶ ἐθαύμασαν. 18. ἐδέξω σὺ τὸ εὐαγγέλιον, οὗτοι δὲ οὐ δέξονται αὐτό. 19. οὐδὲ ἠκούσαμεν τὸν κύριον οὐδὲ ἐπιστεύσαμεν εἰς αὐτόν.

II 1. We did not receive the gospel, because we did not hear the voice of the apostle. 2. In those days we were not believing in the Lord, but this disciple persuaded us. 3. The sinner turned unto the Lord, and already is being taught by Him. 4. The servants have prepared houses for you. 5. This blind man believed in the Lord. 6. The children wondered, and the disciples believed. 7. Thou didst not pray to the Lord, and on account of this He did not heal thee. 8. Those evil men pursued these women into the desert. 9. I have preached the gospel to them. 10. Ye persecuted me, but I did not persecute you. 11. These blind men glorified the Lord, because He had healed[1] them. 12. Through His disciples He proclaimed His gospel to the world. 13. The promises are good, and we received them. 14. Ye have received the same promises and believed on the same Lord. 15. He has not preached the gospel nor does he preach it now. 16. That woman has neither glorified the Lord nor received the children.

---

[1] The English pluperfect is often to be translated by the Greek aorist.

Lesson XV

Second Aorist Active and Middle Indicative.

186. Vocabulary

γάρ, conj., postpositive (see §91), *for*

ἔβαλον, *I threw, I cast*, 2nd aor. of βάλλω

ἐγενόμην, *I became*, dep. 2nd aor. of γίνομαι

εἶδον[1], *I saw*, 2nd aor. of βλέπω (may also be regarded as 2nd aor. of ὁράω)

εἶπον, *I said*, 2nd aor. of λέγω

ἔλαβον, *I took*, 2nd aor. of λαμβάνω

ἤγαγον, *I led*, 2nd aor. of ἄγω

ἦλθον, *I came, I went*, 2nd aor. of ἔρχομαι

ἤνεγκα, *I bore, I brought*, 1st aor. of φέρω (conjugated like the 1st aor. of λύω, but with -κα instead of -σα)

λείπω, 2nd aor. ἔλιπον, *I leave*

ὄψομαι, *I shall see*, dep. fut. of βλέπω (may also be regarded as future of ὁράω)

πίπτω, 2nd aor. ἔπεσον, *I fall*

προσφέρω, *I bring to* (takes the accusative of the thing that is brought and the dative of the person to whom it is brought. Example: προσφέρω τὰ τέκνα τῷ κυρίῳ, *I bring the children to the Lord*)

187. It has already been observed that the second aorist is not a different tense from the first aorist, but only a different way of forming the same tense. Very few verbs, therefore, have both a first aorist and a second aorist, just as very few verbs in English form their preterit both by adding -ed and by making changes within the body of the word.

---

[1] In the New Testament, εἶδον has, in the indicative, almost exclusively first aorist endings, instead of second aorist endings, and in other verbs also first aorist endings are often placed on second aorist stems. See J. H. Moulton, A Grammar of New Testament Greek, Vol. II, 1920, "Accidence and Word Formation" , edited by W . F. Howard, pp. 208f., note 1. It is therefore rather a concession to weakness when εἶδον etc. are here treated as second aorist throughout. But this procedure will probably be better until the nature of the second aorist becomes thoroughly familiar to the student. The first aorist endings can afterwards easily be recognized when they occur. Compare §521.

Thus the preterit of *live* is *lived*, and the preterit of *rise* is *rose*, but *live* has no preterit *love*, nor has *rise* a preterit *rised*. The uses of the tense lived are exactly the same as the uses of the tense rose. So also in Greek the uses of the second aorist are exactly the same as the uses of the first aorist.

188. It cannot be determined beforehand whether a verb is going to have a first aorist or a second aorist, nor if it has a second aorist what the form of that second aorist will be. These matters can be settled only by an examination of the lexicon for each individual verb.

189. The *second aorist system* (consisting of all moods of the second aorist active and middle) differs from the *present system* (consisting of all moods of the present and imperfect active, middle and passive), not by adding -σα or any other tense suffix to the stem of the verb, but by differences, as over against the present, within the body of the word. Usually these differences mean that the second aorist has gotten back nearer to the real, fundamental verb stem than the present has.

Examples: (1) λαμβάνω has a second aorist ἔλαβον, λαβ- being the second aorist stem and λαμβαν- the present stem. (2) βάλλω has a second aorist ἔβαλον, βαλ- being the second aorist stem and βαλλ- the present stem.

190. Upon the second aorist stem are formed the second aorist active and middle. The aorist passive of all verbs is different from the aorist middle, whether the aorist middle is first aorist or second aorist, ἐλιπόμην, therefore, the aorist middle of λείπω, does not mean *I was left*. In order to translate *I was left*, an entirely different form, the aorist passive, would be used.

191. The second aorist, being a secondary tense, has an augment, which is just like the augment of the imperfect. Thus a second aorist stem like λιπ- (of λείπω) , which begins with a consonant, prefixes ἐ to make the augment (the stem λιπ- thus making ἔλιπον), while a second aorist stem like ἐλθ-, which begins with a vowel, lengthens that vowel (the stem ἐλθ- thus making ἦλθον).

192. The second aorist, being a secondary tense, has secondary personal endings. Between these and the stem comes the variable vowel o/ε exactly as in the present and imperfect. The second aorist indicative, therefore, is conjugated exactly like the imperfect, except that the imperfect is formed on the present stem, while the second aorist indicative is formed on the second aorist stem. Thus ἐλείπομεν means we were leaving (imperfect), whereas ἐλίπομεν means *we left* (second aorist). Sometimes a single letter serves to distinguish imperfect from second aorist. ἐβάλλομεν, for example, means *we were throwing* (imperfect), whereas ἐβάλομεν means *we threw* (second aorist).

193. The second aorist active indicative of λείπω, *I leave*, is as follows:

	Sing.		Plur.
1.	ἔλιπον, *I left*	1.	ἐλίπομεν, *we left*
2.	ἔλιπες, *thou leftst*	2.	ἐλίπετε, *ye left*
3.	ἔλιπε(ν), *he left*	3.	ἔλιπον, *they left*

194. The second aorist middle indicative of λείπω is as follows:

	Sing.		Plur.
1.	ἐλιπόμην	1.	ἐλιπόμεθα
2.	ἐλίπου	2.	ἐλίπεσθε
3.	ἐλίπετο	3.	ἐλίποντο

195. Exercises

I 1. καὶ εἴδομεν τὸν κύριον καὶ ἠκούσαμεν τοὺς λόγους αὐτοῦ. 2. οὐδὲ γὰρ εἰσῆλθες εἰς τοὺς οἴκους αὐτῶν οὐδὲ εἶπες αὐτοῖς παραβολήν. 3. ἐν ἐκείνῃ τῇ ὥρᾳ ἐγένοντο μαθηταὶ τοῦ κυρίου. 4. οὗτοι μὲν ἐγένοντο μαθηταὶ ἀγαθοί, ἐκεῖνοι δὲ ἔτι ἦσαν πονηροί. 5. προσέφερον αὐτῷ τοὺς τυφλούς. 6. ἔπεσον ἐκ τοῦ οὐρανοῦ οἱ ἄγγελοι οἱ πονηροί. 7. τὰ μὲν δαιμόνια ἐξεβάλετε, τὰ δὲ τέκνα ἐθεραπεύσατε. 8. τοὺς μὲν πονηροὺς συνηγάγετε ὑμεῖς εἰς τοὺς οἴκους ὑμῶν, τοὺς δὲ ἀγαθοὺς ἡμεῖς. 9. οὐκ ἐκήρυξας τὸ εὐαγγέλιον ἐν τῇ ἐκκλησίᾳ, οὐδὲ γὰρ ἐγένου μαθητής. 10. νῦν μὲν λέγετε λόγους ἀγαθούς, εἶπον δὲ οὗτοι τοὺς αὐτοὺς λόγους καὶ ἐν ταῖς ἡμέραις ἐκείναις. 11. ἐπιστεύσαμεν εἰς τὸν κύριον, οἱ γὰρ μαθηταὶ ἤγαγον ἡμᾶς πρὸς αὐτόν. 12. ταῦτα μὲν εἶπον ὑμῖν ἐν τῷ ἱερῷ, ἐκεῖνα δὲ οὔπω λέγω. 13. τότε μὲν εἰσήλθετε εἰς τὴν ἐκκλησίαν, ἐν ἐκείνῃ δὲ τῇ ἡμέρᾳ εἰσελεύσεσθε εἰς τὸν οὐρανόν. 14. τότε ὀψόμεθα τὸν κύριον ἐν τῇ δόξῃ αὐτοῦ· ἐπιστεύσαμεν γὰρ εἰς αὐτόν. 15. ὁ μὲν κύριος ἐξῆλθε τότε ἐκ τοῦ κόσμου, οἱ δὲ μαθηταὶ αὐτοῦ ἔτι μένουσιν ἐν αὐτῷ. 16. ταύτας τὰς ἐντολὰς ἔλαβον ἀπὸ τοῦ κυρίου, ἤμην γὰρ μαθητὴς αὐτοῦ. 17. τότε μὲν παρελάβετε τὴν ἐπαγγελίαν παρὰ τοῦ κυρίου, νῦν δὲ καὶ κηρύσσετε αὐτὴν ἐν τῷ κόσμῳ. 18. ἤλθετε πρὸς τὸν κύριον καὶ παρελάβετε παρ' αὐτοῦ ταῦτα. 19. συνήγαγεν ἡμᾶς αὐτὸς εἰς τὴν ἐκκλησίαν αὐτοῦ. 20. εἶδον οἱ ἄνθρωποι τὸν υἱὸν τοῦ θεοῦ· ἐγένετο γὰρ αὐτὸς ἄνθρωπος καὶ ἔμενεν ἐν τούτῳ τῷ κόσμῳ.

II 1. We did not see Him, for we were not yet disciples of Him. 2. The apostle brought the sinners to Him. 3. Ye did not hear me, but ye came to my disciples. 4. Ye entered into this house, but the others went out of it. 5. The sinners were going into their houses, but the apostles saw the Lord. 6. In those days we shall see the Lord, but in the evil days we did not see Him. 7. Thy brothers were taking gifts from the children, but the apostles took the children from them. 8. You became a servant of the apostle, but the apostle became to you even a brother. 9. Ye have become a church of God, for ye have believed on His Son. 10. He has gathered together His disciples into His kingdom. 11. The faithful teacher said that the Lord is good. 12. They believed in the Lord and brought others also to Him. 13. They heard the children and came to them. 14. We received joy and peace from God, because we were already entering into His kingdom. 15. The disciples say that the apostles saw the Lord and received this from Him. 16. You went out into the desert, but the apostle said these things to his brethren.

Lesson XVI

Aorist Passive Indicative. Future Passive Indicative.

196. Vocabulary

ἀναλαμβάνω, *I take up*

ἐβλήθην, *I was thrown, I was cast*, aor. pass. of βάλλω

ἐγενήθην, *I became*, aor., pass. in form, of γίνομαι

ἐγνώσθην, *I was known*, aor. pass. of γινώσκω

ἐδιδάχθην, *I was taught*, aor. pass. of διδάσκω

ἐκηρύχθην, *I was preached, I was proclaimed*, aor. pass. of κηρύσσω

ἐλήμφθην, *I was taken*, aor. pass. of λαμβάνω

ἐπορεύθην, *I went*, aor., passive in form of πορεύομαι

ἠγέρθην, *I was raised*, aor. pass. of ἐγείρω

ἠκούσθην, *I was heard*, aor. pass. of ἀκούω

ἠνέχθην, *I was borne, I was brought*, aor. pass. of φέρω

ἤχθην, *I was led*, aor. pass. of ἄγω

ὤφθην, *I was seen*, aor. pass. of βλέπω (may also be regarded as aor. pass. of ὁράω)

197. The aorist passive indicative and the future passive indicative are formed on the aorist passive stem, which appears in the sixth place among the principal parts. The fourth and fifth of the principal parts will be studied in a subsequent lesson.

198. The aorist passive stem is formed by adding θε to the verb stem. This θε is lengthened throughout the indicative to θη. Thus the aorist passive stem of λύω appears as λυθη-.

199. The aorist being a secondary tense, the augment, formed exactly as in the case of the imperfect (see §124-§126), is prefixed to the tense stem, and the secondary personal endings are added. These personal endings are of the *active* form (see §127), and are like those which are used in the imperfect active indicative except that in the third person plural the alternative ending -σαν is chosen instead of -ν. In the aorist passive indicative, the personal endings are added directly to the tense stem, without any variable vowel intervening.

77

200. The future passive indicative is formed by adding -σ o/ε to the aorist passive stem (with its θε lengthened to θη), which, however, since the future is a primary not a secondary tense, has in the future no augment. To this future passive stem, λυθησ o/ε, the middle primary endings are added, and the future passive is conjugated exactly like the future middle except that the stem is λυθησ o/ε instead of λυσ o/ε.

201. The aorist passive indicative of λύω is as follows:

Sing.			Plur.		
1.	ἐλύθην	I was loosed	1.	ἐλύθημεν	we were loosed
2.	ἐλύθης	thou wast loosed	2.	ἐλύθητε	ye were loosed
3.	ἐλύθη	he was loosed	3.	ἐλύθησαν	they were loosed

202. The future passive indicative of λύω is as follows:

Sing.			Plur.		
1.	λυθήσομαι	I shall be loosed	1.	λυθησόμεθα	we shall be loosed
2.	λυθήσῃ	thou wilt be loosed	2.	λυθήσεσθε	ye will be loosed
3.	λυθήσεται	he will be loosed	3.	λυθήσονται	they will be loosed

203. The uses of the parts of the verb which have been studied so far may be summarized as follows:

Present Indicative	Active.	λύω	=	I loose. or I am loosing.
	Middle.	λύομαι	=	I loose for myself. or I am loosing for myself.
	Passive.	λύομαι	=	I am being loosed.

Imperfect Indicative	Active.	ἔλυον	=	I was loosing.
	Middle.	ἐλυόμην	=	I was loosing for myself.
	Passive.	ἐλυόμην	=	I was being loosed.

Future	Active.	λύω	= *I shall loosed.*
Indicative	Middle.	λύομαι	= *I shall loose for myself.*
	Passive.	λύομαι	= *I shall be loosed.*
Aorist	Active.	λύω	= *I loosed.*
Indicative	Middle.	λύομαι	= *I loosed for myself.*
	Passive.	λύομαι	= *I was loosed.*

Formation of Aorist Passive Stems of Verbs Whose Verb Stems End in a Consonant

204. Before the θ of the aorist passive tense-suffix, a final π or β of the verb stem is changed to φ, a final κ or γ is changed to χ, and a final τ, δ, or θ is changed to σ. The changes in the case of π, β, κ, γ can be remembered if it be observed that θ is equivalent to th and that what the changes amount to is adding on an h to the preceding letters so as to make them conform to the th. Thus before th, p or b becomes ph, and k or g becomes ch.

Examples: The aorist passive of πέμπω is ἐπέμφθην, of ἄγω, ἤχθην, of πείθω, ἐπείσθην.

205. Like the other principal parts, however, the aorist passive of a Greek verb cannot be formed with any certainty on the basis of general rules, but must be noted for each verb separately.

206. Second Aorist Passive

Some verbs have a *second aorist passive* instead of a first aorist passive. This second aorist passive is conjugated in the indicative exactly like a first aorist passive. But it has no θ in the tense stem.

Example: The second aorist passive indicative of γράφω is ἐγράφην, ἐγράφης, ἐγράφη, ἐγράφημεν, ἐγράφητε, ἐγράφησαν. Aorist and Future of Deponent Verbs

207. Some deponent verbs have passive, not middle, forms. Example: The aorist of ἀποκρίνομαι, *I answer*, is ἀπεκρίθην, *I answered*[1].

208. Some deponent verbs have both middle and passive forms.

---

[1] But occasionally ἀποκρίνομαι has middle forms.

Example: The aorist of γίνομαι, I become, is either ἐγενόμην, *I became*, or ἐγενήθην, *I became*, ἐγενόμην and ἐγενήθην mean exactly the same thing, both the middle and the passive forms having active meaning.

209. Exercises

I 1. ἐπιστεύσαμεν εἰς τὸν κύριον καὶ ἐγνώσθημεν ὑπ᾽ αὐτοῦ. 2. ταῦτα ἐγράφη ἐν τοῖς βιβλίοις. 3. ἐδιδάξατε τὰ τέκνα, ἐδιδάχθητε δὲ καὶ αὐτοὶ ὑπὸ τοῦ κυρίου. 4. ἐλήμφθησαν οἱ πιστοὶ εἰς τὸν οὐρανόν, ἐξεβλήθησαν δὲ ἐξ αὐτοῦ οἱ ἄγγελοι οἱ πονηροί. 5. ἐγερθήσονται οἱ νεκροὶ τῷ λόγῳ τοῦ κυρίου. 6. οὗτοι οἱ τυφλοὶ συνήχθησαν εἰς τὴν ἐκκλησίαν. 7. ἐξεβλήθη τὰ δαιμόνια· ὁ γὰρ κύριος ἐξέβαλεν αὐτά. 8. πέμπονται μὲν καὶ νῦν οἱ μαθηταί, ἐπέμφθησαν δὲ τότε οἱ ἀπόστολοι καὶ πεμφθήσονται ἐν ἐκείνῃ τῇ ἡμέρᾳ καὶ οἱ ἄγγελοι. 9. εἰσῆλθες εἰς τὴν ἐκκλησίαν καὶ ἐβαπτίσθης. 10. ἐπιστεύθη ἐν κόσμῳ[1],ἀνελήμφθη ἐν δόξῃ. 11. οἱ ἁμαρτωλοὶ ἐσώθησαν ἐν ἐκείνῃ τῇ ὥρᾳ καὶ ἐγενήθησαν μαθηταὶ τοῦ κυρίου. 12. ἐπορεύθημεν εἰς ἕτερον τόπον· οὐ γὰρ δέξονται ἡμᾶς οὗτοι. 13. ἐδοξάσθη ὁ θεὸς ὑπὸ τοῦ υἱοῦ, ἐδόξασε δὲ αὐτόν. 14. τὸ εὐαγγέλιον ἐκηρύχθη ἐν ταῖς ἡμέραις ἐκείναις, κηρυχθήσεται δὲ καὶ νῦν. 15. ἑτοιμασθήσεται ἡμῖν τόπος ἐν οὐρανῷ κατὰ τὴν ἐπαγγελίαν τοῦ κυρίου. 16. τὰ τέκνα προσηνέχθησαν τῷ κυρίῳ. 17. εἶδον οὗτοι τὸ πρόσωπον τοῦ κυρίου καὶ ἤκουσαν τῆς φωνῆς αὐτοῦ. 18. ἐν τῷ μικρῷ οἴκῳ ἀκουσθήσεται ἡ φωνὴ τοῦ ἀποστόλου. 19. πρῶτός εἰμι τῶν ἁμαρτωλῶν, ἐσώθην δὲ καὶ ἐγώ. 20. ὀψόμεθα μὲν τοὺς ἀγγέλους, ὀφθησόμεθα δὲ καὶ ὑπ᾽ αὐτῶν.

II 1. This is the Church of God, but the sinners were brought into it. 2. This man was cast out on account of the gospel. 3. I was sent to the sinners, but you were being sent to your brothers. 4. Thou didst not receive the gospel, but the others received it and were saved. 5. These words have been written by the apostles. 6. The servants will come into the house, but the sons were baptized in that hour. 7. Ye will see the Lord in heaven, but the apostles were taught by Him. 8. The disciples brought the blind men to the Lord, but the children were led by others. 9. The gifts were being received from the servants, but the law was

---

[1] The article is often omitted with κόσμος. See §311

80

proclaimed to the world. 10. A place was prepared for the brethren. 11. We went to the sea, but our sons will go into the temple. 12. After these things, they were taken up into glory. 13. The Son of Man was raised up from the dead[1] and was glorified. 14. The promises of God were heard in the world.

---

[1] From the dead, ἐκ νεκρῶν.

Lesson XVII

The Third Declension.

210. Vocabulary

ἅγιος, α, ον, adj., *holy*;
οἱ ἅγιοι, *the saints*
αἷμα, αἵματος, τό, *blood*
αἰών, αἰῶνος, ὁ, *an age*; εἰς
    τὸν αἰῶνα, *for ever*; εἰς τοὺς
    αἰῶνας τῶν αἰώνων, *for
    ever and ever*
ἄρχων, ἄρχοντος, ὁ, *a ruler*
γράμμα, γράμματος, τό, *a
letter*

ἐλπίς, ἐλπίδος, ἡ, *a hope*
θέλημα, θελήματος, τό, *a will*
νύξ, νυκτός, ἡ, *a night*
ὄνομα, ὀνόματος, τό, *a name*
πνεῦμα, πνεύματος, τό, *a
    spirit, the Spirit*
ῥῆμα, ῥήματος, τό, *a word*
σάρξ, σαρκός, ἡ, *flesh*
σῶμα, σώματος, τό, *a body*

211. The declensions of (1) ἐλπίς, ἐλπίδος, ἡ, *a hope*, (2) νύξ, νυκτός, ἡ, *a night*, and (3) ἄρχων, ἄρχοντος, ὁ, *a ruler*, are as follows:

ἐλπίς, ἡ, stem ἐλπιδ- νύξ, ἡ, stem νυκτ- ἄρχων, ὁ stem ἀρχοντ-
Sing. N

Sing.	N.	ἐλπίς	νύξ	ἄρχων
	G.	ἐλπίδος	νυκτός	ἄρχοντος
	D.	ἐλπίδι	νυκτί	ἄρχοντι
	A.	ἐλπιδα	νύκτα	ἄρχοντα
	V.	ἐλπί	νύξ	ἄρχων
Plur.	N.V.	ἐλπίδες	νύκτες	ἄρχοντες
	G.	ἐλπίδων	νυκτῶν	ἀρχόντων
	D.	ἐλπίσι	νυξί(ν)	ἄρχουσι(ν)
	A.	ἐλπίδας	νύκτας	ἄρχοντας

212. The case endings in the third declension are as follows:

	Sing.		Plur.
N.	-ς or none	N.V.	-ες
G.	-ος	G.	-ων
D.	-ι	D.	-σι
A.	-α	A.	-ας
V.	Like nominative or		
	none.		

213. These case endings are added to the stem, and the stem can be discovered, not from the nominative, as is possible in the first and second declensions, but only by dropping off the -ος of the genitive singular. Thus the genitive singular must be known before any third declension noun can be declined.

214. It will be observed that both in the accusative singular ending and in the accusative plural ending the α is short. The dative plural -σι(ν) may have the movable ν. (See §44.)

215. The nominative is formed in various ways, which it will probably be most convenient not to try to classify.

216. The vocative also is formed differently in different nouns. It is very often like the nominative.

217. In the dative plural the combination of consonants formed by the -σι of the case ending coming after the final consonant of the stem causes various changes, which are in general the same as those set forth in §156. But where two consonants, as ντ, are dropped before the following σ, the preceding vowel is lengthened, ο, however, being lengthened not to ω but to ου. So in ἄρχουσι(ν), the dative plural of ἄρχων.

218. The gender of third declension nouns, except in the case of certain special classes like the nouns in -μα, -ματος , cannot easily be reduced to rules, and so must be learned for each noun separately.

219. Thus if the student is asked what the word for *flesh* is, it is quite insufficient for him to say that it is σάρξ. What he must rather say is that it is σάρξ, σαρκός, feminine. Without the genitive singular, it would be impossible to determine the stem; and unless the stem is known, of course the noun cannot be declined. And without knowing the gender, one could not use the word correctly. One could not tell, for example, whether ὁ σάρξ or ἡ σάρξ or τὸ σάρξ would be correct.

220. These two difficulties, coupled with the difficulty of the dative plural, make the third declension more difficult than the first and second. Otherwise the declension is easy, when once the case endings have been thoroughly mastered and have been distinguished clearly from those of the other two declensions.

221. Monosyllables of the Third Declension

Monosyllabic nouns of the third declension have the accent on the ultima in the genitive and dative of both numbers. In the genitive plural it is the circumflex.

Example: σάρξ, σαρκός, σαρκῶν.

This rule is an exception to the rule of noun accent. In accordance with the rule of noun accent, the accent would remain on the same syllable as in the nominative singular so nearly as the general rules of accent would permit.

222. Nouns in -μα

An important class of nouns in -μα, with stems ending in -ματ, are declined like ὄνομα. These nouns are all neuter. The declension of ὄνομα, ὀνόματος, τό, *a name*, is as follows:

	Sing.		Plur.
N.A.V.	ὄνομα	N.A.V.	ὀνόματα
G.	ὀνόματος	G.	ὀνομάτων
D.	ὀνόματι	D.	ὀνόμασι(ν)

Since ὄνομα is a neuter noun, it has its accusative and vocative of both numbers like the nominative, and its nominative, accusative, and vocative plural ending in α. (See §42.)

223. The declensions of other third-declension nouns will be found in §559-§566, and can be referred to as they are needed.

224. Exercises

I 1. ἐλπίδα οὐκ ἔχουσιν οὐδὲ τὸ πνεῦμα τὸ ἅγιον. 2. διὰ τὴν ἐλπίδα τὴν καλὴν ἤνεγκαν ταῦτα οἱ μαθηταὶ τοῦ κυρίου. 3. ταῦτά ἐστιν τὰ ῥήματα τοῦ ἁγίου πνεύματος. 4. ἐγράφη τὰ ὀνόματα ὑμῶν ὑπὸ τοῦ θεοῦ ἐν τῷ βιβλίῳ τῆς ζωῆς. 5. τῷ λόγῳ τοῦ κυρίου ἔσωσεν ἡμᾶς ὁ θεός. 6. οἱ ἄρχοντες οἱ πονηροὶ οὐκ ἐπίστευσαν εἰς τὸ ὄνομα τοῦ κυρίου. 7. ταῦτα εἶπον ἐκεῖνοι τοὺς ἄρχουσιν τούτου τοῦ αἰῶνος. 8. ὄψεσθε ὑμεῖς τὸ πρόσωπον τοῦ κυρίου εἰς τὸν αἰῶνα, ἀλλ' οὐκ ὄψονται αὐτὸ οἱ πονηροί, ὅτι οὐκ ἐπίστευσαν εἰς τὸ ὄνομα αὐτοῦ. 9. οὐκέτι κατὰ σάρκα γινώσκομεν τὸν κύριον. 10. ἐν τῇ σαρκὶ ὑμῶν εἴδετε τὸν θάνατον, ἀλλὰ διὰ τοῦ ἁγίου πνεύματος ἔχετε ἐλπίδα καλήν. 11. τὸ μὲν γράμμα ἀποκτείνει, ἐν τῷ δὲ πνεύματι ἔχετε ζωήν. 12. βλέπομεν τὸ πρόσωπον τοῦ κυρίου καὶ ἐν νυκτὶ[1] καὶ ἐν ἡμέρᾳ. 13. ἐδίδαξαν οἱ μαθηταὶ καὶ τοὺς ἄρχοντας καὶ τοὺς δούλους. 14. ἐν ἐκείνῃ τῇ νυκτὶ εἴδετε τὸν ἄρχοντα τὸν πονηρόν. 15. μετὰ τῶν ἀρχόντων ἤμην ἐν ἐκείνῳ τῷ οἴκῳ. 16. μετὰ δὲ ἐκείνην τὴν νύκτα ἦλθεν οὗτος ἐν τῷ πνεύματι εἰς τὴν ἔρημον. 17. ταῦτά ἐστιν ῥήματα ἐλπίδος καὶ ζωῆς. 18. ἤγαγεν αὐτὸν τὸ ἅγιον πνεῦμα εἰς τὸ ἱερόν. 19. ταῦτα τὰ ῥήματα ἐκηρύχθη ἐν ἐκείνῃ τῇ νυκτὶ τοῖς δούλοις τοῦ ἄρχοντος. 20. ἠγέρθησαν τὰ σώματα τῶν ἁγίων.

II 1. By the will of God we believed on the name of the Lord. 2. The rulers did not receive this hope from the apostle, because they did not believe in the Lord. 3. We shall know the will of God for ever. 4. In this age we have death, but in that age hope and life. 5. In our flesh we remain in this age, but through the Spirit of God we have a good hope. 6. By the will of God we were saved from our sins through the blood of the Lord. 7. In those days ye saw the rulers. 8. This age is evil, but in it we have hope. 9. These words we wrote to the rulers. 10. We came to the good ruler and to the apostle of the Lord. 11. In our bodies we shall see death, but we shall be raised up according to the word of God. 12. Ye were persecuted by the ruler, but the blood of the Lord saves you from sin. 13. We wrote those good words to the evil ruler. 14. This night became to them an hour of death, but they believed on the name of the Lord. 15. The evil spirits were cast out by the word of the Lord.

---

[1] In phrases such as ἐν νυκτί and ἐν ἡμέρᾳ, the article is often omitted.

Lesson XVIII

Present Participles. Use of Participles.

225. Vocabulary

προσέρχομαι, dep., *I come to, I go to*, with dative.

ὤν, οὖσα, ὄν, *being*, present participle of εἰμί (for declension, see §580)

226. The declension of λύων, λύουσα, λῦον, *loosing*, the present active participle of λύω, is as follows:

	Sing.		
	M.	F.	N.
N.V.	λύων	λύουσα	λῦον
G.	λύοντος	λυούσης	λύοντος
D.	λύοντι	λυούσῃ	λύοντι
A.	λύοντα	λύουσαν	λῦον

	Plur.		
N.V.	λύοντες	λύουσαι	λύοντα
G.	λυόντων	λυουσῶν	λυόντων
D.	λύουσι(ν)	λυούσαις	λύουσι(ν)
A.	λύοντας	λυούσας	λύοντα

227. This declension, like the declension of other adjectives, should be learned across, and not down the columns. See §61.

228. It will be observed that the masculine and neuter are declined according to the third declension (the masculine exactly like ἄρχων) and the feminine according to the first declension (like δόξα). The accent in the genitive plural feminine follows the *noun* rule for the first declension, not the adjective rule (see §51, §62).

229. It will be remembered that in the accusative plural the α in the ending is short in the third declension but long in the first declension.

230. The declension of λυόμενος, η, ον, *loosing for himself*, the present middle participle, and of λυόμενος, η, ον, *being loosed*, the present passive participle of λύω, is as follows:

	Sing.		
	M.	F.	N.
N.V.	λυόμενος	λυομένη	λυόμενον
G.	λυομένου	λυομένης	λυομένου
D.	λυομένῳ	λυομένη	λυομένῳ
A.	λυόμενον	λυομένην	λυόμενον

	Plur.		
N.V.	λυόμενοι	λυόμεναι	λυόμενα
G.	λυομένων	λυομένων	λυομένων
D.	λυομένοις	λυομέναις	λυομένοις
A.	λυομένους	λυομένας	λυόμενα

It will be observed that this declension is like that of adjectives of the second and first declension.

231. The present participles are formed on the present stem of the verb (see §151). The present participles of any regular verb can be made by adding -ων, -ουσα, -ον, and -όμενος -ομένη, -όμενον to the present stem of that verb.

232. Use of Participles

The participles are verbal adjectives. Being adjectives, they have gender, number, and case; and like other adjectives they agree in gender, number, and case with the nouns that they modify. On the other hand, since they partake of the nature of verbs, (a) they have tense and voice, (b) they receive, like other parts of a verb, adverbial modifiers, and (c) if they be participles of a transitive verb they can take a direct object.

Examples: (1) ὁ ἀπόστολος λέγων ταῦτα ἐν τῷ ἱερῷ βλέπει τὸν κύριον, *the apostle, saying these things in the temple, sees the Lord*. Here the participle λέγων, which means *saying*, agrees with ἀπόστολος, which is in the nominative case and singular number and is a masculine noun. The participle, therefore, must be nominative singular masculine. On the other hand, the participle is enough of a verb to have tense and voice. It is in the present tense because the action which it denotes is represented as going on at the same time as the action of the leading verb βλέπει; it is in the active voice because it represents the *apostle* as doing something, not as having something done to him. And it has the adverbial modifier ἐν τῷ ἱερῷ and the direct object ταῦτα. On the other hand, it has no subject, as a finite verb (e.g. an indicative) would have; for the noun ἀπόστολος, which denotes the person represented as performing the action denoted by the participle, is not the subject of the participle, but the noun with which the participle, like any other adjective, agrees.

(2) βλέπομεν τὸν ἀπόστολον λέγοντα ταῦτα ἐν τῷ ἱερῷ, *we see the apostle saying these things in the temple.* Here the noun with which the participle agrees is accusative singular masculine. Therefore the participle must also be accusative singular masculine. But its direct object and its adverbial modifier are the same as in (1).

(3) προσερχόμεθα τῷ ἀποστόλῳ λέγοντι ταῦτα ἐν τῷ ἱερῷ, *we come to the apostle while he is saying these things in the temple.* Here the participle λέγοντι agrees with a masculine noun in the dative singular and must therefore itself be dative singular masculine. But in this example it is quite impossible to translate the participle literally. The translation, *we come to the apostle saying these things in the temple,* would not do at all, for in that English sentence the participle *saying* would be understood as agreeing not with *the apostle* but with the subject of the sentence, we. It is necessary, therefore, to give up all attempts at translating the participle "literally". Instead, we must express the idea which is expressed by the Greek participle in an entirely different way— by the use of a temporal clause. When such temporal clauses are used to translate a Greek *present* participle they are usually introduced by *while.* Such a free translation would have been better than the literal translation even in Example (1), although there the literal translation was not absolutely impossible. It would have been rather better to translate ὁ ἀπόστολος λέγων ταῦτα ἐν τῷ ἱερῷ βλέπει τὸν κύριον by *while the apostle is saying these things in the temple, he sees the Lord.*

(4) διδασκομένῳ ὑπὸ τοῦ ἀποστόλου προσέρχονται αὐτῷ οἱ δοῦλοι, *while he is being taught by the apostle, the servants are coming to him.* Here διδασκομένῳ agrees with αὐτῷ, which, like τῷ ἀποστόλῳ

in the preceding example, is dative with the verb προσέρχομαι. διδασκομένῳ is the present passive participle of διδάσκω.

233. The Tense of the Participle

The tense of the participle is relative to the time of the leading verb.

The present participle, therefore, is used if the action denoted by the participle is represented as taking place at the same time as the action denoted by the leading verb, no matter whether the action denoted by the leading verb is past, present or future.

Examples: (1) διδασκομένῳ ὑπὸ τοῦ ἀποστόλου προσῆλθον αὐτῷ οἱ δοῦλοι, *while he was being taught by the apostle, the servants came to him*. Here the action denoted by the participle διδασκομένῳ, though it is past with reference to the time when the sentence is spoken or written, is present with reference to the time of the leading verb— that is, the teaching was going on at the same time as the coming of the servants. Hence the present participle is used.

(2) πορευομένῳ ἐν τῇ ὁδῷ προσῆλθον αὐτῷ οἱ μαθηταὶ αὐτοῦ, *while he was going in the way, his disciples came to him*. It will be observed that the participles of the deponent verb πορεύομαι, like other parts of that verb, are active in meaning though passive in form. Otherwise this example is like (1).

(3) πορευόμενος ἐν τῇ ὁδῷ εἶδεν τυφλόν, *while he was going in the way, he saw a blind man*. Here it will be observed that the participle frequently agrees with the unexpressed subject of a verb. Similarly λέγων ταῦτα εἶδεν τυφλόν, means *while he was saying these things, he saw a blind man*, and λέγοντες ταῦτα εἴδετε τυφλόν means *while ye were saying these things, ye saw a blind man*.

234. The Attributive Participle

The participle, like any other adjective, can stand in the attributive position.

Examples: (1) It will be remembered (see §70) that ὁ ἀγαθὸς ἀπόστολος means *the good apostle*. In exactly the same way ὁ λέγων ταῦτα ἐν τῷ ἱερῷ ἀπόστολος means *the saying-these-things-in-the-temple apostle*. The participle (with its modifiers) is here an adjective in the attributive position; it takes the exact place of the attributive adjective ἀγαθός in the phrase ὁ ἀγαθὸς ἀπόστολος. It is more usual, however, to place the attributive participle (with its modifiers) in the second of the two alternative positions in which the attributive adjective can stand. Thus the usual order would be ὁ ἀπόστολος ὁ λέγων ταῦτα ἐν τῷ ἱερῷ. Here the λέγων ταῦτα ἐν τῷ ἱερῷ takes the exact place of ἀγαθός in the phrase ὁ ἀπόστολος ὁ ἀγαθός, which is one of the two ways in which *the good apostle* can be expressed.

Of course the "literal" translation, *the saying-these-things-in-the-temple apostle*, is not good English. The idiomatic English way of expressing the same idea is *the apostle who is saying these things in the temple*. The difference between this attributive use of the participle and the use which appears in Example (1) in §232 should be noticed very carefully. In the sentence ὁ ἀπόστολος λέγων ταῦτα ἐν τῷ ἱερῷ βλέπει τὸν κύριον, the participle λέγων, being in the *predicate*, not in the attributive, position, goes only somewhat loosely with ὁ ἀπόστολος (though it agrees with it), and really modifies also the verb βλέπει— that is, it tells when the action denoted by βλέπει took place. But the addition of the one little word ὁ before λέγων makes an enormous difference in the meaning. When that word is added we have the sentence ὁ ἀπόστολος ὁ λέγων ταῦτα ἐν τῷ ἱερῷ βλέπει τὸν κύριον, *the apostle who says these things in the temple sees the Lord*. Here λέγων stands in the attributive position, and does not in any way modify the verb βλέπει; but it tells *what* apostle is being spoken of. Suppose some one asks us what apostle we are talking about. We could reply, "Not the good apostle or the bad apostle, or the great apostle or the small apostle, but *the saying-these-things-in-the-temple apostle*." It will be seen that the attributive participle identifies the particular apostle that we are talking about.

(2) Compare εἶδον τοὺς ἀποστόλους λέγοντας ταῦτα, *I saw the apostles while they were saying these things* or *I saw the apostles saying these things*, with εἶδον τοὺς ἀποστόλους τοὺς λέγοντας ταῦτα, *I saw the apostles {that/who} were saying these things*. In the latter case the (attributive) participle tells *what* apostles we are talking about.

235. Substantive Use of the Participle

The participle, like any other adjective, can be used substantively with the article.

It will be remembered that ὁ ἀγαθός means *the good man*; ἡ ἀγαθή, *the good woman*; τὸ ἀγαθόν, *the good thing*; οἱ ἀγαθοί, *the good men*, etc.

In exactly the same way ὁ λέγων ταῦτα ἐν τῷ ἱερῷ means *the saying-these-things-in-the-temple man*. The participle (with its modifiers), just like the adjective, tells *what* man we are talking about. But how shall the same idea be expressed in idiomatic English? There are various closely related ways— for example, *the man who* {says/is saying} *these things in the temple*, or *the one who* {says/is saying} *these things in the temple or he who* {says/is saying} *these things in the temple*. It should be observed, however, that none of these English phrases is a literal translation of the Greek. The Greek ὁ does not mean *the man* or *the one* or *he*. It means *the*, and it is just as simple an article as the article in the phrase *the cat* or *the dog* or *the house*. But in English we do not use the article with the substantive participle. Therefore we have to reproduce the idea of the Greek ὁ λέγων by a phrase of which the individual parts have absolutely nothing to do with the individual parts of the Greek phrase. It is only the total meaning of the English phrase which is the same as the total meaning of the Greek phrase.

The following examples should also be examined:

(1) εἶδον τὸν λέγοντα ταῦτα ἐν τῷ ἱερῷ, *I saw the one who was saying these things in the temple*. Here the Greek uses the present participle because the time of the action denoted by the participle is the same as that of the action denoted by the leading verb, even though the action denoted by the leading verb here happens to be in past time.

(2) εἶδον τοὺς λέγοντας ταῦτα, *I saw those who were saying these things*.

(3) ὁ ἀδελφὸς τῆς λεγούσης ταῦτα δοῦλός ἐστιν, *the brother of the woman who is saying these things is a servant*.

(4) ὁ πιστεύων εἰς τὸν ἐγείροντα τοὺς νεκροὺς σώζεται, *he who believes on the One who raises the dead is being saved*.

(5) τὸ σῶζον τοὺς ἀνθρώπους τὸ θέλημα τοῦ θεοῦ ἐστιν, *the thing that saves (or that which saves) men is the will of God*.

(6) τὰ βλεπόμενα οὐ μένει εἰς τὸν αἰῶνα, *the things that are seen do not remain for ever*.

236. The following summary may be found useful:

Present Participles

Act λύων   = *loosing*
Mid λυόμενος   = *loosing for himself*
Pass λυόμενος   = *being loosed*

Present Participles with Article

Act. ὁ λύων, *the loosing man*

$$= \begin{cases} \textit{the man who looses} \\ \textit{the one who looses} \\ \textit{he who looses.} \end{cases}$$

Mid. ὁ λυόμενος, *the loosing-for-himself man*

$$= \begin{cases} \textit{the man who looses for himself} \\ \textit{the one who looses for himself} \\ \textit{he who looses for himself.} \end{cases}$$

ὁ λυόμενος, *the being-loosed man*

$$= \begin{cases} \textit{the man who is being loosed} \\ \textit{the one who is being loosed} \\ \textit{he who is being loosed.} \end{cases}$$

τὸ λῦον, *the loosing thing*

$$= \begin{cases} \textit{the thing that looses} \\ \textit{that which looses} \end{cases}$$

οἱ λύοντες, *the loosing men the men who loose*

$$= \begin{cases} \textit{the men who loose} \\ \textit{the ones who loose} \\ \textit{those who loose} \end{cases}$$

237. It should be noticed that the English word *he* in the phrase *he who looses is not a real*— certainly not an ordinary— personal pronoun, but merely the light antecedent of the relative pronoun *who*. *He* has no value of its own but goes in the closest possible way with *who*, so as to form the phrase *he who*. The Greek language, rather strangely as it may seem to us, possesses no such light antecedent of the relative. The ordinary Greek way, therefore, of expressing the idea *he who looses* is to use article with participle and say *the loosing man*, ὁ λύων. Similarly, the English word *that* in the phrase *that which looses*, and the English word *those* in the phrase *those who loose*, are not really demonstrative adjectives or pronouns; they do not really "point out" anything. They are very different, for example, from the demonstratives in the phrases *that house across the street* or *those trees over there on the campus*. The *that* and the *those* in these sentences could be accompanied by a pointing finger; they are real demonstratives. But the *that* and the *those* in the phrases *that which looses* or *those that loose* are simply light antecedents of the relative, and for them the Greek has no equivalent. Such phrases, therefore, must be cast into an entirely different mold before they can be translated into Greek.

238. The English word *that* has a number of widely different uses. It is (1) a conjunction, (2) a demonstrative adjective or pronoun, (3) a light antecedent of the relative, and (4) a relative pronoun like *which*.

Example: *I know that that which saves the men that receive that gospel is the will of God.* Here the first that is a conjunction; the second, the light antecedent of the relative; the third, a relative pronoun; the fourth, a real demonstrative. The Greek language has a different way of expressing each of these uses of that. The sentence in Greek would be as follows: γινώσκω ὅτι τὸ σῷζον τοὺς δεχομένους ἐκεῖνο τὸ εὐαγγέλιον τὸ θέλημα τοῦ θεοῦ ἐστιν.

The two uses of the English word *those* may be illustrated by the sentence, *those who believe will receive those good men*, οἱ πιστεύοντες δέξονται ἐκείνους τοὺς ἀγαθούς.

239. The importance of this lesson and the two following lessons can hardly be overestimated. Unless the student understands thoroughly the use of participles, it will be quite impossible for him ever to master the later lessons or to read the Greek Testament. The participle is quite the crucial matter in the study of Greek.

240. Exercises

I 1. διωκόμενοι ὑπὸ τοῦ ἄρχοντος προσευχόμεθα τῷ θεῷ. 2. ὁ σὲ δεχόμενος δέχεται καὶ τὸν κύριον. 3. ταῦτα λέγομεν τοῖς πορευομένοις εἰς τὸν οἶκον περὶ τοῦ ἐγείροντος τοὺς νεκρούς. 4. ἐξερχομένοις ἐκ τῆς ἐκκλησίας λέγει ἡμῖν ταῦτα. 5. αἱ ἐκκλησίαι αἱ διωκόμεναι ὑπὸ τῶν ἀρχόντων πιστεύουσιν εἰς τὸν κύριον. 6. οἱ πιστεύοντες εἰς τὸν κύριον σῴζονται. 7. γινώσκει ὁ θεὸς τὰ γραφόμενα ἐν τῷ βιβλίῳ τῆς ζωῆς. 8. ἐξήλθομεν πρὸς αὐτοὺς ἄγοντες τὰ τέκνα. 9. εἴδομεν τοὺς λαμβάνοντας τὰ δῶρα ἀπὸ τῶν τέκνων. 10. οὗτός ἐστιν ὁ ἄρχων ὁ δεχόμενός με εἰς τὸν οἶκον αὐτοῦ. 11. ἅγιοί εἰσιν οἱ πιστεύοντες εἰς τὸν κύριον καὶ σωζόμενοι ὑπ' αὐτοῦ. 12. τοῦτό ἐστι τὸ πνεῦμα τὸ σῶζον ἡμᾶς. 13. ἦσαν ἐν τῷ οἴκῳ τῷ λυομένῳ ὑπὸ τοῦ ἄρχοντος. 14. ἦσαν ἐν τῷ οἴκῳ λυομένῳ ὑπὸ τοῦ ἄρχοντος. 15. αὕτη ἐστὶν ἡ ἐκκλησία ἡ πιστεύουσα εἰς τοῦ κύριον. 16. διδασκόμενοι ὑπὸ τοῦ κυρίου ἐπορεύεσθε ἐν τῇ ὁδῷ τῇ ἀναβαινούσῃ εἰς τὴν ἔρημον. 17. ἐκηρύχθη ὑπ' αὐτῶν τὸ εὐαγγέλιον τὸ σῶζον τοὺς ἁμαρτωλούς. 18. τοῦτό ἐστιν τὸ εὐαγγέλιον τὸ κηρυσσόμενον ἐν τῷ κόσμῳ καὶ σῶζον τοὺς ἀνθρώπους. 19. ἦλθον πρὸς αὐτὸν βαπτίζοντα τοὺς μαθητάς. 20. ἔτι ὄντα ἐν τῷ ἱερῷ εἴδομεν αὐτόν.

II 1. While he was still in the[1] flesh the Lord was saving those who were believing on Him. 2. While we were being taught in the temple we were being persecuted by the ruler. 3. Those who are being saved by the Lord know Him who saves them. 4. Those who were proclaiming these things received, themselves also, the things which were being proclaimed by them. 5. She who is receiving the Lord into her house sees the face of the One who saves her. 6. While He was still teaching in the temple we saw Him. 7. While we were teaching in the temple we saw the One who saves us. 8. The hope that is seen is not hope. 9. The Lord said to those who were believing on Him that God saves sinners. 10. The brothers of those who persecute the disciples have not hope. 11. Those who say these things do not know the One who saves the Church. 12. We were cast out by the ruler who persecutes the Church. 13. This is the voice which is being heard by those who believe in the Lord. 14. While I was remaining in the house, I saw the women who were taking gifts from the disciples. 15. Being preached by those who believe in the Lord, the gospel will lead men into the Church. 16. The faithful ones will see the Lord going up into heaven.

---

[1] In such phrases, the article is often omitted in Greek.

Lesson XIX

Aorist Participles Active and Middle. Use of Participles
(continued). The Negatives οὐ and μή.

241. Vocabulary

ἀγαγών, *having led*, 2nd aor.
    act. part. of ἄγω
ἀπέθανον, *I died*, 2nd aor. of
    ἀποθνῄσκω
ἀπεκρίθην, *I answered*, aor.
    indic., pass. in form, of
    ἀποκρίνομαι
εἰπών, *having said*, 2nd aor.
    act. part. of λέγω

ἐλθών, *having come*, 2nd aor.
    part. of ἔρχομαι
ἐνεγκών, *having borne, having
    brought*, 2nd aor. act. part. of
    φέρω (the 1st aorist,
    ἤνεγκα, is commoner in the
    indicative)
ἰδών, *having seen*, 2nd aor. act.
    part. of βλέπω (or ὁράω)

242. The declension of λύσας, λύσασα, λυσαν, having loosed, the
aorist active participle of λύω, is as follows:

Sing.

	M.	F.	N.
N.V.	λύσας	λύσασα	λῦσαν
G.	λύσαντος	λυσάσης	λύσαντος
D.	λύσαντι	λυσάσῃ	λύσαντι
A.	λύσαντα	λύσασαν	λῦσαν

Plur.

N.V.	λύσαντες	λύσασαι	λύσαντα
G.	λυσάντων	λυσασῶν	λυσάντων
D.	λύσασι(ν)	λυσάσαις	λύσασι(ν)
A.	λύσαντας	λυσάσας	λύσαντα

243. Like the present active participle, the aorist active participle is
declined according to the third declension in the masculine and neuter,
and according to the first declension in the feminine.

244. The characteristic σα, which, it will be remembered is the sign
of the aorist system (the third of the principal parts), appears

throughout. This σα, as in the rest of the aorist system, is added to the verb stem.

245. The augment, however, appears only in the indicative mood. Thus, although the aorist active indicative of λύω is ἔλυσα, the aorist active participle is not ἐλύσας, but λύσας, and although the aorist active indicative of ἀκούω is ἤκουσα the aorist active participle is not ἤκούσας but ἀκούσας.

246. The declension of λυσάμενος, η, ον, *having loosed for himself*, the aorist middle participle of λύω, is as follows:

	Sing.		
	M.	F.	N.
N.V.	λυσάμενος	λυσαμένη	λυσάμενον
G.	λυσαμένου	λυσαμένης	λυσαμένου
D.	λυσαμένῳ	λυσαμένη	λυσαμένῳ
A.	λυσάμενον	λυσαμένην	λυσάμενον
	Plur.		
N.V.	λυσάμενοι	λυσάμεναι	λυσάμενα
G.	λυσαμένων	λυσαμένων	λυσαμένων
D.	λυσαμένοις	λυσαμέναις	λυσαμένοις
A.	λυσαμένους	λυσαμένας	λυσάμενα

247. Like the present middle and passive participle, the aorist middle participle (the aorist passive is quite different) is declined like an ordinary adjective of the second and first declension.

248. Like the aorist active participle and the rest of the aorist system, the aorist middle participle is formed on the aorist stem. The characteristic σα appears throughout.

249. The declension of ἰδών, ἰδοῦσα, ἰδόν, having seen, the second aorist active participle of βλέπω (it may also be regarded as coming from ὁράω), is as follows:

	M.	**Sing.** **F.**	**N.**
N.V.	ἰδών	ἰδοῦσα	ἰδόν
G.	ἰδόντος	ἰδούσης	ἰδόντος
D.	ἰδόντι	ἰδούσῃ	ἰδόντι
A.	ἰδόντα	ἰδοῦσαν	ἰδόν
		Plur.	
N.V.	ἰδόντες	ἰδοῦσαι	ἰδόντα
G.	ἰδόντων	ἰδουσῶν	ἰδόντων
D.	ἰδοῦσι(ν)	ἰδούσαις	ἰδοῦσι(ν)
A.	ἰδόντας	ἰδούσας	ἰδόντα

250. It will be observed that the second aorist active participle is declined like the present active participle except that it has an irregular accent. The accent on the first form does not follow the verb rule of recessive accent, but is on the ultima. Thereafter the noun rule is followed, the accent remaining on the same syllable throughout, except in the genitive plural feminine, where §51 comes into play.

251. It will be remembered that the augment appears only in the indicative mood. It must therefore be dropped from the third of the principal parts before the aorist participle can be formed. In irregular verbs like βλέπω (ὁράω) the dropping of the augment in the second aorist sometimes gives difficulty. The third of the principal parts of βλέπω (ὁράω) is εἶδον. Without the augment the second aorist stem is ἰδ-, for ι was here irregularly augmented to ει. On the other hand, the second aorist participle of λέγω is εἰπών (εἶπον being the second aorist indicative), because here εἰπ- was the second aorist stem and being regarded as long enough already was not changed at all for the augment.

252. Except in the case of a few such verbs, where the dropping of the augment from the third of the principal parts in order to get the aorist stem to which the -ων is added to form the participle, might give difficulty, the student is expected to perform the necessary processes for himself. Thus if a form ἀποθανών is found in the exercises, the student is expected to see that this form is the participle of a second aorist of which the indicative (with the augment) is ἀπέθανον. This form, since the verb is irregular, will be found in the general vocabulary.

253. The second aorist middle participle is declined exactly like the present middle participle, and differs from the present middle participle only because it is formed on the second aorist stem instead of on the present stem. Thus λαβόμενος is the second aorist middle participle of λαμβάνω, ἔλαβον being the second aorist active indicative (third of the principal parts).

254. Use of the Aorist Participle

In accordance with the principle formulated in §233, that the tense of the participle is relative to the time of the leading verb, the aorist participle denotes action prior to the action denoted by the leading verb, whether the action denoted by the leading verb is past, present or future.

Examples:

(1) ὁ ἀπόστολος εἰπὼν ταῦτα ἐν τῷ ἱερῷ βλέπει τὸν κύριον, *the apostle having said these things in the temple is seeing the Lord*. Here εἰπὼν, the aorist participle, denotes action prior to the action denoted by βλέπει. Compare Example (1) in §232.

(2) εἰπὼν ταῦτα ἀπῆλθεν, *having said these things he went away*. The literal translation of the participle is here perfectly possible. But it would be more idiomatic English to translate, *when he had said these things he went away*, or *after he had said these things he went away*. Compare λέγων ταῦτα ἀπῆλθεν, *he went away saying these things* or *while he was saying these things he went away*. Notice that when a Greek present participle is translated by a temporal clause in English, the English word that introduces the temporal clause is naturally *while*, and when it is an aorist participle that is to be translated into English, the English word introducing the temporal clause is naturally *when* or *after*. In the case of the aorist participle, the verb in the English temporal clause will often be perfect ("has seen", etc.) or pluperfect ("had seen", etc.)—perfect when the leading verb is present or future, and pluperfect when the leading verb is past.

(3) εἰπὼν ταῦτα ἀπέρχεται, *having said these things he goes away, or after he has said these things he goes away*.

99

(4) προσῆλθον αὐτῷ εἰπόντι ταῦτα, *they came to him after he had said these things*. Here the literal translation of the participle would be absolutely impossible in English, because in the English sentence *they came to him having said these things*, the *having said* would agree not with him but with the subject of the sentence, they, and the sentence would be a translation, not of προσῆλθον αὐτῷ εἰπόντι ταῦτα but of προσῆλθον αὐτῷ εἰπόντες ταῦτα. Compare with προσῆλθον αὐτῷ εἰπόντι ταῦτα the sentence προσῆλθον αὐτῷ λέγοντι ταῦτα, which means *they came to him while he was saying these things*.

(5) ἐλθόντες πρὸς τὸν κύριον ὀψόμεθα αὐτόν, *having come to the Lord we shall see Him*, or *when* (or *after*) *we have come to the Lord we shall see Him*.

255. The aorist participle can of course be used attributively or substantively with the article (see §234, §235).

Examples: (1) ὁ μαθητὴς ὁ ἀκούσας ταῦτα ἐν τῷ ἱερῷ ἦλθεν εἰς τὸν οἶκον, *the having-heard-these-things-in-the-temple disciple went into the house*, or *the disciple who {heard/had heard} these things in the temple went into the house*. On the other hand, ὁ μαθητὴς ἀκούσας ταῦτα ἐν τῷ ἱερῷ ἦλθεν εἰς τὸν οἶκον would mean *the disciple, when he had heard these things in the temple, went into the house*.

(2) ὁ ἀκούσας ταῦτα ἀπῆλθεν, *the having-heard-these-things man went away*, or *{he/the one/the man} who {heard/had heard} these things went away*. On the other hand ἀκούσας ταῦτα ἀπῆλθεν would mean *having heard these things he went away* or *when he had heard these things he went away*. In the former sentence ὁ ἀκούσας tells what man we are talking about, while ἀκούσας without the article merely adds a detail about a person who is designated in some other way or not designated at all.

(3) εἶδον τοὺς εἰπόντας ταῦτα, *I saw the having-said-these-things men*, or *I saw {those/the ones/the men} who had said these things*.

The student should compare with these examples the corresponding examples given for the present participle.

256. The Negatives

οὐ is the negative of the indicative, μή is the negative of the other moods, including the infinitive and the participle.

100

Example: ὁ μή πιστεύων οὐ σῴζεται, the not-believing one is not saved, or he who does not believe is not saved. Here μή negatives the participle πιστεύων, and οὐ negatives the indicative σῴζεται.

257. Exercises

I 1. λαβόντες ταῦτα παρὰ τῶν πιστευόντων εἰς τὸν κύριον ἐξήλθομεν εἰς τὴν ἔρημον. 2. πισταί εἰσιν αἱ δεξάμεναι τοὺς διωκομένους ὑπὸ τοῦ ἄρχοντος. 3. εἴδομεν αὐτοὺς καὶ μένοντας ἐν τῷ οἴκῳ καὶ ἐξελθόντας ἐξ αὐτοῦ. 4. οἱ ἰδόντες τὸν κύριον ἦλθον πρὸς τοὺς ἀγαγόντας τὸν μαθητὴν ἐκ τοῦ ἱεροῦ. 5. ταῦτα εἴπομεν περὶ τοῦ σώσαντος ἡμᾶς. 6. οὗτοί εἰσιν οἱ κηρύξαντες τὸ εὐαγγέλιον, ἀλλ' ἐκεῖνοί εἰσιν οἱ διώξαντες τοὺς πιστεύοντας. 7. προσενεγκόντες τῷ κυρίῳ τὸν διωκόμενον ὑπὸ τοῦ ἄρχοντος τοῦ πονηροῦ ἀπήλθετε εἰς ἄλλον τόπον. 8. προσῆλθον τῷ κυρίῳ ἐλθόντι εἰς τὸ ἱερόν. 9. ἐπίστευσας εἰς αὐτόν εἰπόντα ταῦτα. 10. ταῦτα εἶπον ἐξελθὼν ἐκ τῆς ἐκκλησίας. 11 ὁ μὴ ἰδὼν τὸν κύριον οὐκ ἐπίστευσεν εἰς αὐτόν. 12. ταῦτα εἶπεν ὁ κύριος ἔτι ὢν ἐν τῇ ὁδῷ τοῖς ἐξελθοῦσιν ἐκ τοῦ οἴκου καὶ πορευομένοις μετ' αὐτοῦ. 13. ἀκούσαντες τὰ λεγόμενα ὑπὸ τοῦ κυρίου ἐπίστευσαν εἰς αὐτόν. 14. εἴδομεν τοὺς γενομένους μαθητὰς τοῦ κυρίου καὶ ἔτι μένοντας ἐν τῇ ἐλπίδι αὐτῶν τῇ πρώτῃ. 15. τὰ τέκνα τὰ λαβόντα ταῦτα ἀπὸ τῶν ἀκουσάντων τοῦ κυρίου εἶδον αὐτὸν ἔτι ὄντα ἐν τῷ οἴκῳ. 16. ἰδοῦσαι αὗται τὸν κηρύξαντα τὸ εὐαγγέλιον ἐκεῖνο ἦλθον πρὸς αὐτὸν ἐρχόμενον εἰς τὸν οἶκον. 17. οἱ ἄγγελοι οἱ πεσόντες ἐκ τοῦ οὐρανοῦ πονηροὶ ἦσαν. 18. ἰδόντες τοὺς ἔτι ὄντας ἐν τῷ ἱερῷ ἐκήρυξαν αὐτοῖς τὴν βασιλείαν τοῦ θεοῦ. 19. ταῦτα ἀπεκρίθη τοῖς προσενεγκοῦσιν αὐτῷ τὰ τέκνα. 20. ἀπήλθομεν μὴ ἰδόντες τὸν διδάξαντα ἡμᾶς.

II 1. Those who have not seen the apostle do not know him. 2. I did not see him who had believed on the Lord. 3. I saw him after he had believed on the Lord, but ye saw him while he was still in the kingdom of the Evil One. 4. Having heard these things we believed on Him who had died in behalf of us. 5. We came to those who were going in the way. 6. We shall see the apostle after we have gone into this house. 7. Those men said to those who had gone into the house that the Lord is good. 8. While we were saying these things we were going into our house. 9. When they had received these gifts from the ones who had brought them, they came together into the church. 10. These are the women who received the one who had taught them. 11. When these men had seen the Lord, they were brought to the rulers. 12. The disciples who had come into the church were baptized by the apostles who had seen the Lord. 13. The blind man who had received this man was with those who were persecuting him. 14. The demons that were being cast out said this to him who was casting them out. 15. As we were going through the desert, we taught those who were with us. 16. We saw the servant when he had believed on the Lord and was still in the house.

Lesson XX

Aorist Passive Participle. Genitive Absolute.

258. Vocabulary

γραφείς, *having been written*,
2nd aor. pass. part. of
γράφω (declined like a 1st
aor. pass. part.)
ἐκεῖ, adv., *there*
εὐθέως or εὐθύς, adv.,
immediately

ἱμάτιον, τό, *a garment*
οἰκία, ἡ, *a house* (a synonym of
οἶκος)
παιδίον, τό, *a little child*
συναγωγή, ἡ, *a synagogue*
στρατιώτης, ου, ὁ, *a soldier*
φυλακή, ἡ, a guard, *a prison*

259. The declension of λυθείς, λυθεῖσα, λυθέν, having been loosed,
the aorist passive participle of λύω, is as follows:

	Sing.		
	M.	F.	N.
N.V.	λυθείς	λυθεῖσα	λυθέν
G.	λυθέντος	λυθείσης	λυθέντος
D.	λυθέντι	λυθείσῃ	λυθέντι
A.	λυθέντα	λυθεῖσαν	λυθέν

	Plur.		
N.V.	λυθέντες	λυθεῖσαι	λυθέντα
G.	λυθέντων	λυθεισῶν	λυθέντων
D.	λυθεῖσι(ν)	λυθείσαις	λυθεῖσι(ν)
A.	λυθέντας	λυθείσας	λυθέντα

260. Like the present active participle and the aorist active participle,
the aorist passive participle is declined according to the third
declension in the masculine and neuter, and according to the first
declension in the feminine.

261. The characteristic -θε, which it will be remembered is the sign
of the aorist passive system (the sixth of the principal parts), appears
throughout. This -θε, as in the rest of the aorist passive system, is
added to the verb stem.

103

262. The augment, of course, must be dropped (from the sixth of the principal parts) before the aorist passive participle can be formed. Compare §251, §252.

263. The aorist passive participle has an irregular accent, the accent in the nominative singular masculine not being recessive. In the other forms of the declension the rule of noun accent is followed, except of course in the genitive plural feminine, where §51, §228 come into play.

264. Like the other aorist participles, the aorist passive participle denotes action prior to the time of the leading verb; and to it applies also all that has been said about the attributive and substantive uses of the participle.

Examples:

(1) ἐκβληθέντα τὰ δαιμόνια ὑπὸ τοῦ κυρίου ἀπηλθεν εἰς τὴν θάλασσαν, the demons, *having been cast out by the Lord, went away into the sea*, or {*when/after*} *the demons had been cast out by the Lord, they went away into the sea.*

(2) ἐγερθέντι ἐκ νεκρῶν προσῆλθον αὐτῷ, *they came to Him after He had been raised from the dead.*

(3) οἱ διδαχθέντες ὑπὸ τοῦ ἀποστόλου ἦλθον εἰς τὸν οἶκον, *the having-been-taught-by-the-apostle men came into the house*, or {*the men/the ones/those*} *who had been taught by the apostle came into the house.*

265. The following summary will serve for the review of what has been learned thus far about the participles:

I. The Participles

Present	Act. λύων	=	loosing
	Mid. λυόμενος	=	loosing for himself
	Pass. λυόμενος	=	being loosed
Aorist	Act. λύσας	=	loosing
	Mid. λυσάμενος.	=	loosing for himself
	Pass. λυσάμενος	=	being loosed

II. Article with Participle

Present	Act. ὁ λύων *the loosing man.*	=	the man who looses. the one who looses. he who looses.
	Mid. ὁ λυόμενος *the loosing-for- himself-man.*	=	*the man who looses for himself.* *the one who looses for himself.* *he who looses for himself.*
	Pass. ὁ λυόμενος *the being-loosed man.*	=	*the man who is being loosed.* *the one who is being loosed.* *he who is being loosed.*
Aorist	Act. ὁ λύσας *the having-loosed man.*	=	*the man who (has)loosed.* *the one who (has) loosed.* *he who (has) loosed.*
	Mid. ὁ λυσάμενος *the having-loosed- for-himself man.*	=	*the man who (has) loosed for himself.* *the one who (has) loosed for himself.* *he who (has) loosed for himself.*
	Pass. ὁ λυθείς *the having-been- loosed man.*	=	*the man who ($has\ been \atop was$) loosed.* *the one who ($has\ been \atop was$) loosed.* *he who ($has\ been \atop was$) loosed.*

266. The Genitive Absolute

A noun or pronoun with a participle often stands out of connection with the rest of the sentence in the construction called the *genitive absolute*.

Examples: (1) εἰπόντων ταῦντα τῶν ἀποστόλων οἱ μαθηταὶ ἀπῆλθον, *the apostles having said these things, the disciples went away.* Here εἰπόντων and τῶν ἀποστόλων stand in the genitive absolute.

ἀποστόλων is not the subject of any verb, the subject of the only finite verb in the sentence being μαθηταί, nor has it any other connection with the framework of the sentence. It is therefore *absolute* (the word means "loosed" or "separated"). In the English translation, *the apostles having said* is in the absolute case, which in English grammar is called the nominative absolute. But this nominative absolute is very much less common in English than the genitive absolute is in Greek. Usually, therefore, it is better to translate the Greek genitive absolute by a clause, thus giving up any attempt at a "literal" translation. For example, instead of the "literal" translation of the sentence just given, it would have been better to translate, *when* (or *after*) *the apostles had said these things, the disciples went away*. Of course all that has already been said about the tense of the participle applies to the participle in the genitive absolute as well as in other constructions.

It should be noticed that the genitive absolute is normally used only when the noun or pronoun going with the participle is different from the subject of the finite verb. Thus in the sentence, εἰπόντες ταῦτα οἱ ἀπόστολοι ἀπῆλθον, *the apostles, having said these things, went away*, or *when the apostles had said these things they went away*, the word ἀπόστολοι has a construction in the sentence; it is the subject of the leading verb ἀπῆλθον. Therefore it is not "absolute." But in the former example it is not the apostles but some one else that is represented as performing the action denoted by the leading verb. Hence, in that former example ἀποστόλων is not the subject of the sentence but genitive absolute.

(2) λέγοντος αὐτοῦ ταῦτα οἱ μαθηταὶ ἀπῆλθον, *while he was saying these things, the disciples went away*. Compare λέγων ταῦτα ἀπῆλθεν, *while he was saying these things he went away or he went away saying these things*.

(3) τῶν μαθητῶν διδαχθέντων ὑπὸ τοῦ κυρίου ἐξῆλθον εἰς τὴν ἔρημον οἱ δοῦλοι, *when the disciples had been taught by the Lord, the servants went out into the desert*. Compare οἱ μαθηταὶ διδαχθέντες ὑπὸ τοῦ κυρίου ἐξῆλθον εἰς τὴν ἔρημον, *when the disciples had been taught by the Lord, they went out into the desert*.

106

267. Exercises

I 1. πορευθέντος τοῦ ἄρχοντος πρὸς τὸν κύριον οἱ δοῦλοι εἶπον ταῦτα τοῖς μαθηταῖς. 2. πορευθεὶς πρὸς αὐτοὺς ὁ ἄρχων ἐπίστευσεν εἰς τὸν κύριον. 3. πιστευσάντων ὑμῶν εἰς τὸν κύριον εὐθὺς ἐπίστευσε καὶ ὁ ἄρχων. 4. εἰσελθόντος εἰς τὴν οἰκίαν τοῦ ἐγερθέντος ὑπὸ τοῦ κυρίου οἱ μαθηταὶ ἐθαύμασαν. 5. ἐκβληθέντος αὐτοῦ ἐκ τῆς συναγωγῆς συνήχθησαν οἱ ἄρχοντες. 6. ἐκβληθέντα ἐκ τῆς συναγωγῆς ἐδίδαξεν αὐτὸν ὁ κύριος. 7. εἰπόντος ταῦτα τοῦ πνεύματος τοῦ ἁγίου οἱ μαθηταὶ ἐκήρυξαν τὸν λόγον τοῦ θεοῦ. 8. τοῖς θεραπευθεῖσιν ὑπ' αὐτοῦ εἴπετε ῥήματα ἐλπίδος καὶ ζωῆς. 9. ἐλθόντος τούτου εἰς τὴν οἰκίαν αὐτοῦ εὐθέως εἴπομεν τοῖς ἄλλοις τὰ ῥήματα τὰ παραλημφθέντα ἀπὸ τοῦ κυρίου. 10. βληθέντες εἰς φυλακὴν διὰ τὸ εὐαγγέλιον τὸ κηρυχθὲν αὐτοῖς ὑπὸ τοῦ ἀποστόλου ἐδόξασαν ἐκεῖ τὸν σώσαντα αὐτούς. 11. ἀναλημφθέντος αὐτοῦ εἰς οὐρανὸν εἰσῆλθον οἱ μαθηταὶ εἰς τὴν οἰκίαν αὐτῶν. 12. ἐδέξασθε τοὺς ἐκβληθέντας ἐκ τῆς συναγωγῆς καὶ τὰς δεξαμένας αὐτοὺς εἰς τὰς οἰκίας αὐτῶν. 13. αὗταί εἰσιν αἱ διωχθεῖσαι καὶ ἔτι διωκόμενοι ὑπὸ τῶν ἀρχόντων. 14. αὕτη ἐστὶν ἡ ἐλπὶς ἡ κηρυχθεῖσα ἐν τῷ κόσμῳ ὑπὸ τῶν ἰδόντων τὸν κύριον. 15. τῶν στρατιωτῶν διωξάντων ἡμᾶς εἰς τὴν οἰκίαν ἐδέξαντο ἡμᾶς οἱ ὄντες ἐκεῖ. 16. διωχθέντας ἡμᾶς ὑπὸ τῶν στρατιωτῶν ἐδέξαντο οἱ ὄντες ἐν τῇ οἰκίᾳ. 17. εἰσερχομένῳ σοι εἰς τὴν οἰκίαν προσῆλθον οἱ ἄρχοντες, εἰσελθόντα[1] δὲ ἐξέβαλον. 18. ταῦτα μὲν εἶπον αὐτοῖς προσφέρουσι τὰ παιδία τῷ κυρίῳ, ἐκεῖνα δὲ προσενεγκοῦσιν. 19. πορευομένου μὲν τοῦ κυρίου μετὰ τῶν μαθητῶν αὐτοῦ ἔλεγον οἱ ἀπόστολοι ταῦτα, ἐλθόντος δὲ εἰς τὴν οἰκίαν ἐκεῖνα. 20. ταῦτα εἶπον ὑμῖν ἔτι οὖσιν μετ' ἐμοῦ.

II 1. When the soldiers had taken the garments from the children, the disciples were cast out of the house. 2. When the disciples had been cast out of the synagogue, they came to us. 3. While we were coming into our house, the Lord said these things to the rulers. 4. The Lord said those things to you, both while ye were with Him in the way and after ye had come to the ruler. 5. Those who had heard the apostle saying these things saw the house which had been destroyed by the

---

[1] What noun or pronoun is naturally to be supplied as that with which εἰσελθόντα agrees?

soldiers. 6. When the rulers had heard the things which were being said by the Lord, they persecuted the disciples. 7. While the disciples were being persecuted by the rulers, the apostles were going into another house. 8. Those who went into the house of the ruler were my brothers. 9. When our names have been written into the book of life, we shall see the Lord. 10. Having been brought to the Lord by these disciples we see Him for ever. 11. These are the rulers who have become disciples of Thee. 12. When the apostle had been cast into prison, the disciples who had heard these things went away into another place. 13. After those women had been cast into prison, we went away into the desert. 14. When those who had been cast into prison had seen the man who had been raised up, they marveled and believed on the Lord. 15. When the disciples had led to the Lord those who had been persecuted on account of Him, those servants came to us bringing good gifts. 16. Those who have not received this hope from God will not enter into the kingdom of heaven. Answer Guide is located at the end of this book.

Lesson XXI

The Subjunctive Mood.

268. Vocabulary

ἁμαρτάνω, *I sin*

δικαιοσύνη, ἡ, *righteousness*

ἐάν, conditional particle, with subjunctive, *if*

εἰ, with indicative, *if*

εὐαγγελίζομαι, dep. with middle forms, *I preach the gospel, I preach the gospel to* (with acc. of the thing preached and either acc. or dat. of the person to whom it is preached)

ἵνα, conj., with subjunctive, *in order that*

λαός, ὁ, *a people*

λοιπός, ή, όν, adj. *remaining;* οἱ λοιποί, *the rest* (= the remaining persons)

μακάριος, α, ον, adj., *blessed*

μαρτυρία, ἡ, *a witnessing, a testimony, a witness*

μηδέ, *and not, nor, not even* (with moods other than the indicative); μηδέ..........μηδέ, *neither..........nor*

μηκέτι, *no longer* (with moods other than the indicative)

ὄχλος, ὁ, *a crowd, a multitude*

269. The subjunctive mood occurs only in the present and aorist tenses (except for very rare occurrences of the perfect). It has *primary* personal endings throughout, even in the aorist (which, it will be remembered, is a secondary tense). The personal endings are preceded throughout by a long variable vowel ω/η instead of the short variable vowel o/ε which occurs in the present indicative.

270. The present active subjunctive of λύω is as follows:

	Sing.		Plur.
1.	λύω	1.	λύωμεν
2.	λύῃς	2.	λύητε
3.	λύῃ	3.	λύωσι(ν)

271. The present middle and passive subjunctive of λύω is as follows:

	Sing.		Plur.
1.	λύωμαι	1.	λυώμεθα
2.	λύῃ	2.	λύησθε
3.	λύηται	3.	λύωνται (ν)

272. It will be observed that these present subjunctive forms are like the present indicative forms except that a long vowel comes immediately after the stem, while in the indicative there is a short vowel— ω of the subjunctive standing instead of the ο of the indicative, and η of the subjunctive standing instead of the ε of the indicative. The only exceptions are (1) in the present active, third person plural, where ω in the subjunctive stands instead of ου in the indicative, and (2) in the present middle and passive, second person singular, where the indicative already has η (in λύῃ).

273. The -ωσι(ν) of the third person plural active may have the movable ν.

274. The aorist active subjunctive is as follows:

	Sing.		Plur.
1.	λύσω	1.	λύσωμεν
2.	λύσῃς	2.	λύσητε
3.	λύσῃ	3.	λύσωσι(ν)

275. The aorist middle subjunctive is as follows:

	Sing.		Plur.
1.	λύσωμαι	1.	λυσώμεθα
2.	λύσῃ	2.	λύσησθε
3.	λύσηται	3.	λύσωνται

276. It will be observed that the endings (with variable vowel) are exactly the same in the aorist active and middle subjunctive as they are in the present active and middle subjunctive. But these endings (with variable vowel) are in the aorist added to the aorist stem, whereas in the present they are added to the present stem. The σ makes all the difference.

277. There is in the aorist subjunctive of course no augment (see §245).

278. The second aorist active and middle subjunctive is conjugated exactly like the first aorist subjunctive. Of course, however, it is formed on the second aorist stem.

279. The aorist passive subjunctive is as follows:

	Sing.		Plur.
1.	λυθῶ	1.	λυθῶμεν
2.	λυθῇς	2.	λυθῆτε
3.	λυθῇ	3.	λυθῶσι(ν)

280. The aorist passive subjunctive, like the aorist passive indicative, has active personal endings. The endings (with the variable vowel) are exactly like those in the present active subjunctive. But the rule of verb accent seems to be violated— the accent does not seem to be recessive. This apparent irregularity is due to the fact that there has been *contraction*, the -θε of the aorist passive stem having been contracted with the following vowels in accordance with the rules which will be given in §316. But for present purposes the peculiarity of the accent may simply be learned without any further attention being given to the reason for it.

281. Before the aorist subjunctives can be formed from the principal parts given in the vocabulary, the augment must be dropped in the manner explained in §251, §252.

282. Present Subjunctive of εἰμί.

Learn the present subjunctive of εἰμί in §602.

283. The Tenses in the Subjunctive

In the subjunctive mood there is absolutely no distinction of time between the tenses; the aorist tense does not refer to past time and the present subjunctive does not necessarily refer to present time. The distinction between the present and the aorist concerns merely the manner in which the action is regarded. The aorist subjunctive refers to the action without saying anything about its continuance or repetition, while the present subjunctive refers to it as continuing or as

111

being repeated. Thus ἵνα λύσω means simply *in order that I may loose*, while ἵνα λύω means *in order that I may be loosing*, or the like. But ordinarily it is quite impossible to bring out the difference in an English translation. The present and the aorist subjunctive will usually have to be translated exactly alike. The student should use the aorist in the exercises unless he sees some reason for using the present, since the aorist presents the action in a simpler way, without any added thought of its duration.

284. The Negative of the Subjunctive

The negative of the subjunctive is μή, in accordance with the rule given in §256.

285. The Hortatory Subjunctive

The first person plural of the subjunctive is used in exhortations.

Example: πιστεύσωμεν εἰς τὸν κύριον, *let us believe on the Lord.*

286. The Subjunctive in Purpose Clauses

Purpose is expressed by ἵνα with the subjunctive.

Examples:

(1) ἐρχόμεθα ἵνα ἴδωμεν αὐτόν, *we come in order that we may see him.*

(2) ἤλθομεν ἵνα ἴδωμεν αὐτόν, *we came in order that we might see him.*

287. ἵνα, *in order that*, with the subjunctive, must be distinguished sharply from ὅτι, *that*, with the indicative. The latter introduces indirect discourse.

Example: Compare λέγουσιν ὅτι γινώσκουσι τὸν κύριον, *they say that they know the Lord*, with τοῦτο λέγουσιν ἵνα ἀκούωσιν οἱ μαθηταί, *they say this in order that the disciples may hear.*

The Subjunctive in Future Conditions

288. Future conditions are expressed by ἐάν with the subjunctive; other conditions by εἰ with the indicative.[1]

---

[1] This simple rule does not cover all of the facts. For example, it takes no account of "present general" conditions, which are expressed, like future conditions, by ἐάν with the subjunctive. But present general conditions are

Examples: (1) ἐὰν εἰσέλθωμεν εἰς τὴν οἰκίαν ὀψόμεθα τὸν κύριον, *if we go into the house, we shall see the Lord.* Here ἐὰν εἰσέλθωμεν clearly refers to the future. Compare εἰ μαθηταί ἐσμεν τοῦ κυρίου σωθησόμεθα, *if we are disciples of the Lord, we shall be saved.* Here the meaning is, *if it is now a fact that we are disciples of the Lord, we shall be saved.* Hence εἰ . . . . . ἐσμεν refers to present time.

(2) ἐὰν διδάσκητε τοὺς ἀδελφοὺς πιστοί ἐστε διδάσκαλοι, *if you teach the brethren, you are faithful teachers.* Here the meaning is, *if at any time you shall be engaged in teaching the brethren, you are faithful teachers,* ἐὰν διδάσκητε here refers to an indefinite future. Compare εἰ διδάσκετε τοὺς ἀδελφοὺς πιστοί ἐστε διδάσκαλοι, *if you are teaching the brethren, you are faithful teachers.* Here the meaning is, *if the work in which you are now engaged is that of teaching the brethren, you are faithful teachers.* It should be observed that in order to distinguish εἰ with the indicative from ἐάν with the subjunctive, it is often advisable to choose the periphrastic present in English to translate the present indicative after εἰ. Thus *if you are teaching is a present condition,* while *if you teach is usually a future condition.*

289. The above examples will show that the difference between the two kinds of conditions here treated concerns only the *protasis* (the if-clause). Various moods and tenses can stand in the *apodosis* (the conclusion) after either kind of protasis. A hortatory subjunctive, for example, can stand after a simple present condition. For example, εἰ μαθηταί ἐσμεν τοῦ κυρίου διδάσκωμεν τοὺς ἀδελφούς, *if we are disciples of the Lord* [i. e., *if that is now a fact*], *let us teach the brethren.*

290. It should also be noticed that one cannot always tell from the mere form of the English sentence whether a condition is present or future. Thus in modern colloquial English we often use the present

---

closely allied to future conditions. In the sentence, if any one does wrong he suffers, which is a present general condition, the contemplated possibility of one's doing wrong stretches out into the future; what is meant is that at any time when a man does wrong or shall do wrong he will suffer for it. It is perhaps unnecessary, therefore, to trouble the beginner with this additional category. In general, the simple rule given in the text will serve fairly well for New Testament Greek. The exceptions can be noted as they occur. Conditions contrary to fact will be treated in §551.

indicative to express a future condition. For example, in the sentence, *if it rains tomorrow, we shall not go to the picnic, if it rains* clearly refers to the future and would be ἐάν with the subjunctive in Greek. It is the meaning of the English sentence, then, and not the mere form, which should be noticed in determining what the Greek shall be.

291. Exercises

I 1. ἐὰν εὐαγγελισώμεθα ὑμᾶς, λήμψεσθε σωτηρίαν καὶ ἐλπίδα. 2. ἐὰν μὴ δέξησθε τὴν μαρτυρίαν ἡμῶν, οὐ σωθήσεσθε. 3. ἐάν μὴ ἴδῃ οὗτος τὸν κύριον, οὐ πιστεύσει εἰς αυτόν. 4. εἰ κηρύσσεται ἡμῖν ὅτι ἀγαθός ἐστιν ὁ κύριος, ἀγαθοὶ ὦμεν καὶ ἡμεῖς, ἵνα διδάσκωμεν τοὺς λοιπούς. 5. εὐηγγελισάμην αὐτοὺς ἵνα σωθῶσιν καὶ ἔχωσιν ζωήν. 6. μηκέτι ἁμαρτάνωμεν, ἵνα γενώμεθα μαθηταὶ πιστοί. 7. μακάριοί εἰσιν οἱ ὄχλοι, ἐὰν ἀκούσωσιν τὰ ῥήματά μου. 8. ἐὰν εἰσέλθωσιν εἰς ἐκείνην τὴν οἰκίαν οἱ πιστεύοντες εἰς τὸν κύριον, εὐαγγελισόμεθα αὐτοὺς ἐκεῖ. 9. ἐκηρύξαμεν τούτῳ τῷ λαῷ τὰ ῥήματα τῆς ζωῆς, ἵνα δέξωνται τὴν ἀλήθειαν καὶ σωθῶσιν. 10. προσέλθωμεν τῷ ἰδόντι τὸν κύριον, ἵνα διδάξῃ ἡμᾶς περὶ αὐτοῦ. 11. ταῦτα εἰπόντων αὐτῶν ἐν τῷ ἱερῷ οἱ ἀκούσαντες ἐδέξαντο τὰ λεγόμενα, ἵνα κηρύξωσιν αὐτὰ καὶ τοῖς λοιποῖς. 12. πιστεύσωμεν εἰς τὸν ἀποθανόντα ὑπὲρ ἡμῶν, ἵνα γράψῃ τὰ ὀνόματα ἡμῶν εἰς τὸ βιβλίον τῆς ζωῆς. 13. ἐλεύσομαι πρὸς τὸν σώσαντά με, ἵνα μὴ λύω τὰς ἐντολὰς αὐτοῦ μηδὲ πορεύωμαι ἐν ταῖς ὁδοῖς τοῦ θανάτου. 14. ταῦτα εἶπον ἐν τῷ ἱερῷ, ἵνα οἱ ἀκούσαντες σωθῶσιν ἀπὸ τῶν ἁμαρτιῶν αὐτῶν καὶ ἔχωσιν τὴν δικαιοσύνην τοῦ θεοῦ. 15. εἰ εἴδετε ταῦτα ἐν ταῖς ἡμεραις ταῖς κακαῖς, ὄψεσθε τὰ αὐτὰ καὶ νῦν καὶ εἰς τὸν αἰῶνα. 16. ἐὰν μὴ διδαχθῇς ὑπὸ τοῦ κυρίου, οὐ γνώσῃ αὐτὸν εἰς τὸν αἰῶνα. 17. ὁ λύων τὰς ἐντολάς τοῦ θεοῦ οὐκ ἔχει ἐλπίδα, ἐὰν μὴ ἐπιστρέψῃ πρὸς τὸν κύριον. 18. ταῦτα παρέλαβεν ἀπὸ τοῦ ἀποθανόντος ὑπὲρ αὐτοῦ, ἵνα παραλαβόντες αὐτὰ οἱ λοιποὶ σωθῶσιν καὶ αὐτοί. 19. συνελθόντες εἰς τὴν οἰκίαν δεξώμεθα τὴν μαρτυρίαν τοῦ εὐαγγελισαμένου ἡμᾶς. 20. διωξάντων τῶν στρατιωτῶν τοὺς ἁγίους ἵνα μὴ πιστεύσωσιν εἰς τὸν σώσαντα αὐτούς, συνῆλθον οὗτοι εἰς τὴν συναγωγήν.

II 1. Let us receive the witness of these men, in order that we may be saved. 2. If we do not turn to the Lord, we shall not know Him. 3. If the Lord prepares a place for us, we shall enter into heaven. 4. If we received this commandment from the Lord, let us preach the gospel to the multitudes. 5. If these men are disciples of the Lord, they will not persecute the saints. 6. If these rulers persecute those who believed on the Lord, they will not come to the Lord in order that they may be saved. 7. If he sees the woman who received the saints, he will take the little children from her. 8. When the disciples had said these things to the saints, they were taught by the Lord in order that they might sin no longer. 9. If the Son of Man came in order that He might save sinners, let us receive His witness. 10. If we know the Lord, let us not persecute His saints nor cast them out of the synagogue. 11. If the crowds who have heard the Lord see Him in that synagogue, they will come to Him in order that He may say to them words of hope. 12. Unless[1] He says these things to the multitudes, they will not be saved. 13. If thou seest in that night the one who saved thee, the ruler will persecute thee, in order that thou mayest not preach the gospel to the others. 14. The Lord came to us, in order that we might preach the gospel to you. 15. The faithful servants came, in order that they might bring to us those garments.

---

[1] The English word unless is another way of saying if not. It is to be translated, therefore, by εἰ μή with the indicative or by ἐὰν μή with the subjunctive. Which is correct here?

Lesson XXII

The Present and Aorist Infinitives. The Articular
Infinitive. Indirect Discourse. Proper Names.

292. Vocabulary

δεῖ, impersonal verb, used
only in third person, *it is
necessary* (takes the
accusative and infinitive)

ἔξεστι(ν), impersonal verb,
used only in third person, *it
is lawful* (with dative of the
person for whom "it is
lawful")

θέλω, *I wish*

Ἰησοῦς, Ἰησοῦ, ὁ, *Jesus*

Ἰουδαῖος, ὁ, *a Jew*

κελεύω, *I command*

κώμη, ἡ, *a village*

μέλλω, *I am about* (*to do
something*), *I am going* (*to do
something*)

ὀφείλω, *I owe, I ought*

πάσχω, *I suffer*

πρό, prep. with gen., *before*

σωτηρία, ἡ, *salvation*

Φαρισαῖος, ὁ, *a Pharisee*

Χριστός, ὁ, *Christ*; ὁ Χριστός,
Christ, or *the Messiah*

293. The present and aorist infinitives of λύω are as follows:

	Present			Aorist	
Act.	λύειν, *to loose*		Act.	λῦσαι, *to loose*	
Mid.	λύεσθαι, *to loose for one's self*		Mid.	λύσασθαι, *to loose for one's self*	
Pass.	λύεσθαι, *to be loosed*		Pass.	λυθῆναι, *to be loosed*	

294. It will be observed that the present infinitives are formed upon the present stem, the aorist active and middle infinitives upon the aorist stem (with the characteristic -σα), and the aorist passive infinitive upon the aorist passive stem (with the characteristic -θε lengthened to -θη).

295. The first aorist active infinitive is accented upon the penult, even where this involves an exception to the rule of verb accent. Thus πιστεῦσαι, *to believe*, not πίστευσαι. The accent of the aorist passive infinitive is also irregular.

296. The second aorist active infinitive of λείπω is λιπεῖν, and the second aorist middle infinitive is λιπέσθαι. These are like the present infinitives in their endings except for the irregular accent. They are formed, of course, upon the second aorist stem.

297. The present infinitive of εἰμί is εἶναι.

298. The infinitive is a verbal noun. In many cases the use of the Greek infinitive is so much like that of the infinitive in English as to call for no comment. Thus θέλω ἀκούειν τὸν λόγον means *I wish to hear the word*. Here the English is a literal translation of the Greek.

299. There is ordinarily no distinction of time between the tenses in the infinitive, but the distinction is the same as that which prevails in the subjunctive. The present infinitive refers to the action in its continuance or as repeated; the aorist infinitive refers to it in no such special way. It is usually impossible to bring out the distinction in an English translation.

300. The negative of the infinitive is μή.

The Articular Infinitive

301. The Greek infinitive, being a verbal noun, can have the article, like any other noun. It is treated as an indeclinable neuter noun and so has the neuter article.

302. The infinitive with the article can stand in most of the constructions in which any other noun can stand. Thus καλόν ἐστι τὸ ἀποθανεῖν ὑπὲρ τῶν ἀδελφῶν, means *the act of dying in behalf of the brethren is good*, or, less literally, *it is good to die in behalf of the brethren*. Here τὸ ἀποθανεῖν is a noun in the nominative case, being the subject of the verb ἐστιν.

303. Of particular importance is the use of the articular infinitive after prepositions.

Examples: μετὰ τὸ λῦσαι, *after the act of loosing*; ἐν τῷ λύειν, *in or during the process of loosing*; διὰ τὸ λυθῆναι, *on account of the fact of being loosed*; μετὰ τὸ λυθῆναι, *after the fact of being loosed*; πρὸ τοῦ λῦσαι, *before the act of loosing*; εἰς τὸ λῦσαι, *into the act of loosing*. This last preposition, εἰς, is very frequently used with the articular infinitive to

117

express purpose. If one act is done so as to get into another act, it is done for the purpose of that other act. Thus εἰς τὸ λῦσαι means *in order to loose*.

304. So far, the infinitive has been viewed as a noun. But it is also part of a verb, and as part of a verb it can have not only, as the participle can, adverbial modifiers and a direct object, but also, unlike the participle, a subject. The subject of the infinitive is in the *accusative* case.

Examples:

(1) ἐν τῷ λέγειν αὐτοὺς ταῦτα, *in* (or *during*) *the circumstance that they were saying these things* = *while they were saying these things*. Here αὐτούς is the subject of the infinitive λέγειν and ταῦτα is the direct object of it.

(2) μετὰ τὸ ἀπόλυθῆναι τὸν ὄχλον ἀπῆλθεν ὁ κύριος, *after the circumstance that the crowd was dismissed, the Lord went away, or after the crowd had been dismissed, the Lord went away.* The same thought might have been expressed by ἀπολυθέντος τοῦ ὄχλου ἀπῆλθεν ὁ κύριος.

(3) διὰ δὲ τὸ λέγεσθαι τοῦτο ὑπὸ τῶν ὄχλων ἀπῆλθεν ὁ ἀπόστολος, *and on account of the circumstance that this was being said by the crowds, the apostle went away,* or *because this was being said by the crowds, the apostle went away.*

(4) ταῦτα δὲ εἶπον ὑμῖν εἰς τὸ μὴ γενέσθαι ὑμᾶς δούλους τῆς ἁμαρτίας, *and these things I said to you, with the tendency toward the result that you should not become servants of sin, or and these things I said to you in order that you might not become servants of sin.*

305. It will be observed that the articular infinitive with prepositions is usually to be translated into English by a clause introduced by a conjunction. But it must not be supposed that the details of such translation have anything to do with the details of the Greek original. It is rather the total idea expressed by the Greek phrase which is transferred into a totally different idiom.

Indirect Discourse

306. Indirect discourse is sometimes expressed by the accusative and infinitive.

Example: ἔλεγον οἱ ἄνθρωποι αὐτὸν εἶναι τὸν προφήτην, *the men were saying that he was the prophet.*

307. But usually indirect discourse is expressed by ὅτι with the indicative. The usage is exactly like that in English except for the following important difference:

308. In indirect discourse in Greek, in part contrary to the English usage, the same mood and tense are retained as those which stood in the direct discourse lying back of the indirect.

Examples: (1) λέγει ὅτι βλέπει τὸν ἀπόστολον, *he says that he sees the apostle.* Here the direct discourse lying back of the indirect is *I see the apostle,* for such are the actual words of the speaker; such are the words which would have stood in the quotation if quotation marks had been used. In this sentence there is no difference between the Greek and the English usage.

(2) εἶπεν ὅτι βλέπει τὸν ἀπόστολον, *he said that he saw the apostle.* Here βλέπει is in the present tense because the direct discourse lying back of the indirect discourse is *I see the apostle* — those were the actual words of the speaker. The tense of the direct discourse, *I see,* is retained in the indirect discourse (though of course the person is changed). English, on the other hand, changes the tense in the indirect discourse, when the leading verb is in past time. Thus, although a perfectly literal translation was possible in (1) it is impossible in (2).

(3) εἶπεν ὁ μαθητὴς ὅτι εἶδεν τὸν ἀπόστολον, *the disciple said that he had seen the apostle.* Here the direct discourse was *I saw the apostle,* or *I have seen the apostle.* English throws the tense in the indirect discourse a step further back (had seen instead of saw or has seen); Greek retains the same tense.

(4) εἶπεν ὅτι ὄψεται τὸν ἀπόστολον, *he said that he would see the apostle.* The direct discourse was *I shall see.* English changes *shall* to *would* (or *should* with the first person); Greek retains the same tense.

Proper Names

309. Proper names (spelled with a capital letter) often have the article. Of course the article must be omitted in an English translation.

310. The declension of Ἰησοῦς, ὁ, Jesus, is as follows:

N. Ἰησοῦς
G. Ἰησοῦ
D. Ἰησοῦ
A. Ἰησοῦν
V. Ἰησοῦ

311. Certain nouns, referring to persons or things which instead of being only one of a class are quite unique, are treated as proper nouns, the article being either inserted or omitted. So θεός or ὁ θεός, God; πνεῦμα or τὸ πνεῦμα, the Spirit; κόσμος or ὁ κόσμος, the world; νόμος or ὁ νόμος, the Law.

312. Exercises

I 1. οὐκ ἔξεστίν σοι ἔχειν αὐτήν. 2. κελεύσας δὲ τοὺς ὄχλους ἀπολυθῆναι ἐξῆλθεν εἰς τὴν ἔρημον. 3. οὐκ ἔστιν καλὸν λαβεῖν τὸν ἄρτον τῶν τέκνων καὶ ἐκβαλεῖν αὐτόν. 4. ἤρξατο δὲ ὁ Ἰησοῦς λέγειν τοῖς Ἰουδαίοις ὅτι δεῖ αὐτὸν ἀπελθεῖν. 5. μέλλει γὰρ ὁ υἱὸς τοῦ ἀνθρώπου ἔρχεσθαι ἐν δόξῃ μετὰ τῶν ἀγγέλων αὐτοῦ. 6. εἰ θέλει μετ᾽ ἐμοῦ ἐλθεῖν, δεῖ αὐτὸν ἀποθανεῖν. 7. καλόν σοί ἐστιν εἰς ζωὴν εἰσελθεῖν. 8. ἐν δὲ τῷ λέγειν με τοῦτο ἔπεσε τὸ πνεῦμα τὸ ἅγιον ἐπ᾽ αὐτούς. 9. μετὰ δὲ τὸ ἐγερθῆναι τὸν κύριον ἐδίωξαν οἱ Ἰουδαῖοι τοὺς μαθητὰς αὐτοῦ. 10. πρὸ δὲ τοῦ βληθῆναι εἰς φυλακὴν τὸν προφήτην ἐβάπτιζον οἱ μαθηταὶ τοῦ Ἰησοῦ τοὺς ἐρχομένους πρὸς αὐτούς. 11. διὰ δὲ τὸ εἶναι αὐτὸν ἐκεῖ συνῆλθον οἱ Ἰουδαῖοι. 12. θέλω γὰρ ἰδεῖν ὑμᾶς, ἵνα λάβητε δῶρον ἀγαθόν, εἰς τὸ γενέσθαι ὑμᾶς μαθητὰς πιστούς. 13. ἀπέθανεν ὑπὲρ αὐτῶν ὁ Ἰησοῦς εἰς τὸ σωθῆναι αὐτούς. 14. ἔπεμψεν ὁ θεὸς τὸν Ἰησοῦν, ἵνα ἀποθάνῃ ὑπὲρ ἡμῶν, εἰς τὸ δοξάζειν ἡμᾶς τὸν σώσαντα ἡμᾶς. 15. εἶπεν ὁ τυφλὸς ὅτι βλέπει τοὺς ἀνθρώπους. 16. εἶπεν ὁ Ἰησοῦς ὅτι ἐλεύσεται ἐν τῇ βασιλείᾳ αὐτοῦ. 17. ταῦτα ἔλεγεν ὁ ἀπόστολος ἔτι ὢν ἐν σαρκί, εἰς τὸ πιστεῦσαι εἰς τὸν Ἰησοῦν τοὺς ἀκούοντας. 18. κελεύσας ἡμᾶς ὁ Ἰησοῦς ἐλθεῖν εἰς τὴν κώμην εὐθὺς ἀπέλυσε τὸν ὄχλον. 19. σωθέντες ὑπὸ τοῦ Ἰησοῦ ὀφείλομεν καὶ πάσχειν διὰ τὸ ὄνομα αὐτοῦ. 20. ἐν τῷ πάσχειν ἡμᾶς ταῦτα ἔλεγον οἱ ἀδελφοὶ ὅτι βλέπουσι τὸν Ἰησοῦν.

II 1. While Jesus was preaching the gospel to the people, the Pharisees were commanding the soldiers to bring Him. 2. After Jesus had commanded the crowds to go away, His disciples came to Him. 3. If we wish to see Jesus, let us go into this village. 4. They said that it was lawful for them to take these garments. 5. They saw that it was necessary for the Son of Man to suffer these things. 6. After Jesus had said these things to the Pharisees, the multitudes went away. 7. On account of our not being disciples of Jesus, the ruler will command us to go away. 8. After salvation had been proclaimed to the people, Jesus taught His disciples. 9. We ought when we suffer these things to pray to the One who has saved us. 10. We shall be saved in that hour, because we have believed on the name of Jesus. 11. Those who had come into that village saw that Jesus was in the house. 12. Let us not sin, for God will not receive into His kingdom those who sin and do not turn to Him. 13. While these men were praying to God, the soldiers were persecuting the Church. 14. And when they had entered into this village, they said that they wished to see Jesus. 15. This woman came to see the works of the Christ. 16. The men were brought to Jesus Christ in order that He might heal them.

Lesson XXIII

Contract Verbs.

313. Vocabulary

ἀγαπάω, *I love* (the most
frequent and the loftiest
word for *I love* in the New
Testament)
ἀκολουθέω, *I follow* (takes the
dative)
Γαλιλαία, ἡ, *Galilee*
δηλόω, *I show, I make manifest*
εὐλογέω, *I bless*
εὐχαριστέω, *I give thanks*
ζητέω, *I seek*
θεωρέω, *I behold*
καλέω, καλέσω, ἐκάλεσα, --,
--, ἐκλήθην, *I call*
λαλέω, *I speak*

παρακαλέω, *I exhort, I comfort*
περιπατέω, *I walk*
ποιέω, *I do, I make*
προσκυνέω, *I worship* (usually
takes the dative)
σταυρόω, *I crucify*
τηρέω, *I keep*
τιμάω, *I honor*
φιλέω, *I love* (denotes a love
akin to friendship. The
word is much less frequent
in the New Testament than
ἀγαπάω)
χώρα, ἡ, *a country*

Rules of Contraction[1]

314. Two vowels or a vowel and a diphthong are often united into a single long vowel or diphthong. The process by which they are united is called contraction.

315. It must not be supposed, however, that contraction *always* takes place when two vowels or a vowel and a diphthong (even in the combinations set forth in the following rules) come together within a word.

316. The rules of contraction are as follows:

---

[1] The following formulation of the rules of contraction is, in essentials, that which is given in White, Beginner's Greek Book, 1895, pp. 75f. It has been used here by kind permission of Messrs. Ginn and Company.

I. Vowel with Vowel

1. An open and a close vowel, when the open vowel comes first, are united in the diphthong which is composed of the two vowels in question.

Example: ε-ι makes ει. It must be observed, however, that when the close vowel comes before the open vowel, a diphthong is never formed. Thus ι-ε (for example, in ἱερόν), is always two syllables, never a diphthong.

2. Two like vowels form the common long.

Examples: α-α makes long α ; ε-η makes η ; ο-ω makes ω.

3. But ε-ε makes ει and ο-ο makes ου.

This rule forms an exception to rule 2.

4. An o-sound (ο or ω) overcomes α, ε, or η (whether the o-sound comes first or second), and forms ω.

Examples: α-ο makes ω ; ε-ω makes ω.

5. But ε-ο and ο-ε make ου. This rule forms an exception to rule 4.

6. When α and ε or η come together, whichever one comes first overcomes the other, and forms its own long.

Examples: α-ε and α-η make long α; ε-α makes η.

II. Vowel with Diphthong

1. A vowel disappears by absorption before a diphthong that begins with the same vowel.

Examples: ε-ει makes ει; ο-ου makes ου.

2. When a vowel comes before a diphthong that does not begin with the same vowel, it is contracted with the diphthong's first vowel. The diphthong's second vowel disappears, unless it is ι, in which case it becomes subscript.

Examples: α-ει makes ᾳ (α is first contracted with ε in accordance with I 6, and then the ι becomes subscript); α-ου makes ω (α is contracted with ο by I 4, and the υ disappears); ε-ου makes ου (ε is contracted with ο by I 5, and υ disappears).

3. But ο-ει and ο-η make οι.

III. Accent of Contract Syllables

1. If either of the contracted syllables had an accent, the resulting syllable receives an accent. If the resulting syllable is a penult or an antepenult, the general rules of accent (see §11) will always tell which kind of accent it has. If the resulting syllable is an ultima it has a circumflex.

Examples: (1) φιλέομεν makes φιλουμεν, in accordance with I 5. Since one of the two syllables that united to make ου had an accent, ου must have an accent. The general rules of accent declare that if the ultima is short, a long penult, if accented at all, must have the circumflex. Hence φιλοῦμεν is correct. (2) τιμαόμεθα makes τιμωμεθα in accordance with I 4. Since one of the two syllables that united to make ω had an accent, ω must have an accent. But in accordance with the general rules of accent only an acute can stand on an antepenult. Therefore τιμώμεθα is correct. (3) δηλόεις makes δηλοις in accordance with II 3. Since one of the two syllables that united to make οι had an accent, οι must have an accent. The general rules of accent will permit either an acute or a circumflex to stand on a long ultima. But the present rule gives special guidance. Therefore δηλοῖς is correct.

2. If neither of the contracted syllables had an accent, the resulting syllable receives none.

Example: ἐφίλεε makes ἐφιλει in accordance with I 3. Since neither of the two syllables that unite to make ει is accented, ει receives no accent, and ἐφίλει is correct.

Present System of Contract Verbs

317. The student should write out in the uncontracted forms the present system (present tense in all moods studied thus far, and imperfect tense) of τιμάω, *I honor*; φιλέω, *I love*, and δηλόω, *I make manifest*, and should then write the contract form opposite to each uncontracted form, applying the rules of contraction. The results can be tested by the conjugation of these verbs which is given in §590-§592.

318. It should be observed that there are two exceptions to the rules: (1) the present active infinitive of verbs in -αω is contracted from -άειν to -ᾶν instead of to -ᾷν , and (2) the present active infinitive of verbs in -οω is contracted from ο-ειν to -οῦν instead of to -οῖν.

319. Contraction is carried out in all the forms of the declension of the participles.

320. In general, the uncontracted forms of these verbs in -άω, -έω and -όω do not occur in the New Testament. The reason why the uncontracted forms, and not the contract forms, of the present active indicative first person singular are given in the lexicons is that the uncontracted forms must be known before the verb can be conjugated, since it makes a great difference for the conjugation whether τιμῶ, for example, is contracted from τιμάω, τιμέω, or τιμόω.

Principal Parts of Verbs in -άω, -έω and -όω

321. Verbs whose stems end in a vowel regularly lengthen that vowel (α as well as ε being lengthened to η) before the tense suffixes (e.g. the -σο/ε of the future system, the -σα of the first aorist system, and the -θε of the aorist passive system). Thus the principal parts of τιμάω, so far as we have learned them, are τιμάω, τιμήσω, ἐτίμησα , — , — , ἐτιμήθην (not τιμάω, τιμάσω, etc.); the principal parts of φιλέω are φιλέω, φιλήσω, etc.; and the principal parts of δηλόω are δηλόω, δηλώσω , etc. It should be observed that this lengthening of the final vowel of the stem of these "contract" verbs has nothing to do with contraction. The contraction appears only in the present system.

322. It is very important that the student should learn to reverse the process involved in this rule. Thus, if a form φανερωθείς be found in the Greek-English exercises, the student should first say to himself that the -θε in φανερωθείς is evidently the sign of the aorist passive system. The verb stem without the tense suffix would be φανερω- . But since the final vowel of the verb stem is lengthened before the tense suffix -θε , the verb stem was φανερο- and the verb was φανερόω. Or if a form ἠρωτήθη be found, the student should first say to himself that the -θη is evidently the ending of the aorist passive indicative, third person singular, like ἐλύθη. But the aorist passive indicative has the augment, which if the verb begins with a vowel consists in the lengthening of that vowel. Therefore, to get the verb, the η at the beginning of ἠρωτήθη must be shortened. But η is the long of either α or ε. It cannot be determined, therefore, whether the verb began with α or ε. Again, the η just before the -θη in ἠρωτήθη was the lengthened form of the verb stem. The verb stem therefore ended in either α or ε. Accordingly there are four possibilities as to the verb from which ἠρωτήθη may be found to have come; ἠρωτήθη may be found to have come from ἀρωτέω, ἀρωτάω, ἐρωτέω, or ἐρωτάω. Trying each of these in the lexicon we discover that the last is correct.

323. καλέω is an exception to the rule just given. It does not lengthen the final ε of the stem before the σ of the future and aorist systems. The aorist passive, moreover, is irregularly formed.

324. Exercises

I 1. οὐκ εὐλογήσει ὁ θεὸς τὸν μὴ περιπατοῦντα κατὰ τὰς ἐντολὰς τοῦ Ἰησοῦ. 2. οἱ ἀγαπώμενοι ὑπὸ τοῦ Ἰησοῦ ἀγαπῶσι τὸν ἀγαπῶντα αὐτούς. 3. λαλοῦντος τοῦ Ἰησοῦ τοῖς ἀκολουθοῦσιν ἤρξατο ὁ ἄρχων παρακαλεῖν αὐτόν ἀπελθεῖν. 4. ἀκολουθήσαντες τῷ λαλήσαντι ταῦτα ζητήσωμεν τὸν οἶκον αὐτοῦ. 5. εἰ ἀγαπῶμεν τὸν θεόν, τηρῶμεν τὰς ἐντολὰς αὐτοῦ καὶ ποιῶμεν τὰ λαλούμενα ἡμῖν ὑπὸ τοῦ Ἰησοῦ. 6. τοῦτο ποιήσαντος τοῦ Ἰησοῦ ἐλάλει περὶ αὐτοῦ ὁ θεραπευθεὶς τῷ ἀκολουθοῦντι ὄχλῳ. 7. ἐθεώρουν οἱ ἀπόστολοι τὰ ἔργα τὰ ποιούμενα ὑπὸ Ἰησοῦ ἐν τῷ περιπατεῖν αὐτοὺς σὺν αὐτῷ. 8. μετὰ τὸ βληθῆναι εἰς φυλακὴν τὸν προφήτην οὐκέτι περιεπάτει ὁ Ἰησοῦς ἐν τῇ χώρᾳ ἐκείνῃ. 9. οἱ ἀγαπῶντες τὸν θεὸν ποιοῦσι τὰς ἐντολὰς αὐτοῦ. 10. ταῦτα ἐποίουν τῷ Ἰησοῦ καὶ οἱ θεραπευθέντες ὑπ' αὐτοῦ. 11. ἐζήτουν αὐτὸν οἱ ὄχλοι, ἵνα θεωρῶσι τὰ ποιούμενα ὑπ' αὐτοῦ. 12. οὐ φιλοῦσι τὸν Ἰησοῦν οἱ μὴ ποιοῦντες τὰς ἐντολὰς αὐτοῦ. 13. ἀγαπῶμεν τὸν θεὸν ἐν ταῖς καρδίαις ἡμῶν ἀγαπῶντες καὶ τοὺς ἀδελφούς. 14. ταῦτα ἐλάλησεν ὁ Ἰησοῦς τοῖς ἀκολουθοῦσιν αὐτῷ ἔτι περιπατῶν μετ' αὐτῶν ἐν τῇ χώρᾳ τῶν Ἰουδαίων. 15. ἐὰν μὴ περιπατῶμεν κατὰ τὰς ἐντολὰς τοῦ Ἰησοῦ, οὐ θεωρήσομεν τὸ πρόσωπον αὐτοῦ. 16. μετὰ τὸ καλέσαι αὐτοὺς τὸν Ἰησοῦν οὐκέτι περιεπάτουν ἐν ταῖς ὁδοῖς τοῦ πονηροῦ οὐδὲ ἐποίουν τὰ πονηρά. 17. ταῦτα ἐποιεῖτε ἡμῖν διὰ τὸ ἀγαπᾶν ὑμᾶς τὸν καλέσαντα ὑμᾶς εἰς τὴν βασιλείαν αὐτοῦ. 18. τῷ Ἰησοῦ λαλήσαντι ταῦτα μετὰ τὸ ἐγερθῆναι ἐκ νεκρῶν προσεκύνησαν οἱ κληθέντες ὑπ' αὐτοῦ. 19. ἐθεώρουν τὸν Ἰησοῦν σταυρούμενον ὑπὸ τῶν στρατιωτῶν αἱ ἀκολουθήσασαι αὐτῷ ἐκ τῆς Γαλιλαίας. 20. οὐ θεωρήσομεν αὐτὸν ἐὰν μὴ ἀκολουθῶμεν αὐτῷ περιπατοῦντι ἐν τῇ Γαλιλαίᾳ.

II 1. Those things spake Jesus to those who were following Him out of Galilee. 2. I was beholding Him who had loved me and died in behalf of me. 3. Let us worship the One who does these things and bless His holy name. 4. Those who were beholding Him as He was walking in Galilee were saying that they did not wish to follow Him. 5. Having followed Jesus as He was walking in Galilee, they beheld Him also after He had been raised up from the dead. 6. Let us seek the One who has spoken to us words of hope. 7. Let us bless the name of the One who walked with us in the world and was crucified in behalf of us. 8. If thou followest Him who does these things, thou wilt behold Him in His glory. 9. If we do not love those who bless us we will not love those who do evil things. 10. He loves us and makes manifest to us His glory, in order that we may bless God for ever. 11. While the multitudes were following Jesus and were hearing the things which were being spoken by Him, the rulers were saying that they did not love Him. 12. I will show to those who have followed me the things which have been shown to me by Jesus. 13. These are those who love Jesus and beheld His works and were called into His kingdom. 14. His brother exhorted him to follow Jesus in order that he might be with Him for ever. 15. This parable we speak to those who love God and keep His commandments. 16. This is the child that blesses God and loves Him.

Lesson XXIV

Future and First Aorist and Middle of Liquid Verbs.
Future of εἰμί. Reflexive Pronouns.

325. Vocabulary

ἀλλήλων, reciprocal pron., *of each other, of one another*

ἀποθανοῦμαι, *I shall die*, dep. fut. of ἀποθνῄσκω

ἀποκτενῶ, ἀπέκτεινα, fut. and aor. of ἀποκτείνω, *I kill*

ἀποστελῶ, ἀπέστειλα, fut. and aor. of ἀποστέλλω, *I send*

ἀρῶ, ἦρα, fut. and aor. of αἴρω, *I take up, I take away*

βαλῶ, *I shall throw, I shall cast*, fut. of βάλλω

ἑαυτοῦ, reflexive pron., *of himself*

ἐγερῶ, ἤγειρα, fut. and aor. of ἐγείρω, *I raise up*

ἐμαυτοῦ, reflexive pron., *of myself*

ἐπί, prep. with gen., *over; on, at the time of*; with dat., *on, on the basis of, at*; with acc., *on, to, against* (ἐπί is an exceedingly common, but a rather difficult, preposition. Its various uses must be learned by observation in reading)

ἔσομαι, *I shall be*, fut. of εἰμί

μενῶ, ἔμεινα, fut. and aor. of μένω, *I remain*

μετανοέω, *I repent*

σεαυτοῦ, reflexive pron., *of thyself*

σπείρω, σπερῶ, ἔσπειρα,--,--, ἐσπάρην, *I sow*

φοβέομαι, dep. with passive forms, *I am afraid, I fear, I am afraid of*

326. Liquid verbs are verbs whose stems end in λ, μ, ν, or ρ, these consonants being called liquids.

327. The Future of Liquid Verbs

The future active and middle of liquid verbs is formed, not by adding -σο/ε, as is the case with other verbs, but by adding -εο/ε, to the verb stem. The ε contracts with the following variable vowel, in accordance with the rules of contraction given in the preceding lesson. Thus the future active and middle of liquid verbs is conjugated exactly like the present of verbs in -εω.

328. The future active indicative of κρίνω, I judge, is as follows:

Sing.		Plur.	
1.	κρινῶ	1.	κρινοῦμεν
2.	κρινεῖς	2.	κρινεῖτε
3.	κρινεῖ	3.	κρινοῦσι(ν)

329. It will be observed that the only way in which the future active indicative in the three persons of the singular and in the third person plural is distinguished (in appearance) from the present active indicative of κρίνω is by the accent.

330. The future middle indicative of κρίνω is as follows:

Sing.		Plur.	
1.	κρινοῦμαι	1.	κρινούμεθα
2.	κρινῇ	2.	κρινεῖσθε
3.	κρινεῖται	3.	κρινοῦνται

331. It will be remembered (see §157) that the verb stem is often disguised in the present system. Thus the future of a liquid verb is often distinguished from the present by something more than the addition of the ε.

Example: The future of βάλλω is βαλῶ, βαλ- and not βαλλ- being the verb stem. Even κρινῶ really differs from the present κρίνω in that the ι is short in the future and long in the present. But even that distinction does not prevail in the case of μένω.

332. Some verbs have liquid stems in the future but not in other tenses.

Example: The future of λέγω is ἐρῶ.

The First Aorist of Liquid Verbs

333. The first aorist active and middle of liquid verbs is formed not by adding -σα to the verb stem but by adding -α alone and making changes within the body of the word, the verb stem usually being lengthened (ε lengthened not to η but to ει). The conjugation, in all the moods, is like the conjugation of other first aorists.

Examples: (1) The first aorist active of μένω, *I remain*, is ἔμεινα (indic.), μείνω (subj.), μεῖναι (infin.) and μείνας (part.). (2) The first aorist active of ἀποστέλλω, *I send*, is ἀπέστειλα (indic.), ἀποστείλω (subj.), ἀποστεῖλαι (infin.) and ἀποστείλας (part.).

334. Of course liquid verbs may have second aorists or irregular aorists. So the aorist of βάλλω is a second aorist ἔβαλον. Some verbs, moreover, may have a present stem ending in a liquid, and yet not be liquid verbs. Thus λαμβάνω is not a liquid verb, the verb stem being λαβ-. The student is reminded again that one cannot always predict what the various tense systems of a Greek verb will be. The lexicon must be consulted.

335. Future Indicative of εἰμί.

The future indicative of εἰμί, *I am*, is as follows:

	Sing.		Plur.
1.	ἔσομαι	1.	ἐσόμεθα
2.	ἔσῃ	2.	ἔσεσθε
3.	ἔσται	3.	ἔσονται

It will be observed that the conjugation is just like that of the future middle of λύω, except that in the third person singular the variable vowel is omitted, ἔσται standing instead of ἔσεται.

336. The English Preparatory Use of "There"

The word *there* is sometimes put before the verb in an English sentence without any special force except as an indication that the subject is to follow the verb. This "preparatory" *there* is not translated at all in Greek.

Examples: (1) χαρὰ ἔσται ἐν οὐρανῷ, there shall be joy in heaven. (2) ἦσαν μαθηταὶ ἐν τῷ οἴκῳ, there were disciples in the house.

Declension of Reflexive Pronouns

337. The declension of ἐμαυτοῦ, ῆς, *of myself*, the reflexive pronoun of the first person, is as follows:

	Sing.			Plur.	
	Masc.	Fem.		Masc.	Fem.
G.	ἐμαυτοῦ	ἐμαυτῆς	G.	ἑαυτῶν	ἑαυτῶν
D.	ἐμαυτῷ	ἐμαυτῇ	D.	ἑαυτοῖς	ἑαυταῖς
A.	ἐμαυτόν	ἐμαυτήν	A.	ἑαυτούς	ἑαυτάς

338. The declension of σεαυτοῦ, ῆς, of thyself, the reflexive pronoun of the second person, is as follows:

	Sing.			Plur.	
	Masc.	Fem.		Masc.	Fem.
G.	σεαυτοῦ	σεαυτῆς	G.	ἑαυτῶν	ἑαυτῶν
D.	σεαυτῷ	σεαυτῇ	D.	ἑαυτοῖς	ἑαυταῖς
A.	σεαυτόν	σεαυτήν	A.	ἑαυτούς	ἑαυτάς

339. The declension of ἑαυτοῦ, ῆς, οῦ, of himself, of herself, of itself, the reflexive pronoun of the third person, is as follows:

	Sing.				Plur.		
	Masc.	Fem.	Neut.		Masc.	Fem.	Neut.
G.	ἑαυτοῦ	ἑαυτῆς	ἑαυτοῦ	G.	ἑαυτῶν	ἑαυτῶν	ἑαυτῶν
D.	ἑαυτῷ	ἑαυτῇ	ἑαυτῷ	D.	ἑαυτοῖς	ἑαυταῖς	ἑαυτοῖς
A.	ἑαυτόν	ἑαυτήν	ἑαυτό	A.	ἑαυτούς	ἑαυτάς	ἑαυτά

340. It will be observed that the declension of the reflexive pronouns is like that of αὐτός, except that there is no nominative case and in the reflexive pronouns of the first and second persons no neuter gender.

341. In the plural, ἑαυτῶν, which originally belonged only to the pronoun ἑαυτοῦ of the third person, is made to do duty for all three persons.

342. Use of Reflexive Pronouns Reflexive pronouns are pronouns that refer back to the subject of the clause.

Examples: (1) οὐ λαλῶ περὶ ἐμαυτοῦ, I do not speak concerning myself; (2) οὐ δοξάζεις σεαυτόν, thou dost not glorify thyself; (3) οὐκ ἔχει ζωὴν ἐν ἑαυτῷ, he has not life in himself; (4) δοξάζετε ἑαυτούς, ye glorify yourselves.

343. Reciprocal Pronoun

The reciprocal pronoun is ἀλλήλων, of one another, of each other. It occurs in the New Testament only in the forms ἀλλήλων, of one another, ἀλλήλοις to or for one another, and ἀλλήλους, one another (βλέπουσιν ἀλλήλους, they see one another).

344. Exercises

I 1. οὐ γὰρ ἑαυτοὺς κηρύσσομεν ἀλλὰ Χριστὸν Ἰησοῦν κύριον, ἑαυτοὺς δὲ δούλους ὑμῶν διὰ Ἰησοῦν 2. ὁ ἐγείρας τὸν κύριον Ἰησοῦν ἐγερεῖ καὶ ἡμᾶς σὺν Ἰησοῦ 3. εἶπεν ὁ μαθητὴς ὅτι ἀποθανεῖται ὑπὲρ τοῦ Ἰησοῦ. 4. οὐκ ἐγεροῦμεν αὐτοὶ ἑαυτούς, ὁ δὲ Ἰησοῦς ἐγερεῖ ἡμᾶς ἐν τῇ ἐσχάτῃ ἡμέρᾳ. 5. εὐθὺς ἦρεν ὁ πονηρὸς τὸ παρὰ τὴν ὁδὸν σπαρέν. 6. ἐὰν ἀγαπᾶτε ἀλλήλους, ἔσεσθε μαθηταὶ τοῦ ἀποθανόντος ὑπὲρ ὑμῶν. 7. ἐὰν πιστεύσητε εἰς τὸν Ἰησοῦν, μετ᾽ αὐτοῦ μενεῖτε εἰς τὸν αἰῶνα. 8. ὁ ἀγαπῶν τὸν υἱὸν ἀγαπᾷ καὶ τὸν ἀποστείλαντα αὐτόν. 9. χαρὰ ἔσται ἐπὶ τῷ ἁμαρτωλῷ τῷ ἐπὶ τῷ ῥήματι τοῦ Ἰησοῦ μετανοήσαντι. 10. οἱ ἀποκτείναντες τὸν Ἰησοῦν καὶ διώξαντες τοὺς μαθητὰς αὐτοῦ ἐκβαλοῦσι καὶ ἡμᾶς. 11. ἐπιστρέψαντες οὗτοι ἐπὶ τὸν θεὸν ἔμειναν ἐν τῇ ἐκκλησίᾳ αὐτοῦ. 12. ἐγείραντος τοῦ θεοῦ τοὺς νεκροὺς ἐσόμεθα σὺν τῷ κυρίῳ εἰς τοὺς αἰῶνας τῶν αἰώνων. 13. οὐκ εἰς ἐμαυτὸν ἐπίστευσα, ἀλλ᾽ εἰς τὸν κύριον. 14. ἔξεστιν ἡμῖν λαβεῖν δῶρα ἀπ᾽ ἀλλήλων, ἀλλ᾽ οὐκ ἀποκτεῖναι οὐδὲ διῶξαι ἀλλήλους. 15. οὗτος μὲν ἐστιν ὁ ἄρχων ὁ ἀποκτείνας τοὺς προφήτας, ἐκεῖνος δέ ἐστιν ὁ ἁμαρτωλὸς ὁ μετανοήσας ἐπὶ τῷ ῥήματι τοῦ Ἰησοῦ. 16. ἐὰν δὲ τοῦτο εἴπωμεν κατ᾽ αὐτοῦ, φοβούμεθα τοὺς ὄχλους, λέγουσι γὰρ εἶναι αὐτὸν προφήτην. 17. ἀποστελεῖ πρὸς αὐτοὺς διδασκάλους καὶ προφήτας, ἵνα μετανοήσωσιν καὶ φοβῶνται τὸν θεόν. 18. μακάριοί εἰσιν οὐχ οἱ ἑαυτοὺς δοξάζοντες ἀλλ᾽ οἱ δοξάζοντες τὸν ἀποστείλαντα τὸν υἱὸν αὐτοῦ εἰς τὸν κόσμον. 19. ἐρχομένου πρὸς αὐτοὺς τοῦ Ἰησοῦ περιπατοῦντος ἐπὶ τῆς θαλάσσης ἐφοβοῦντο οἱ ἰδόντες αὐτὸν μαθηταί. 20. ταῦτα ἐροῦμεν τοῖς ἀποσταλεῖσι πρὸς ἡμᾶς προφήταις.

II 1. When Jesus has taken away our sins we shall be holy for ever. 2. Let us not begin to say[1] in ourselves that we do not know Him. 3. We shall not fear the ruler who killed the prophets, for God will send His angels to us. 4. When the soldiers had killed Jesus our Lord, we were afraid and went away from Him. 5. He said that it was not necessary for us to see each other. 6. If ye persecute and kill those who are being sent to you, ye shall no longer be the people of God. 7. The multitudes

---

[1] With ἄρχομαι, I begin, the present infinitive, not the aorist infinitive, should be used.

went away, but those who remained said that He had the words of life. 8. When Jesus had spoken these things and had sent His disciples into the villages of Galilee, the Pharisees were afraid of the people. 9. Having killed Jesus they will cast out of their synagogues those who have believed on Him. 10. The apostle himself did not save himself, but God was the One who saved him. 11. When the Lord had spoken this parable, those rulers said that they would kill those who had been sent by Him. 12. Unless Jesus himself sends us we shall not be disciples of Him. 13. Unless ye repent ye will remain in sin forever. 14. He who said this word to the One who sent the apostles will say the same word also to those who have been sent by Him. 15. Those good disciples, having loved those who were following Jesus, will love also those who follow His apostles. 16. Those who saw Him as He was walking in Galilee will behold Him in heaven for ever.

Lesson XXV

More Nouns of the Third Declension. Adjectives of the Third Declension in -ης, -ες.

345. Vocabulary

ἀληθής, ές, adj., *true*

ἀνήρ, ἀνδρός, ὁ, *a man* (ἀνήρ
is a man as distinguished
from women and children;
ἄνθρωπος, is a human
being as distinguished from
other beings)

ἀρχιερεύς, ἀρχιερέως, ὁ, *a
chief priest*

βασιλεύς, βασιλέως, ὁ, *a king*

γένος, γένους, τό, *a race, a
kind*

γραμματεύς, γραμματέως, ὁ,
a scribe

ἔθνος, ἔθνους, τό, *a nation;*
plur., τὰ ἔθνη, *the nations,
the Gentiles*

ἱερεύς, ἱερέως, ὁ, *a priest*

μήτηρ, μητρός, ἡ, *a mother*

ὄρος, ὄρους, τό, *a mountain*

πατήρ, ματρός, ὁ, *a father*

πίστις, πίστεως, ἡ, *faith*

πλήρης, ες, *full*

πόλις, πόλεως, ἡ, *a city*

χάρις, χάριτος, ἡ, *grace*

346. Before studying the present lesson, the student should review the paradigms in Lesson XVII.

347. The declension of χάρις, χάριτος, ἡ, *grace*, is follows:

	Sing.		Plur.
N.V.	χάρις	N.V.	χάριτες
G.	χάριτος	G.	χαρίτων
D.	χάριτι	D.	χάρισι(ν)
A.	χάριν	A.	χάριτας

348. This noun differs from those in §211, in that the accusative singular ending is -ν instead of -α. The final τ of the stem (χαριτ-) drops out before the -ν. If χάρις were declined like ἐλπίς the accusative singular would be χάριτα.

134

349. The declension of πόλις, πόλεως (stem πολι-), ἡ, *a city*, is as follows:

	Sing.		Plur.
N.	πόλις	N.V.	πόλεις
G.	πόλεως	G.	πόλεων
D.	πόλει	D.	πόλεσι(ν)
A.	πόλιν	A.	πόλεις
V.	πόλι		

350. The final ι of the stem is changed to ε except in the nominative, accusative and vocative singular. πόλει in the dative singular is contracted from πόλε-ι, and πόλεις in the nominative plural from πόλε-ες, in accordance with the rules of contraction given in Lesson XXIII. The accusative plural has -εις, instead of εας or (as the rules of contraction would require) -ης. The accusative singular has instead of -α the -ν ending which appears in certain other third declension nouns such as χάρις. The genitive singular ending is -ως instead of -ος. The accent in the genitive singular and plural of this class of nouns is the only exception to the rule that if the ultima is long the antepenult cannot be accented (see §11).

351. These third-declension nouns in -ις with genitives in -εως, of which πόλις is an example, form a very important class of nouns in the New Testament. The nouns of this class are declined alike and are all of feminine gender.

352. The declension of γένος, γένους, (stem γενεσ-), τό, *a race*, is as follows:

	Sing.		Plur.
N.A.V.	γένος	N.A.V.	γένη
G.	γένους	G.	γενῶν
D.	γένει	D.	γένεσι(ν)

353. The final σ of the stem (γενεσ-) is dropped except in the nominative singular. The ε which is then left at the end of the stem is contracted with the vowels of the regular third-declension endings, in accordance with the rules of contraction given in Lesson XXIII.

354. These third-declension nouns in -ος, -ους, are declined alike, and are all of neuter gender.

355. The declension of βασιλεύς, βασιλέως, (stem βασιλεύ-), ὁ, *a king*, is as follows:

	Sing.		Plur.
N.	βασιλεύς	N.V.	βασιλεῖς
G.	βασιλέως	G.	βασιλέων
D.	βασιλεῖ	D.	βασιλεῦσι(ν)
A.	βασιλέα	A.	βασιλεῖς
V.	βασιλεῦ		

356. The final υ of the stem is dropped before those endings which begin with a vowel. Contraction takes place in the dative singular and nominative plural. The genitive singular has -ως instead of -ος (compare πόλις.). But the accusative singular has the α-ending, not the ν-ending.

357. These nouns in -ευς, -εως are masculine.

358. Observe the declension of πατήρ and of ἀνήρ in §565.

359. The declension of other third-declension nouns will give little difficulty when once the genitive singular and the gender are known. Only the dative plural is sometimes troublesome, but the forms can at least be easily recognized when they occur.

360. The declension of ἀληθής, ές (stem ἀληθεσ-), *true*, is as follows:

	Sing.			Plur.	
	M.F.	N.		M.F.	N.
N.	ἀληθής	ἀληθές	N.V.	ἀληθεῖς	ἀληθῆ
G.	ἀληθοῦς	ἀληθοῦς	G.	ἀληθῶν	ἀληθῶν
D.	ἀληθεῖ	ἀληθεῖ	D.	ἀληθέσι(ν)	ἀληθέσι(ν)
A.	ἀληθῆ	ἀληθές	A.	ἀληθεῖς	ἀληθῆ
V.	ἀληθές	ἀληθές			

361. The final σ of the stem is dropped in most of the forms, and contraction then takes place. Compare πόλις, γένος, and βασιλεύς.

362. This is the first adjective studied thus far which is declined according to the third declension in the feminine as well as in the masculine and neuter.

363. Exercises

I 1. ἀληθῆ ἐστι τὰ λαλούμενα ὑπὸ τοῦ ἱερέως τούτου. 2. συνελθόντων τῶν ἀρχιερέων καὶ γραμματέων ἵνα ἀποκτείνωσι τὸν ἄνδρα τοῦτον, προσηύξαντο οἱ μαθηταὶ ἐν τῷ ἱερῷ. 3. ἀπεκρίθη ὁ βασιλεὺς ὁ ἀγαθὸς λέγων ὅτι οὐ θέλει ἀποκτεῖναι τοῦτον. 4. χάριτι δὲ ἐσώθησαν ἐκεῖνοι οἱ ἁμαρτωλοὶ καὶ ἠγέρθησαν ἐν δόξῃ. 5. τῇ γὰρ χάριτι σωζόμεθα διὰ πίστεως ἵνα δοξάζωμεν τὸν θεόν. 6. ἰδὼν τὸν πατέρα καὶ τὴν μητέρα αὐτοῦ ἐν τῇ πόλει ἔμεινεν σὺν αὐτοῖς. 7. εἰς τὰ ἔθνη ἀποστελεῖς τοὺς ἀποστόλους σου, ἵνα κηρύσσωσιν αὐτοῖς τὸ εὐαγγέλιον τῆς χάριτός σου. 8. ἀγαθὸς ἦν οὗτος ὁ ἀνὴρ καὶ πλήρης πνεύματος ἁγίου καὶ πίστεως. 9. ἰδόντες δὲ τὴν χάριν τοῦ θεοῦ παρεκάλεσαν τὰ ἔθνη μένειν ἐν τῇ χάριτι σὺν χαρᾷ καὶ ἐλπίδι. 10. καταβαινόντων δὲ αὐτῶν ἐκ τοῦ ὄρους ἐλάλει ταῦτα ὁ Ἰησοῦς. 11. ἀγαπήσωμεν τοὺς πατέρας καὶ τὰς μητέρας ἡμῶν, ἵνα τηρήσωμεν τὴν ἐντολὴν τοῦ θεοῦ. 12. τῶν ἀρχιερέων ἰδόντων τοὺς συνερχομένους εἰς τὸ ἀκούειν τοῦ ἀνδρὸς εἶπον πρὸς ἑαυτοὺς οἱ ἄρχοντες ὅτι δεῖ αὐτὸν ἀποθανεῖν. 13. οἱ βασιλεῖς οἱ πονηροὶ ἀπέκτειναν καὶ τοὺς ἄνδρας καὶ τὰ τέκνα. 14. ὁ δὲ θεὸς ἤγειρεν αὐτούς, ἵνα δοξάζωσιν αὐτὸν εἰς τὸν αἰῶνα. 15. ἐὰν μὴ χάριν ἔχωμεν καὶ πίστιν καὶ ἐλπίδα, οὐ μετανοήσουσι τὰ ἔθνη ἐπὶ τῷ λόγῳ ἡμῶν. 16. τοῖς ἀνδράσι τοῖς πεμφθεῖσιν ὑπὸ τοῦ βασιλέως προσηνέγκαμεν τὸν πατέρα καὶ τὴν μητέρα ἡμῶν. 17. ἐλθὼν πρὸς τὸν βασιλέα ταύτης τῆς χώρας παρεκάλεσας αὐτὸν μὴ ἀποκτεῖναι τὸν ἄνδρα τοῦτον. 18. εἰ ἀληθῆ ἐστι τὰ λεγόμενα ὑπὸ τῶν ἀκολουθησάντων τῷ ἀνδρί ἐν τῇ Γαλιλαίᾳ ἀποκτενοῦσιν αὐτὸν οἱ ἀρχιερεῖς. 19. διὰ πίστεως σώσει τοὺς πιστεύοντας εἰς τὸ ὄνομα αὐτοῦ. 20. ἐδέξαντο δὲ καὶ τὰ ἔθνη τὸ ῥῆμα τοῦ Ἰησοῦ τὸ ἀληθές.

II 1. This is the race that killed those who believe on Jesus. 2. When the scribes had entered into that city, the disciples went away to the mountains. 3. We saw that the word which was being spoken by the

137

man was true. 4. When the Lord had said this to the chief priests, the ruler marveled. 5. The father of him who killed the men will kill also the children. 6. God will raise up from the dead those who have been saved by His grace. 7. Ye shall be saved by God through faith. 8. On account of the faith of the fathers and of the mothers the children will die in the evil city. 9. The city being itself full of sin has also a wicked king. 10. If we enter into those cities having our hearts full of grace and faith and hope, those who repent at our word will see the King in His glory. 11. Jesus said to the scribes who were following that He was going into the holy city. 12. If we love the brethren we shall bless also the One who sent them into the nations. 13. The king said to my father that the chief priests and Pharisees wished to kill those who were following Jesus. 14. While Jesus was speaking these things in that wicked city, the chief priests were gathering together the soldiers in order that they might kill Him. 15. Those who have not the grace of God in their hearts have neither life nor hope. 16. If ye go into those cities and villages, ye shall see the king who killed your fathers and your mothers.

Lesson XXVI

Declension of πᾶς, πολύς, μέγας, and Numerals.
Attributive and Substantive Uses of Prepositional
Phrases and of the Genitive. Accusative of Extent of
Time and Space.

364. Vocabulary

δύο, *two*

εἷς, μία, ἕν, *one*

ἕξ, indecl., *six*

ἔτος, ἔτους, τό, *a year*

ἤ, conj., *or*

ἤθελον, imperfect indic, of
θέλω (with an apparently
irregular augment, but
another form of the verb
was ἐθέλω)

Ἰάκωβος, ὁ, *James*

καθαρός, ά, όν, adj., *clean,
pure*

μέγας, μεγάλη, μέγα, adj.,
great

μηδείς, μηδεμία, μηδέν, *no
one, nothing* (with moods
other than the indicative)

ὀλίγος, η, ον, adj., *little, few*

οὐδείς, οὐδεμία, οὐδέν, *no one,
nothing* (with the indicative)

πᾶς, πᾶσα, πᾶν, adj., *all, every*

πεντακισχίλιοι, αι, α, *five
thousand*

πέντε, indecl., *five*

πλῆθος, πλήθους, τό, *a
multitude*

πολύς, πολλή, πολύ, adj.,
much, many

πούς, ποδός, ὁ, *a foot*

στάδιον, τό, (plural τὰ
στάδια, but also masc. οἱ
στάδιοι), *a stadium, a furlong*

τέσσαρες, α, *four*

τρεῖς, τρία, *three*

ὡς, adv., *as; with numerals,
about*

365. The declension of πᾶς, πᾶσα, πᾶν, adj., all, every, is as follows:

	Sing.				Plur.		
	Masc.	Fem.	Neut.		Masc.	Fem.	Neut.
N.	πᾶς	πᾶσα	πᾶν	N.	πάντες	πᾶσαι	πάντα
G.	παντός	πάσης	παντός	G.	πάντων	πασῶν	πάντων
D.	παντί	πάσῃ	παντί	D.	πᾶσι(ν)	πάσαις	πᾶσι(ν)
A.	πάντα	πᾶσαν	πᾶν	A.	πάντας	πάσας	πάντα

139

366. The masculine and neuter stem is παντ- and the word is declined nearly like the first aorist active participle of λύω. But the accent is slightly irregular in the masculine and neuter, since it follows the rule for monosyllables of the third declension (see §221) in the singular but not in the plural.

The Use of πᾶς

367. πᾶς can stand in the predicate position with a noun that has the article. This usage corresponds so exactly with English as to call for little explanation.

Example: πᾶσα ἡ πόλις, *all the city*.

368. But πᾶς can also stand in the attributive position.

Example: ἡ πᾶσα πόλις, *the whole city*; οἱ πάντες μαθηταί, *the whole body of disciples, all the disciples*.

369. With a singular noun, πᾶς often means *every*.

Example: πᾶν ὄρος, *every mountain*. πᾶς is frequently used with article and participle.

Examples: πᾶς ὁ πιστεύων, *everyone who believes*; πάντες οἱ πιστεύοντες, *all those who believe*; πάντα τὰ ὄντα ἐκεῖ, *all the things that are there*.

370. Declension of πολύς and of μέγας

Learn the declension of πολύς, πολλή, πολύ, *much, many, great*, and of μέγας, μεγάλη, μέγα, *great*, in §574, §575. It will be observed that except for the short forms in the nominative, vocative and accusative, masculine and neuter singular, these two adjectives are declined like ordinary adjectives of the second and first declension.

Numerals

371. The declension of εἷς, μία, ἕν, *one*, is as follows:

	M.	F.	N.
N.	εἷς	μία	ἕν
G.	ἑνός	μιᾶς	ἑνός
D.	ἑνί	μιᾷ	ἑνί
A.	ἕνα	μίαν	ἕν

The slight irregularities should be noticed.

372. The declension of οὐδείς, οὐδεμία, οὐδέν, *no one*, and μηδείς, μηδεμία, μηδέν, *no one*, is like that of εἷς.

373. δύο, *two*, is indeclinable (the same for all cases and genders) except that it has a dative form δυσί(ν).

374. The declension of τρεῖς, τρία, *three*, and of τέσσαρες, τέσσαρα, *four*, may be found in §588.

375. The other cardinal numerals up to διακόσιοι, two hundred, are indeclinable.

Attributive and Substantive Uses of Prepositional Phrases and of the Genitive

376. Prepositional phrases are frequently treated as attributive adjectives, being placed after the article.

Example: οἱ ἐν ἐκείνῃ τῇ πόλει μαθηταί, or οἱ μαθηταὶ οἱ ἐν ἐκείνῃ τῇ πόλει, *the in-that-city disciples*, or (by a free translation) *the disciples who are* [or, if the leading verb is past, *were*] *in that city*. Here the prepositional phrase takes the exact place of an attributive adjective. It will be remembered that οἱ ἀγαθοὶ μαθηταί or οἱ μαθηταὶ οἱ ἀγαθοί means *the good disciples* (see §70). If in these two Greek phrases ἐν τῇ πόλει be substituted for the attributive adjective ἀγαθοί we have the idiom now under discussion.

377. Like other attributive adjectives, these prepositional phrases can be used substantively.

Example: As οἱ ἀγαθοί means *the good men*, so οἱ ἐν τῇ πόλει means *the in-the-city men*, or *the men who are* (or *were*) *in the city*.

378. A noun in the genitive case can be used in this same way.

Example: As οἱ ἀγαθοί means *the good men*, so οἱ τοῦ Ἰησοῦ means *the of-Jesus men, the belonging-to-Jesus men,* $\begin{cases} \textit{the ones} \\ \textit{the men} \\ \textit{those} \end{cases}$ *who belong to Jesus.*

379. The genitive in this usage may indicate various relationships. Sometimes it indicates sonship. Thus ὁ τοῦ Ζεβεδαίου may mean *the son of Zebedee*. The context must determine. All that is certainly implied in the Greek is that the person spoken of is connected in some way with Zebedee. The literal meaning of the phrase is *the belonging-to-Zebedee man.*

380. Notice that *the disciples who are in the city* may be expressed by οἱ μαθηταὶ οἱ ὄντες ἐν τῇ πόλει, *the being-in-the-city disciples*. But the ὄντες is not needed. So also *those who are in the city* might be οἱ ὄντες ἐν τῇ πόλει, *the being-in-the-city people*. But again the ὄντες is not needed. The prepositional phrase can be used as an attributive adjective just as well as the participle (with its modifiers) can.

381. All three of the idioms just discussed (οἱ ἐν τῇ πόλει μαθηται, οἱ ἐν τῇ πόλει, and οἱ τοῦ Ἰησοῦ) are important. It should now be increasingly evident how much of Greek syntax is dependent on the distinction between the attributive and the predicate position. See §68-§74.

382. Accusative of Extent of Space and Time

The accusative is used to express extent of space or time, answering the question *how far?* or *how long?*

Examples: ἐπορεύθην μετ' αὐτοῦ στάδιον ἕν, *I went with him one furlong*; ἔμεινα μίαν ἡμέραν, *I remained one day*.

383. Exercises

I 1. μείνας σὺν αὐτῷ ἔτη τρία ἦλθεν εἰς ἐκείνην τὴν πόλιν. 2. ἰδὼν δὲ τοὺς ἐν τῇ μεγάλῃ πόλει ἔγραψε καὶ τοῖς ἐν τῇ μικρᾷ¹. 3. πορευθέντες δὲ οἱ τοῦ Ἰακώβου σταδίους ὡς πέντε εἶδον τὸν Ἰησοῦν καὶ πάντας τοὺς μετ' αὐτοῦ μαθητάς. 4. ἀκούσαντες δὲ ταῦτα πάντα οἱ ἐν τῇ συναγωγῇ εἶπον ὅτι θέλουσιν ἰδεῖν τὸν ταῦτα ποιοῦντα. 5. ἐθαύμασεν πᾶν τὸ πλῆθος ἐν τῷ βλέπειν αὐτοὺς τὰ ποιούμενα ὑπὸ τοῦ Ἰησοῦ. 6. οὐκ ἔμεινε μίαν ἡμέραν ὁ μετὰ δύο ἔτη ἰδὼν τὸν ἀπόστολον τὸν εὐαγγελισάμενον αὐτόν. 7. τῶν ἀρχιερέων ὄντων ἐν ἐκείνῃ τῇ μεγάλῃ πόλει ἔμεινεν ὁ Ἰησοῦς ἐν τῇ κώμῃ

---

¹ What noun is naturally to be supplied with τῇ μικρᾷ?

ἡμέρας ὡς πέντε ἢ ἕξ. 8. δεῖ τοὺς ἐν ταῖς πόλεσιν ἐξελθεῖν εἰς τὰ ὄρη. 9. θεραπευθέντος ὑπὸ τοῦ Ἰησοῦ τοῦ ὑπὸ τῶν τεσσάρων προσενεχθέντος αὐτῷ ἐδόξασαν πάντες οἱ ἐν τῇ οἰκίᾳ τὸν ποιήσαντα τὰ μεγάλα ταῦτα. 10. πρὸ δὲ τοῦ ἐλθεῖν τοὺς ἐκ τῶν πόλεων ἦν ὁ Ἰησοῦς μετὰ τῶν μαθητῶν αὐτοῦ ἐν τῇ ἐρήμῳ. 11. ἐποιήθη μὲν δι' αὐτοῦ ὁ κόσμος καὶ πάντα τὰ ἐν αὐτῷ, αὐτὸς δὲ ἐγένετο δι' ἡμᾶς ὡς δοῦλος. 12. τοῦτο ἐποίησεν ἵνα σώσῃ πάντας τοὺς πιστεύοντας εἰς αὐτόν. 13. πᾶς ὁ ἀγαπῶν τὸν θεὸν ἀγαπᾷ καὶ τοὺς ἀδελφούς. 14. συνήχθησαν πάντες οἱ ἐν τῇ πόλει ἵνα ἀκούσωσι τὰ λεγόμενα ὑπὸ τῶν ἀποστόλων. 15. ταῦτα ἔλεγον οἱ ἐν τῷ οἴκῳ πᾶσι τοῖς ἀρχιερεῦσι καὶ γραμματεῦσι διὰ τὸ γινώσκειν αὐτοῖς πάντα τὰ περὶ τοῦ Ἰησοῦ. 16. ταῦτα ἐποίει ὁ βασιλεὺς τῶν Ἰουδαίων, ἤθελε γὰρ ἀποκρεῖναι τὰ ἐν τῇ κώμῃ παιδία. 17. οὐδεὶς γινώσκει πάντα τὰ ἐν τῷ κόσμῳ εἰ μὴ[1] ὁ ποιήσας τὰ παντα. 18. σωθήσεται οὐδεὶς ἐὰν μὴ διὰ πίστεως· ἐτήρησε γὰρ οὐδεὶς πάσας τὰς ἐντολὰς τοῦ θεοῦ. 19. προσευχώμεθα ὑπὲρ τῶν διωκόντων ἡμᾶς, ἵνα γενώμεθα υἱοὶ τοῦ πατρὸς ἡμῶν τοῦ ἐν οὐρανοῖς. 20. μακάριοι οἱ καθαροί, αὐτοὶ γὰρ τὸν θεὸν ὄψονται.

II 1. The chief priests saw that all the things which were being spoken by Jesus were true. 2. In that place there were about five thousand men with many gifts and many garments. 3. Many are those that go down into the evil way, but few are those who walk in the ways of life. 4. If ye become disciples of me I will show you all things. 5. By the grace of God all we have become disciples of Jesus. 6. Through faith we have become children of our Father who is in heaven, for Jesus has saved us. 7. Let us do all the things that are in the law, according to the things that are being said to us by the prophets. 8. In that great city we saw three disciples of the Lord praying to their Father in heaven[2]. 9. When Jesus had called one of the three men who were in the boat, he spake to him all the things concerning the Kingdom of God. 10. We were in the same city one year, but Jesus sent us into all the villages which are in Galilee. 11. When Jesus had done all these great things, the Pharisees said that a demon was in Him. 12. When Jesus had

---

[1] εἰ μή and ἐὰν μή are often to be translated except.

[2] With what is in heaven to be construed? If it is to be construed with Father, it should be put in the attributive position. The meaning then is our in-heaven Father, our Father who is in heaven.

spoken all these things to the multitudes who were in the cities and villages, He sent the disciples in order that they might preach in the other cities also. 13. All the churches shall see the One who saved them through His grace and sent to them the apostles. 14. Many kings and priests shall say that all the things which have been spoken by Jesus are true. 15. We saw no one in that great city except one disciple and a few children. 16. Those who belonged to Jesus died on account of their faith.

Lesson XXVII

Interrogative, Indefinite, and Relative Pronouns.
Deliberative Questions. Conditional Relative Clauses.

384. Vocabulary

αἰτέω, *I ask, I request*

εἰ, *whether* (in indirect questions) ; the common meaning, *if*, has already been given

ἐπερωτάω, *I ask a question of, I question*

ἐρωτάω, *I ask a question, I ask a question of, I question, I ask* (Originally ἐρωτάω meant *to ask* in the sense of *to question*, and αἰτέω meant *to ask* in the sense of *to request*. But in New Testament Greek ἐρωτάω is frequently used in the latter sense as well as in the former)

καρπός, ὁ, *a fruit*

κρίσις, κρίσεως, ἡ, *a judgment*

ὅπου, adv., *where* (relative)

ὅς, ἥ, ὅ, rel. pron., *who, which*

ὅταν, for ὅτε ἄν, *whenever* (with subjunctive)

ὅτε, adv., *when* (relative)

οὖν, conj., *accordingly, therefore, then* (postpositive, like δέ and γάρ. See §91)

πίνω, πίομαι (very irregular future), ἔπιον, *I drink*

ποῦ, adv., *where?* (interrogative)

πῶς, adv., *how?* (interrogative)

τίς, τί, interrogative pron., *who? which? what?*

τις, τι, indefinite pron., *someone, something, a certain one, a certain thing*

φάγομαι, fut. (very irregular), ἔφαγον, 2nd aor., of ἐσθίω, *I eat*

Interrogative and Indefinite Pronouns

385. The declension of the interrogative pronoun, τίς, τί, *who? which? what?*, is as follows:

	Sing. M.F.	N.		Plur. M.F.	N.
N.	τίς	τί	N.V.	τίνες	τίνα
G.	τίνος	τίνος	G.	τίνων	τίνων
D.	τίνι	τίνι	D.	τίσι(ν)	τίσι(ν)
A.	τίνα	τί	A.	τίνας	τίνα

145

386. The declension is according to the third declension in all three genders, the masculine and feminine being alike throughout, and the neuter differing from the masculine and feminine only in the nominative and accusative.

387. The acute accent in the interrogative pronoun is never changed to the grave.

Example: τί λέγει; *what does he say?*

388. The declension of the indefinite pronoun, τις, τι, *some one, something, a certain one, a certain thing,* is as follows:

	Sing.				Plur.	
	M.F.	N.			M.F.	N.
N.	τις	τι	N.V.		τινές	τινά
G.	τινός	τινός	G.		τινῶν	τινῶν
D.	τινί	τινί	D.		τισί(ν)	τισί(ν)
A.	τινά	τι	A.		τινάς	τινά

389. The indefinite pronoun is declined like the interrogative pronoun except that all the forms of the indefinite pronoun are enclitic and receive an accent only when the rules in §92 so prescribe.

390. Both the interrogative and the indefinite pronouns can be used either with a noun or separately.

Examples: (1) τίνα καρπὸν ἔχετε; *what fruit have ye?* (2) τί λέγεις; *what dost thou say?* (3) ἄνθρωπός τις, *a certain man;* (4) εἶπέν τις, *a certain man said.*

391. The accusative singular neuter, τί, of the interrogative pronoun is often used adverbially to mean *why.*

Example: τί ποιεῖτε ταῦτα; *why do ye do these things?*

Indirect Questions

392. Indirect questions, like the ordinary form of indirect discourse (see §308), retain the same mood and tense as those which would have been found in the direct discourse lying back of the indirect.

393. The same interrogative words are commonly used in indirect questions as those which are used in direct questions.

Examples: (1) ἠρώτησεν αὐτὸν τίς ἐστιν, he asked him who he was. The direct question lying back of the indirect was, τίς εἶ; *who art thou?* (2) εἶπεν αὐτοῖς ποῦ μένει, *he told them where he was abiding.* The direct question which he was answering was ποῦ μένεις; *where art thou abiding?*

394. Deliberative Questions

The subjunctive is used in deliberative questions. A deliberative question is a question that expects an answer in the imperative mood.

Examples: (1) ποιήσωμεν τοῦτο ἢ μὴ ποιήσωμεν; *shall we do this or shall we not do it?* The answer expected is in the imperative — *do it or do not do it.* (2) τί ποιήσωμεν, *what shall we do?* The natural answer is *do this* or *do that*, or the like.

The Relative Pronoun

395. The declension of the relative pronoun, ὅς, ἥ, ὅ, *who, which,* is as follows:

	Sing.				Plur.		
	Masc.	Fem.	Neut.		Masc.	Fem.	Neut.
N.	ὅς	ἥ	ὅ	N.V.	οἵ	αἵ	ἅ
G.	οὗ	ἧς	οὗ	G.	ὧν	ὧν	ὧν
D.	ᾧ	ᾗ	ᾧ	D.	οἷς	αἷς	οἷς
A.	ὅν	ἥν	ὅ	A.	οὕς	ἅς	ἅ

396. It will be observed that except for ὅ instead of ὅν in the nominative and accusative singular neuter (compare αὐτός and ἐκεῖνος) the declension of the relative pronoun is like that of a regular adjective of the second and first declension. The nominative singular feminine and the nominative plural masculine and feminine are like the corresponding forms of the article except that the article in those forms is proclitic.

397. Like other pronouns, the relative pronoun agrees with its antecedent in gender and number but has its own case in its own clause.

147

Example: (1) ὁ ἀπόστολος ὃν εἶδες ἀπῆλθεν, *the apostle whom you saw went away;* (2) ἀληθῆ ἦν πάντα ἃ εἶπεν ὁ Ἰησοῦς, *all things which Jesus said were true;* (3) ὁ μαθητὴς ὃν ἠγάπησεν ὁ Ἰησοῦς ἦν ἐν τῷ οἴκῳ, *the disciple whom Jesus loved was in the house.*

398. But where the antecedent of the relative pronoun is in the genitive or dative case and the relative pronoun itself would naturally be in the accusative case as the object of the verb in the relative clause, it is regularly *attracted* to the case of its antecedent.

Examples: πάντων δὲ θαυμαζόντων ἐπὶ πᾶσιν οἷς ἐποίει εἶπεν πρὸς τοὺς μαθητὰς αὐτοῦ ...., *but when all were wondering at all the things which He was doing, He said to his disciples........* Here οἷς would have been accusative if it had retained the case which it would have had in its own clause. But it is attracted to the case of πᾶσιν.

399. The antecedent of the relative pronoun is frequently left unexpressed. Thus ὅς can mean *he who;* ἥ, *she who;* ὅ, *that which, what;* οἵ, *the men who,* or *they who;* αἵ, *the women who;* ἅ, *the things which.*

Examples: (1) οὐκ ἔξεστίν μοι ὃ θέλω ποιῆσαι, *it is not lawful for me to do that which I wish (or to do what I wish).* (2) ὃς γὰρ οὐκ ἔστιν καθ’ ὑμῶν ὑπὲρ ὑμῶν ἐστιν, *for he who is not against you is for you.* In such a case essentially the same thought is expressed as by the article with participle— ὃς οὐκ ἔστιν is almost like ὁ μὴ ὤν. But in many cases only the article with participle could be used. For example *in the one who has* could hardly be expressed in any way but by ἐν τῷ ἔχοντι. (3) ἔχω ὃ θέλω, *I have what I wish.* Here the English word *what* is a short way of saying the *thing which* or *that which* and so is correctly translated by ὅ. Compare λέγω αὐτῷ τί ἔχω, *I tell him what I have.* Here the English word *what* is an interrogative word in an indirect question, and so is correctly translated by τί.

Conditional Relative Clauses

400. The indefinite relative clauses which in English are marked by the suffix -ever added to the relative word (e. g., *whoever, whichever, whatever, wherever, whenever*), have in Greek ordinarily the subjunctive with the particle ἄν or ἐάν. This is one of the commonest uses of the subjunctive.

Examples: (1) ὃς γὰρ ἐὰν θέλῃ τὴν ψυχὴν αὐτοῦ σῶσαι οὐ σώσει αὐτήν, *for whoever wishes to save his life shall not save it*; (2) ὃς ἂν πιστεύσῃ σωθήσεται, *whoever believes [or shall believe] shall be saved*; (3) εἰς ἣν δ' ἂν πόλιν εἰσέλθητε ὄψεσθε ἐν αὐτῇ μαθητάς, *and into whatever city ye enter [or shall enter] ye shall see disciples in it*; (4) ὅπου ἐὰν ᾖ ὁ διδάσκαλος ἐκεῖ ἔσονται καὶ οἱ διδασκόμενοι ὑπ' αὐτοῦ, *wherever the teacher is there will be also those who are being taught by him.*

401. It will be observed that the verb in the English translation of these conditional relative clauses can be either future indicative or present indicative. It often makes little difference which is used. In such clauses the present indicative in English frequently refers to future time.

402. Exercises

I 1. ὃς ἐὰν μὴ δέξηται ὑμᾶς τοῦτον οὐ δέξεται ὁ βασιλεύς. 2. ἃ ἐὰν ποιήσωμεν ὑμῖν, ποιήσετε καὶ ὑμεῖς ἡμῖν. 3. ἐρωτήσαντός τινος αὐτοὺς τί φάγῃ ἀπεκρίθησαν αὐτῷ λέγοντες ὅτι δεῖ αὐτὸν φαγεῖν τὸν ἄρτον τὸν ἐν τῷ οἴκῳ. 4. τίνος[1] ἔσται ταῦτα πάντα ἐν τῇ ἐσχάτῃ ἡμέρᾳ; 5. ὅταν ἔλθῃ ὁ υἱὸς τοῦ ἀνθρώπου τίνες ἔσονται οἱ πιστεύοντες; 6. ὃς ἂν λύσῃ μίαν τῶν ἐντολῶν ποιεῖ ὃ οὐκ ἔξεστιν ποιεῖν. 7. ἃ εἶπεν ὑμῖν ὁ προφήτης ἔτι ὢν μεθ' ὑμῶν ταῦτα ἐροῦσι καὶ οἱ εὐαγγελισάμενοι ἡμᾶς. 8. ἐάν τις ἀπὸ νεκρῶν πορευθῇ πρὸς αὐτούς, μετανοήσουσιν. 9. ὃς ἐὰν μὴ ἀκούσῃ τῶν προφητῶν οὐδὲ μετανοήσει ἐάν τινα ἴδῃ τῶν νεκρῶν. 10. οἳ ἂν εἴπωσιν ἃ οὐκ ἔστιν ἀληθῆ οὐ λήμψονται καρπόν τινα τοῦ ἔργου αὐτῶν. 11. ἔλεγεν ὅτι ἐάν τις ἐγερθῇ ἐκ νεκρῶν μετανοήσουσιν. 12. ἠρώτησαν τὸν προφήτην οἱ ἐν τῇ Γαλιλαίᾳ εἰ οἱ νεκροὶ ἀκούσουσι τῆς φωνῆς τοῦ κυρίου. 13. εἶπεν οὖν αὐτοῖς ὅτι ἐν τῇ κρίσει ἀκούσουσιν πάντες τοῦ κυρίου. 14. ἐλθόντες οἱ φαρισαῖοι εἴς τινα κώμην ἐπηρώτησαν τοὺς ἐν αὐτῇ λέγοντες Ποῦ εἰσιν οἱ τοῦ προφήτου· ἃ γὰρ λέγουσι περὶ αὐτῶν οἱ ἐν τῇ Γαλιλαίᾳ οὐκ ἔστιν ἀληθῆ. 15. ἔλεγε δὲ ὁ ἐπερωτηθεὶς Τί ἐπερωτᾷς με; οὐ γὰρ θέλω ἀποκρίνεσθαί σοι

---

[1] A noun or pronoun in the genitive case may stand in the predicate with the verb to be. Thus ἡ βασιλεία ἐστὶ τοῦ θεοῦ or θεοῦ ἐστιν ἡ βασιλεία means the kingdom is God's or the kingdom belongs to God.

οὐδέν[1]. 16. ἔλεγεν οὖν τῶν μαθητῶν τις τῷ ἀποστόλῳ Τί ποιήσει οὗτος; ὁ δὲ ἀπόστολος εὐθὺς ἀπεκρίθη αὐτῷ λέγων Ποιήσει ὁ θεὸς ἃ θέλει καὶ πάντα ἃ θέλει ἐστίν ἀγαθά. 17. ἃ ἔβλεπε τὸν κύριον ποιοῦντα ταῦτα ἤθελε καὶ αὐτὸς ποιεῖν.

II 1. We did what those who were in the same city asked. 2. The priests whom we saw while they were still there asked us who those disciples were. 3. Whoever does not do what I say shall not receive from me what he asks. 4. A certain scribe went into the city in order that he might take the books which the prophets had written. 5. Into whatever nation we go, let us seek the disciples who are in it. 6. What shall we say concerning all these things? 7. They asked us what they should say concerning those in the city. 8. A certain man having come to Jesus said that he wished to be healed. 9. Whoever shall ask anything shall receive what he asks. 10. They asked Jesus what the will of God was. 11. Whoever kills his brother will come into the judgment. 12. Why then do you eat what it is not lawful to eat? 13. Whoever is not taught by the Lord will not know Him. 14. When the chief priests had seen what Jesus was doing they sent a certain messenger to the Pharisees. 15. Where shall we abide? For the night is coming and no one has said to us what we shall do.

---

[1] The Greek language frequently uses a double negative where it is not allowable in English. Thus οὐ λέγω οὐδέν means *I do not say anything, or I say nothing.*

Lesson XXVIII

The Imperative Mood.

403. Vocabulary

ἁγιάζω, *I hallow, I sanctify*

ἀγρός, ὁ, *a field*

γῆ, ἡ, *earth, land* (γῆ has the circumflex accent throughout, because there has been contraction)

ἐγγύς, adv., *near*

ἐλεέω, *I have mercy on, I pity*

ὅσος, η, ον, rel. adj., *as great as, as much as, as many as*

ὅστις, ἥτις, ὅτι, (plural οἵτινες), indef. rel. pron.,

whoever, whichever, whatever (scarcely used except in the nominative case; sometimes used almost like the simple relative pronoun ὅς)

οὖς, ὠτός, τό, *an ear*

ὀφθαλμός, ὁ, *an eye*

σκότος, σκότους, τό, *darkness*

ὕδωρ, ὕδατος, τό, *water*

φῶς, φωτός, τό, *light*

404. The imperative mood occurs in the New Testament almost exclusively in the present and aorist tenses.

405. The present imperative, active, middle, and passive, is formed on the present stem; the aorist imperative, active and middle, on the aorist stem; and the aorist passive imperative, on the aorist passive stem. There is of course no augment. See §245.

406. The imperative mood has no first person, but only second and third.

407. The present active imperative of λύω is as follows:

	Sing.		Plur.
2.	λῦε, *loose (thou)*	2.	λύετε, *loose (ye)*
3.	λυέτω, *let him loose*	3.	λυέτωσαν, *let them loose*

408. The present middle imperative of λύω is as follows:

Sing.		Plur.	
2.	λύου, *loose (thou) for thyself*	2.	λύεσθε, *loose (ye) for yourselves*
3.	λυέσθω, *let him loose for himself*	3.	λυέσθωσαν, *let them loose for themselves*

409. The present passive imperative of λύω is as follows:

Sing.		Plur.	
2.	λύου, *be (thou) loosed*	2.	λύεσθε, *be (ye) loosed*
3.	λυέσθω, *let him be loose*	3.	λυέσθωσαν, *let them be loosed*

410. It will be observed that the present active and the present middle and passive imperative have the variable vowel o/ε.

411. The aorist active imperative of λύω is as follows:

Sing.		Plur.	
2.	λῦσον, *loose (thou)*	2.	λύσατε, *loose (ye)*
3.	λυσάτω, *let him loose*	3.	λυσάτωσαν, *let them loose*

412. The aorist middle imperative of λύω is as follows:

Sing.		Plur.	
2.	λῦσαι, *loose (thou) for thyself*	2.	λύσασθε, *loose (ye) for yourselves*
3.	λυσάσθω, *let him loose for himself*	3.	λυσάσθωσαν, *let them loose for themselves*

413. It will be observed that the aorist active and the aorist middle imperative have the characteristic -σα of the aorist stem. This -σα is disguised only in λῦσον, the second aorist active imperative, second person singular.

414. The aorist passive imperative of λύω is as follows:

Sing.		Plur.	
2.	λύθητι, *be (thou) loosed*	2.	λύθητε, *be (ye) loosed*
3.	λυθήτω, *let him be loosed*	3.	λυθήτωσαν, *let them be loosed*

415. It will be observed that the aorist passive imperative has the characteristic -θε of the aorist passive stem. This -θε is lengthened to -θη.

416. The second aorist active imperative of λείπω, I leave, is as follows:

Sing.		Plur.	
2.	λίπε, *leave (thou)*	2.	λίπετε, *leave (ye*
3.	λιπέτω, *let him leave*	3.	λιπέτωσαν, *let them leave*

417. The second aorist middle imperative of λείπω is as follows:

Sing.		Plur.	
2.	λιποῦ	2.	λίπεσθε
3.	λιπέσθω	3.	λιπέσθωσαν

418. It will be observed that the second aorist active and the second aorist middle imperative are formed on the second aorist stem. They have the same endings as the present imperative.

419. The second aorist middle imperative second person singular (e. g. λιποῦ) always has an irregular accent, instead of following the rule of recessive accent.

Further, the forms εἰπέ, ἐλθέ, from λέγω and ἔρχομαι, have an irregular accent.

420. The Tenses in the Imperative Mood

There is no distinction of time between the tenses in the imperative mood. The aorist imperative refers to the action without saying anything about its duration or repetition, while the present imperative refers to it as continuing or as being repeated. Thus λῦσον means simply loose, while λῦε means continue loosing, or the like. Ordinarily

153

it is impossible to bring out the difference in an English translation. Compare §283.

421. The Use of the Imperative

The imperative mood is used in commands.

Examples: ἀκούσατε τοὺς λόγους μου, *hear my words*; ὁ ἔχων ὦτα ἀκούσατε, *let him who has ears hear*. It will be observed that the English language has, properly speaking, no imperative of the third person. Hence in translating the Greek imperative of the third person we have to use the helping verb let, so that the noun or pronoun that is the subject of the imperative in Greek becomes the object of the helping verb in English.

422. Prohibition

Prohibition (the negative of a command) is expressed by the present imperative with μή or by the aorist subjunctive with μή.

Examples: (1) μὴ λῦε or μὴ λύσῃς, *do not loose* (μὴ λύῃς or μὴ λῦσον would be wrong); (2) μὴ λυέτω or μὴ λύσῃ, *let him not loose*; (3) μὴ λύετε or μὴ λύσητε, *do not loose*; (4) μὴ λυέτωσαν or μὴ λύσωσιν, *let them not loose*.

423. Present Imperative of εἰμί

The present imperative of εἰμί, I am, is as follows:

	Sing.		Plur.
2.	ἴσθι, *be (thou)*	2.	ἔστε, *be (ye)*
3.	ἔστω, *let him be*	3.	ἔστωσαν, *let them be*

424. Exercises

I 1. ἐὰν δὲ μὴ ἀκούσῃ, παράλαβε μετὰ σοῦ ἔτι ἕνα ἢ δύο. 2. ὃ ἐὰν ἴδητε τὸν Χριστὸν ποιοῦντα, τοῦτο ποιήσατε καὶ ὑμεῖς. 3. κύριε, ἐλέησον ἡμᾶς, οὐ γὰρ ἐποιήσαμεν ἃ ἐκέλευσας. 4. μὴ εἰσέλθῃ εἰς τὴν πόλιν ὁ ἐν τῷ ὄρει. 5. οὕτως οὖν προσεύχεσθε ὑμεῖς Πάτερ ἡμῶν ὁ ἐν τοῖς οὐρανοῖς· Ἁγιασθήτω τὸ ὄνομά σου· ἐλθάτω[1] ἡ

---

[1] A first aorist ending is here placed on a second aorist stem, as very frequently in New Testament Greek. See §186, footnote 16, and §521.

βασιλεία σου· γενηθήτω[1] τὸ θέλημά σου, ὡς ἐν οὐρανῷ καὶ ἐπὶ γῆς. 6. ἀπόλυσον οὖν, κύριε, τὰ πλήθη· ἤδη γὰρ ἔρχεται ἡ νύξ. 7. μηδεὶς ἐξέλθῃ εἰς τὰ ὄρη, προσευξάσθωσαν δὲ πάντες τῷ πατρὶ αὐτῶν τῷ ἐν τοῖς οὐρανοῖς. 8. λαβὼν αὐτὸν ἄγε πρὸς ἡμᾶς. 9. μηδενὶ εἴπητε ὃ εἴδετε. 10. ἐγέρθητε[2] καὶ μὴ φοβεῖσθε· ὁ γὰρ κύριος σώσει ὑμᾶς. 11. πάντα οὖν ὅσα ἐὰν εἴπωσιν ὑμῖν ποιήσατε καὶ τηρεῖτε, κατὰ δὲ τὰ ἔργα αὐτῶν μὴ ποιεῖτε· λέγουσιν γὰρ καὶ οὐ ποιοῦσιν. 12. ἔλεγεν αὐτῷ μαθητής τις Κύριε, κέλευσόν με ἐλθεῖν πρὸς σὲ ἐπὶ τὰ ὕδατα. ὁ δὲ Ἰησοῦς εἶπεν Ἐλθέ. 13. ὅσα ἐὰν ἀκούσητε τοῖς ὠσὶν ὑμῶν καὶ ἴδητε τοῖς ὀφθαλμοῖς ὑμῶν εἴπετε καὶ τοῖς ἔθνεσιν. 14. ἃ ἐὰν ἀκούσητε ἐν τῷ σκότει κηρύξατε ἐν τῷ φωτί. 15. μακάριος ὅστις φάγεται ἄρτον ἐν τῇ βασιλείᾳ τοῦ θεοῦ. 16. ἐν ἐκείνῃ τῇ πόλει εἰσὶν ἱερεῖς πονηροί, οἵτινες οὐ ποιοῦσι τὸ θέλημα τοῦ θεοῦ. 17. ἐξελθόντες εἴπετε πᾶσι τοῖς ἔθνεσι τοῖς ἐπὶ πάσης τῆς γῆς ἃ ἐποίησεν ὁ θεὸς τοῖς ἀγαπῶσιν αὐτόν. 18. ὅταν κληθῇς ὑπὸ τινος, πορεύθητι. 19. ὅταν ἴδητε ταῦτα γινόμενα, γνώσεσθε ὅτι ἐγγύς ἐστιν ἡ κρίσις. 20. ἴδετε πάντες ὑμεῖς τὰς χεῖράς μου· οὐ γὰρ ἐποίησαν αὗται αἱ χεῖρες ὧν λέγουσιν ἐκεῖνοι οὐδέν.

II 1. Speak ye to all the Gentiles the things which I have spoken to you. 2. Do not say in your heart that ye do not wish to do the things which the king commands. 3. Let no one fear those evil priests, for whoever does the will of God shall go out with joy. 4. Let Him who has saved us through His blood have mercy on us in these evil days. 5. Whosoever loves God shall come to the light, but he who does not love Him shall walk in the darkness. 6. As manysoever things as ye do, do in the light, in order that the name of God may be hallowed. 7. Let these men be baptized, for Christ has saved them through His word. 8. Pray to thy Father in heaven, for He will do whatsoever things thou askest. 9. Let not the king say this, for we are all faithful men. 10. Let us not do the things which the evil men said to us. 11. Have mercy on all men, for the Lord has had mercy on you. 12. As many as are good, do; but as many things as are evil, do not even speak concerning these. 13. The disciples asked the apostle what they should eat, and the

---

[1] The aorist passive of γίνομαι is the same in meaning as the aorist middle, the verb being deponent throughout. The meaning of the verb here is to take place, to be done.
[2] The passive of ἐγείρω is frequently used as a deponent meaning I arise, I rise.

apostle said to them, "Go into the villages and eat the bread which is in them." 14. Do not begin to say in yourselves that you do not know the truth. 15. Let those who are in the fields not return into their houses. 16. Lord, save me, for I have broken thy commandments.

Lesson XXIX

The Perfect Tense. Review of λύω

425. Vocabulary

ἀκήκοα, perf. act. indic. of
ἀκούω, I hear
βεβάπτισμαι, perf. pass. indic.
of βαπτίζω, I baptize
γέγονα, perf. indic. of
γίνομαι, I become (γίνεται,
it comes to pass, it happens)
γέγραφα, γέγραμμαι, perf.
act. and perf. pass. indic. of
γράφω, I write
γεννάω, I beget
ἐγγίζω, I come near
ἐγήγερται, perf. pass. indic.,
third pers. sing., of ἐγείρω,
I raise up
ἔγνωκα, perf. act. indic. of
γινώσκω, I know

ἐλήλυθα, perf. indic. of
ἔρχομαι, I come, I go
ἐρρέθην, aor. pass. indic.(aor.
pass. part. ῥηθείς) of λέγω,
I say
ἑώρακα, perf. act. indic. of
βλέπω (ὁράω), I see
θνήσκω, I die (used only in the
perfect, τέθνηκα, I am dead,
and in the pluperfect. In
other tenses ἀποθνήσκω is
used)
μαρτυρέω, I bear witness
Πέτρος, ὁ, Peter
πληρόω, I fulfill

426. The perfect active indicative of λύω is as follows:

	Sing.		Plur.
1.	λέλυκα	1.	λελύκαμεν
2.	λέλυκας	2.	λελύκατε
3.	λέλυκε(ν)	3.	λελύκασι (or λέλυκαν)

427. The perfect active infinitive of λύω is λελυκέναι. The irregular accent should be noticed.

428. The perfect active participle of λύω is λελυκώς, λελυκυῖα, λελυκός. The irregular accent should be noticed.

157

429. The forms given above constitute the *perfect system*, which is formed from the fourth of the principal parts, λέλυκα.

430. The perfect system is formed by adding κ (in the indicative κα) to the verb stem, and by prefixing the *reduplication*. The reduplication consists in the first consonant of the verb stem followed by ε.

431. The perfect, being a primary tense, might be expected to have primary personal endings. But in the indicative the endings are exactly like the (secondary) endings of the first aorist, except in the third person plural, and even in the third person plural λέλυκαν sometimes stands instead of λελύκασι(ν).

432. The perfect active subjunctive is so rare that it need not be learned.

433. The declension of the perfect active participle is as follows:

Sing.

	M.	F.	N.
N.	λελυκώς	λελυκυῖα	λελυκός
G.	λελυκότος	λελυκυίας	λελυκότος
D.	λελυκότι	λελυκυίᾳ	λελυκότι
A.	λελυκότα	λελυκυῖαν	λελυκός

Plur.

	M.	F.	N.
N.	λελυκότες	λελυκυῖαι	λελυκότα
G.	λελυκότων	λελυκυιῶν	λελυκότων
D.	λελυκόσι(ν)	λελυκυίαις	λελυκόσι(ν)
A.	λελυκότας	λελυκυίας	λελυκότα

434. It will be observed that the perfect active participle, like the other active participles and like the aorist passive participle, is declined according to the third declension in the masculine and neuter and according to the first declension in the feminine.

Formation of the Perfect Stem in Various Verbs

435. If the verb stem begins with a vowel or diphthong, the reduplication consists in the lengthening of that vowel or diphthong. In this case the reduplication is like the augment.

Examples: The perfect active of ἐλπίζω is ἤλπικα, and of αἰτέω, ἤτηκα.

436. If the verb stem begins with two consonants the reduplication in certain cases (by no means always) consists in the prefixing of an ἐ (like the augment) instead of the repetition of the first consonant with ε.

Examples: ἔγνωκα is the perfect of γινώσκω. But γέγραφα is the perfect of γράφω.

437. Verb stems beginning with φ, θ or χ, are reduplicated with π, τ and κ, respectively.

Examples: πεφίληκα is the perfect of φιλέω; τέθνηκα, *I am dead*, is the perfect of θνήσκω (the present does not occur in the New Testament).

438. If the verb stem ends with a vowel that vowel is regularly lengthened before the κ of the perfect active, just as it is before the σ of the future and first aorist.

Examples: ἠγάπηκα from ἀγαπάω, πεφίληκα from φιλέω.

439. If the verb stem ends with τ, δ or θ, the τ, δ or θ is dropped before the κ of the perfect.

Example: ἤλπικα from ἐλπίζω (stem ἐλπίδ-).

440. Some verbs have a *second perfect*, which is conjugated like the first perfect except that there is no κ.

Examples: γέγραφα from γράφω; ἀκήκοα from ἀκούω.

441. In general, the student should remember what was said in §159 about the variety in the formation of the tense systems of the Greek verb.

Perfect Middle and Passive

442. The perfect middle and passive indicative of λύω is as follows:

	Sing.		Plur.
1.	λέλυμαι	1.	λελύμεθα
2.	λέλυσαι	2.	λέλυσθε
3.	λέλυται	3.	λέλυνται

443. The perfect middle and passive infinitive of λύω is λελύσθαι. The irregular accent should be noticed.

444. The perfect middle and passive participle of λύω is λελυμένος, η, ον, (declined like a regular adjective of the second and first declension).

The irregular accent should be noticed.

445. The forms given above constitute the perfect middle system, which is formed from the fifth of the principal parts, λέλυμαι.

446. The reduplication is the same as in the perfect active.

447. In the indicative, the primary middle endings (see §111) are added directly to the stem, without intervening variable vowel. They are not modified at all. So in the infinitive and participle -σθαι and -μενος are added directly to the stem.

448. If the verb stem ends with a vowel, that vowel is regularly lengthened before the endings in the perfect middle and passive, as before the tense suffixes in the future, first aorist, perfect active, and aorist passive.

Example: μεμαρτύρημαι from μαρτυρέω.

449. If the verb stem ends with a consonant, various changes occur when the endings of the perfect middle and passive are put on. These changes are best learned by observation in the individual verbs.

Example: γέγραμμαι (third person singular γέγραπται) from γράφω.

450. Pluperfect Tense

The pluperfect tense is so rare that its forms need not be learned. It is a secondary tense. The pluperfect active forms a part of the perfect system; and the pluperfect middle and passive, of the perfect middle system.

Use of the Perfect Tense

451. There is no English tense corresponding to the Greek perfect. The translations I have loosed for λέλυκα, *I have loosed for myself* for λέλυμαι (middle), and *I have been loosed* for λέλυμαι (passive) may often serve in the exercises. But they are makeshifts at the best. It has already been observed (see §169) that these same English expressions may often translate the aorist tense rather than the perfect.

452. The Greek perfect tense denotes the present state resultant upon a past action.

Examples: (1) Suppose someone asks an official, "What is your relation to that prisoner?", and he replies, "I have released him," the verb in this answer of the official would be λέλυκα. The perfect would express the present state of the official (with reference to the prisoner) resultant upon his past action of releasing. But if, on the other hand, someone should ask an official, "What is the history of your dealings with that prisoner?" and he should answer, "I have released the prisoner three times and imprisoned him again three times," the first verb of this answer of the official would be ἔλυσα, not λέλυκα, because there is here no thought of the present state resultant upon the past action. Indeed the act of releasing had no result continuing into the present. But even if it had a permanent result the verb referring to it would be aorist, not perfect, unless the present result rather than merely the past action were specially in view. Thus even if, after the question, "What have you done?" the official said merely, "I have released the prisoner," and even if as a matter of fact the releasing had a permanent result, still the aorist tense ἔλυσα might very well be used; for the point under consideration might be the history of the official's dealings with the prisoner and not the official's present relation to him. The distinction is often a fine one. But the perfect should not be used in the exercises unless we can see some clear reason for deserting the aorist.

(2) The perfect passive is often much easier to translate into English than the perfect active. Thus γέγραπται means *it is written* (in the Scriptures). Here the English *it is written* is not a perfect tense at all, but reproduces the Greek perfect very well; the meaning is *it stands written*. Both English and Greek here refer to a present state resultant upon an act of writing which took place long ago.

(3) The perfect passive participle can often be translated neatly by the simple English passive participle. Thus λόγος γεγραμμένος means *a written word*, ἠγαπημένος *means beloved*, etc. But the Greek

perfect active participle is very hard to translate. The student should carefully avoid thinking that *having loosed* is specially connected with the perfect. On the contrary, in the overwhelming majority of cases, *having loosed* is the literal translation of the aorist, not of the perfect— the participle *having* merely indicating that the action has taken place prior to the action of the main verb in the sentence. In general, it should be observed that the Greek aorist is vastly commoner than the perfect.

(4) ἐλήλυθα, the perfect of ἔρχομαι, means *I am come*, and γέγονα means *I am become*. It so happens that because of the peculiar nature of the verbs *to come* and *to become* in English we have a neat way of translating the Greek perfect of ἔρχομαι and γίνομαι. Of course the student should not think that *I am come* has anything to do with the passive voice. It is not at all like *I am loosed*.

453. The conjugation of λύω has now been completed. The student should review it thoroughly as a whole, using the paradigm given in §589. The verb should be learned in columns, strictly in the order given. Thus "present-active" should form one idea in the student's mind, and under it should be subsumed the various moods. It should be noticed particularly how the various parts of the verb are connected with the several principal parts.

454. Exercises

I 1. οὐδείς ἐστιν δίκαιος κατὰ τὸν νόμον εἰ μὴ ὁ ποιήσας πάντα τὰ γεγραμμένα ἐν τῷ βιβλίῳ τοῦ νόμου. 2. εὐηγγελίσατο πάντα τὸν λαόν λέγων ὅτι ἤγγικεν ἡ βασιλεία τῶν οὐρανῶν. 3. ὃ ἑωράκαμεν καὶ ἀκηκόαμεν λέγομεν καὶ ὑμῖν, ἵνα καὶ ὑμεῖς πιστεύσητε εἰς τὸν Χριστόν. 4. καὶ ἐν τούτῳ γινώσκομεν ὅτι ἐγνώκαμεν αὐτόν, ἐὰν τὰς ἐντολὰς αὐτοῦ τηρῶμεν. 5. ὁ ἀγαπῶν τὸν γεννήσαντα ἀγαπᾷ τὸν γεγεννημένον ἐξ αὐτοῦ. 6. πᾶς ὁ γεγεννημένος ἐκ τοῦ θεοῦ οὐχ ἁμαρτάνει, ἀλλ' ὁ γεννηθεὶς ἐκ τοῦ θεοῦ τηρεῖ αὐτόν. 7. τοῦτο γέγονεν[1], ὅτι οὕτως γέγραπται διὰ τοῦ προφήτου. 8. τὸ γεγεννημένον ἐκ τῆς σαρκος σάρξ ἐστιν, καὶ τὸ γεγεννημένον ἐκ τοῦ πνεύματος πνεῦμά ἐστιν. 9. αὕτη δέ ἐστιν ἡ κρίσις, ὅτι τὸ φῶς ἐλήλυθεν εἰς τὸν κόσμον καὶ ἠγάπησαν οἱ ἄνθρωποι τὸ σκότος. 10. ἔλεγον οὖν οἱ Ἰουδαῖοι τῷ τεθεραπευμένῳ οὐκ ἔξεστιν ποιῆσαι

---

[1] γίνομαι here means to take place, to come to pass, to happen.

τοῦτο. 11. ἐγὼ ἐλήλυθα ἐν τῷ ὀνόματι τοῦ πατρός μου καὶ οὐ δέχεσθέ με. 12. ἀλλ' εἶπον ὑμῖν ὅτι καὶ ἑωράκατέ με καὶ οὐ πιστεύετε. 13. ἐὰν μὴ φάγητε τὴν σάρκα τοῦ υἱοῦ τοῦ ἀνθρώπου καὶ πίητε αὐτοῦ τὸ αἷμα, οὐκ ἔχετε ζωὴν ἐν ἑαυτοῖς. 14. τὰ ῥήματα ἃ ἐγὼ λελάληκα ὑμῖν πνεῦμά ἐστιν καὶ ζωή ἐστιν. 15. ἀπεκρίθη αὐτῷ Πέτρος Κύριε, πρὸς τίνα ἀπελευσόμεθα; ῥήματα ζωῆς ἔχεις, καὶ ἡμεῖς πεπιστεύκαμεν καὶ ἐγνώκαμεν ὅτι σὺ εἶ ὁ ἅγιος τοῦ θεοῦ. 16. ταῦτα αὐτοῦ λαλοῦντος πολλοὶ ἐπίστευσαν εἰς αὐτόν. 17. γέγραπται ὅτι δύο ἀνθρώπων ἡ μαρτυρία ἀληθής ἐστιν. 18. ταῦτα εἶπεν πρὸς τοὺς πεπιστευκότας εἰς αὐτὸν Ἰουδαίους. 19. νῦν δὲ ζητεῖτέ με ἀποκτεῖναι, ἄνθρωπον ὃς τὴν ἀλήθειαν ὑμῖν λελάληκα,[1] ἣν ἤκουσα παρὰ τοῦ θεοῦ. 20. εὐλογημένος ὁ ἐρχόμενος ἐν ὀνόματι κυρίου.

II 1. Where is the priest? He is already come. 2. All the baptized disciples are in the small city. 3. The priests having been baptized came together into the same house. 4. Where is the multitude? It has already come near. 5. What is in thy heart? I have believed on the Lord. 6. Art thou faithful? I have kept the faith. 7. It is written through the prophet that the Messiah is coming in these days, and we know that His kingdom is come near. 8. Children beloved by your Father, enter ye into the joy kept in heaven for those who have believed on Christ. 9. Who is this man? He is a child begotten by God. 10. Having been crucified by the soldiers the Lord died, but now He is risen. 11. Brethren beloved by all the disciples, why do ye not pity the little ones? 12. Those who are come out of the darkness into the light know that God will do all the things written in the Law and the prophets. 13. All the things written or spoken through this prophet are true. 14. This is come to pass in order that that which was said by the Lord through the prophet might be fulfilled. 15. If thou art already loosed, give thanks

---

[1] The relative pronoun agrees with its antecedent in person as well as in gender and number. In this sentence, the antecedent of ὅς is ἄνθρωπον, which is first person because it is in apposition with the personal pronoun of the first person, με.

to Him who loosed you. 16. Where is the prophet whom the soldiers persecuted? He is become king of many cities.

Lesson XXX

Comparison of Adjectives. Declension of μείζων. Genitive of Comparison and Use of ἤ. Adverbs. Genitive with Adverbs of Place. Genitive of Time. Genitive of the Articular Infinitive Expressing Purpose. Dative of Respect. Accusative of Specification. Dative of Time. Possessive Adjectives, μή Used as a Conjunction, ἵνα with the Subjunctive in Various Uses, μή with the Indicative in Questions Expecting a Negative Answer.

455. Vocabulary

ἐμός, ή, όν, poss. adj., *belonging to me, my*

ἔμπροσθεν, adv., in front, *in the presence of* (with gen.)

ἐνώπιον, adv., before, *in the sight of, in the presence of* (with gen.)

ἔξω, adv., outside, *outside of* (with gen.)

ἐχθρός, ὁ, *an enemy*

ἤ, than (the meaning or has already been given)

ἡμέτερος, α, ον, poss. adj., *belonging to us, our*

ἴδιος, α, ον, *belonging to one's self, one's own*

ἱκανός, ή, όν, *sufficient, worthy, considerable*

ἰσχυρότερος, α, ον, *stronger, comparative of*

ἰσχυρός, α, ον, *strong*

καλῶς, adv., *well*

κρείσσων, ον, *better, comparative of ἀγαθός*

μᾶλλον, adv., *more, rather*

μείζων, ον, *greater, comparative of* μεγας

μή, conj., *lest, in order that not* (the adverbial use of μή = not has already been given).

μήποτε, *lest perchance*

ὅπως, in order that (takes the subjunctive. Used very much as ἵνα is used)

πάλιν, adv., *again*

πλείων, ον, *more,* comparative of πολύς

σάββατον, τό, *sabbath* (the plural τὰ σάββατα, with irregular dative τοῖς σάββασι(ν), is often used in the singular sense)

σός, ή, όν, poss. adj., *belonging to thee, thy*

ὑμέτερος, α, ον, poss. adj., *belonging to you, your*

165

Comparison of Adjectives

456. The comparative degree of adjectives ends sometimes in -τερος, α, ον, (declined like a regular adjective of the second and first declension) and sometimes in -ιων, -ιων, -ιον (declined according to the third declension in all three genders).

457. The superlative degree ends in -τατος, η, ον, or -ιστος, η, ον, But in the New Testament the superlative is rather rare.

458. A number of adjectives have irregular comparative and superlative forms. These can be learned from the lexicon as they occur. Example: μικρός, *little*; ἐλάσσων, *less*; ἐλάχιστος, least.

459. The declension of μείζων, ον, *greater*, the comparative of μέγας, is as follows:

	Sing.			Plur.	
	M.F.	N.		M.F.	N.
N.	μείζων	μεῖζον	N.V.	μείζονες	μείζονα
G.	μείζονος	μείζονος	G.	μειζόνων	μειζόνων
D.	μείζονι	μείζονι	D.	μείζοσι(ν)	μείζοσι(ν)
A.	μείζονα	μεῖζον	A.	μείζονας	μείζονα

460. σώφρων, wise, ἄφρων, foolish, ἐλάσσων, less, πλείων, more, κρείσσων, better, etc., are similarly declined.

461. The shortened form, μείζω, can stand for μείζονα in the accusative singular masculine and feminine and neuter plural nominative and accusative, and the shortened form, μείζους, in the nominative and accusative plural masculine and feminine.

462. Genitive of Comparison and Use of ἤ, *than*

Where English uses than after a comparative word, Greek uses either (1) the genitive of comparison or (2) ἤ followed by the same case as that which stands in the other member of the comparison.

Examples: (1) μείζονα τούτων ποιήσει, *greater things than these will he do.* (2) ἠγάπησαν οἱ ἄνθρωποι μᾶλλον τὸ σκότος ἤ τὸ φῶς, *men*

166

loved darkness more than light. Here φῶς is accusative. The meaning is *men loved darkness more than they loved light.*

Adverbs

463. Many adverbs are formed from adjectives by substituting ς for ν at the end of the genitive plural masculine and neuter.

Example: καλός, good; genitive plural, καλῶν; adverb, καλῶς, well.

464. The comparative degree of adverbs is like the accusative singular neuter of the comparative degree of the corresponding adjective; and the superlative degree of the adverb is like the accusative plural neuter of the superlative degree of the corresponding adjective.

465. Many adverbs, however, are of diverse forms which must be learned by observation.

466. The Genitive with Adverbs of Place

Adverbs of place take the genitive.

Example: ἔξω, *outside*; ἔξω τῆς πόλεως, *outside of the city*; ἐγγὺς τῆς πόλεως, *near the city.*

467. Genitive of Time Within Which

The genitive is occasionally used to express time within which.

Example: παρέλαβε τὸ παιδίον καὶ τὴν μητέρα αὐτοῦ νυκτός, *he took the young child and His mother by night.*

468. Genitive of the Articular Infinitive Expressing Purpose

The genitive of the articular infinitive, without any preposition, is sometimes used to express purpose. Example: ἦλθεν πρὸς τὸν προφήτην τοῦ βαπτισθῆναι ὑπ' αὐτοῦ, *he came to the prophet in order to be baptized by him.* It will be remembered that for the most part the articular infinitive is used in the same constructions as those in which an ordinary noun with the article can be used. This use of the genitive to express purpose, however, would not be possible for an ordinary noun.

469. The Dative of Respect The dative is used to indicate the respect in which anything exists or is true.

Example: γινωσκόμενος τῷ προσώπῳ, *being known by face* (i. e. *being known so far as the face is concerned*); καθαρὸς τῇ καρδίᾳ, *pure in heart* (i. e. *pure so far as the heart is concerned*); ἀνὴρ ὀνόματι Ἰάκωβος, *a man by name James* (i. e. *a man who is James so far as the name is concerned*).

470. Accusative of Specification

The accusative of specification is very much the same in meaning as the dative of respect, but is less frequently used.

Example: τὸν ἀριθμὸν ὡς πεντακισχίλιοι, *about five thousand in number*.

The Dative of Time

471. The dative is sometimes used to express time when. Example: ἐθεράπευσε τῷ σαββάτῳ, *he healed on the sabbath*.

472. Usually, however, time when is expressed by prepositional phrases. So *on the sabbath* could be ἐν τῷ σαββάτῳ.

Possessive Adjectives

473. The possessive adjectives ἐμός, *my*, σός, *thy*, ἡμέτερος, *our*, ὑμέτερος, *your*, are sometimes used instead of the genitive case of the personal pronouns when emphasis is desired. These possessive adjectives are declined like regular adjectives of the second and first declension. They can stand in the attributive position with the article.

Examples: ὁ ἐμὸς λόγος, *the belonging-to-me word* (i. e., *my word*); ἡ χαρὰ ἡ ἐμή, *my joy*; τὰ θέλημα τὸ ἐμόν, *my will*; τὰ ἐμὰ πάντα σά ἐστιν, *all the belonging-to-me things are thine* (i. e., *all my things are thine*); ὁ ἡμέτερος λόγος, *our word*; ὁ ὑμέτερος λόγος, *your word*.

474. This usage is comparatively infrequent. The common way of saying *my word* is not ὁ ἐμὸς λόγος or ὁ λόγος ὁ ἐμός, but ὁ λόγος μου (*the word of me*).

μή Used as a Conjunction

475. Words denoting fear are followed by μή, *lest*, with the subjunctive. μή is here not an adverb, as is the case when it means not, but a conjunction.

Example: φοβοῦμαι μὴ ἔλθῃ, *I fear lest he come.*

476. Negative clauses of purpose may also be introduced by the simple μή instead of by ἵνα μή.

Example: τοῦτο ποιεῖτε μὴ εἰσέλθητε εἰς κρίσιν, do this lest you come into judgment.

477. ἵνα with the Subjunctive

in Various Uses In addition to the use by which it expresses purpose, ἵνα with the subjunctive is very frequently used after words of exhorting, wishing, striving, and in various ways that are not easily classified.

Examples: (1) εἰπὲ τῷ λίθῳ τούτῳ ἵνα γένηται ἄρτος, *say to this stone that it become bread.* (2) αὕτη ἐστιν ἡ ἐντολὴ ἡ ἐμὴ ἵνα ἀγαπᾶτε ἀλλήλους, *this is my commandment, that you should love one another.*

Questions Expecting a Negative Answer

478. Questions expecting a negative answer are expressed by μή with the indicative.

479. This rule constitutes an important exception to the general rule for the use of οὐ and μή (see §256). Questions expecting a positive answer have οὐ the indicative.

Example: μὴ ἰσχυρότεροι αὐτοῦ ἐσμεν; *are we stronger than he?* The answer expected is "No, of course not." Compare οὐκ ἰσχυρότεροί ἐσμεν αὐτοῦ; *are we not stronger than he?* Here the answer expected is "Yes, certainly we are."

480. Exercises

I 1. παρακαλῶ δὲ ὑμᾶς ἵνα τὸ αὐτὸ λέγητε πάντες. 2. ὅσα ἐὰν θέλητε ἵνα ποιῶσιν ὑμῖν οἱ ἄνθρωποι, οὕτως καὶ ὑμεῖς ποιεῖτε· οὗτος γάρ ἐστιν ὁ νόμος καὶ οἱ προφῆται. 3. κέλευσον οὖν τηρηθῆναι τὸ σῶμα ὑπὸ τῶν στρατιωτῶν, μήποτε ἐλθόντες οἱ μαθηταὶ λάβωσιν αὐτὸ καὶ εἴπωσιν τῷ λαῷ ὅτι ἠγέρθη ἐκ τῶν νεκρῶν. 4. οὐκ ἔστι δοῦλος μείζων τοῦ πέμψαντος αὐτόν. 5. μείζονα

169

ταύτης ἀγάπην οὐδεὶς ἔχει, ἵνα τις ἀποθάνῃ ὑπὲρ τῶν ἄλλων. 6. πάλιν ἀπέστειλεν ἄλλους δούλους πλείονας τῶν πρώτων. 7. εἰ δίκαιόν ἐστιν ἐνώπιον τοῦ θεοῦ ὑμῶν ἀκούειν μᾶλλον ἢ τοῦ θεοῦ, κρίνατε. 8. ἐγὼ δὲ λέγω ὑμῖν Ἀγαπᾶτε τοὺς ἐχθροὺς ὑμῶν καὶ προσεύχεσθε ὑπὲρ τῶν διωκόντων ὑμᾶς, ὅπως γένησθε υἱοὶ τοῦ πατρὸς ὑμῶν τοῦ ἐν οὐρανοῖς. 9. εἶπεν αὐτοῖς ὁ Ἰησοῦς ὅτι ἔξεστι τοῖς σάββασι καλῶς ποιεῖν. 10. ἔμεινεν δὲ ὁ Ἰησοῦς ἐκεῖ διὰ τὸ εἶναι τὸν τόπον ἐγγὺς τῆς πόλεως. 11. τότε συναχθήσονται ἔμπροσθεν αὐτοῦ πάντα τὰ ἔθνη. 12. μὴ ποίει τοῦτο· οὐ γὰρ ἱκανός εἰμι ἵνα εἰς τὴν οἰκίαν μου εἰσέλθῃς. 13. ἐλθόντες οἱ στρατιῶται νυκτὸς ἔλαβον τὸν ἄνδρα καὶ ἀγαγόντες αὐτὸν ἔξω ἀπέκτειναν. 14. τῇ μὲν σαρκὶ οὔκ ἐστε μεθ᾽ ἡμῶν, τῇ δὲ καρδίᾳ ἐστὲ ἐγγύς. 15. μὴ περιπατοῦμεν κατὰ σάρκα; οὐκ ἔχομεν τὸ πνεῦμα τοῦ θεοῦ; 16. εἰσῆλθεν εἰς τὴν οἰκίαν τοῦ ἀρχιερέως τοῦ εἶναι ἐγγὺς τοῦ τόπου ὅπου ἦν ὁ Ἰησοῦς. 17. εἰς τὰ ἴδια ἦλθεν καὶ οἱ ἴδιοι αὐτὸν οὐ παρέλαβον. 18. ἐγὼ ἐλήλυθα ἐν τῷ ὀνόματι τοῦ πατρός μου, καὶ οὐ λαμβάνετέ με· ἐὰν ἄλλος ἔλθῃ ἐν τῷ ὀνόματι τῷ ἰδίῳ, ἐκεῖνον λήμψεσθε. 19. μὴ ἐποίησα τὸ ἴδιον θέλημα; οὐ μᾶλλον ἐποίησα τὸ σόν; 20. εἰ ἐμὲ ἐδίωξαν, καὶ ὑμᾶς διώξουσιν· εἰ τὸν λόγον μου ἐτήρησαν, καὶ τὸν ὑμέτερον τηρήσουσιν.

II 1. Those who have done one work well will do also greater things. 2. He who rules his own house well does a greater thing than he who takes many cities. 3. Why do ye do these things? Are ye kings and priests? Are ye not servants? 4. Those who were in the darkness besought us that we should pity them and not cast them out. 5. Those who belong to me are in the city and those who belong to thee are outside of it, but we shall all be in the presence of God. 6. Art thou stronger than the One who made the earth and the sea and all the things that are in them? 7. Do not fear him who kills the body, but fear rather Him who has made all things. 8. When ye have seen your own brethren ye shall go also to the Gentiles. 9. We have more servants than you, but ours are not sufficient to evangelize[1] all the Gentiles. 10. Those who worship the Lord by day and by night shall be stronger than those who persecute them. 11. More are those who are with us than those

---

[1] What construction has been used after ἱκανός to express the idea *sufficient* (or *worthy*) *that they should*......?

who are with them. 12. Being with you in heart, not in countenance, we exhorted you that ye should do well all the things which we had commanded you. 13. The priests went out of the city, lest perchance the scribes might see them doing that which it is not lawful to do. 14. If anyone stronger than we comes against us we shall not remain in our city. 15. Jesus having healed a certain man on the sabbath, the scribes were afraid lest the people should make Him a king. 16. It is better to die in behalf of the brethren than to do what the apostles exhorted us that we should not do.

Lesson XXXI

Conjugation of δίδωμι. Second Aorist of γινώσκω. The Article before μέν and δέ. The Aorist Participle Denoting the Same Act as the Leading Verb. First Aorist Endings on Second Aorist Stems.

481. Vocabulary

αἰώνιος, ον, adj. of two terminations, the feminine being like the masculine throughout, *eternal*

ἀντί, prep. with gen., *instead of*

ἀποδίδωμι, I give back, *I give what is owed or promised, I render, I pay*

γυνή, γυναικός, ἡ, (with an irregular accent in some forms, see §566), *a woman*

δίδωμι, *I give*

ἔγνων, 2nd aor. (of μι form) of γινώσκω, *I know*

ἐξουσία, ἡ, *authority*

ἔσχον, 2nd aor. of ἔχω, *I have*

ζάω, (has η instead of α in the present system. E. g. ζῇς, ζῇ instead of ζᾷς, ζᾷ), *I live*

ἰδού, demonstrative particle, *behold! lo!*

μόνος, η, ον, adj., *alone, only*

μυστήριον, τό, *a mystery, a secret*

ὁράω, *I see* (The present system of this verb is very much less common than the present system of βλέπω. The common verb to see in the New Testament is βλέπω, ὄψομαι, εἶδον, ἑώρακα, (ὦμμαι), ὤφθην. Yet since βλέπω also has a future βλέψω and a first aorist ἔβλεψα, it will perhaps be more convenient to give ὄψομαι etc. as the principal parts of ὁράω rather than of βλέπω)

παραδίδωμι, *I deliver over*

πειράζω, *I tempt*

ποῖος, α, ον, interrogative pron., *what sort of?*

Σίμων, Σίμωνος, ὁ, *Simon*

χείρ, χειρός, ἡ, *a hand*

482. The verbs which have been studied so far, with the exception of the irregular verb εἰμί, all belong to the same conjugation. They have various ways of forming their principal parts, but the endings that are appended to the principal parts all belong to the same type. There is in Greek only one other conjugation. It is called the *μι conjugation* (to distinguish it from the ω conjugation which has been studied thus far), because its first person singular present active indicative ends in μι.

483. Verbs in μι differ from verbs in ω only in the present and second aorist systems.

484. The principal parts of the μι verb, δίδωμι, I give, are as follows: δίδωμι, δώσω, ἔδωκα, δέδωκα, δέδομαι, ἐδόθην.

485. The stem of δίδωμι is δο-. If it were an ω verb, its first form would be δόω.

486. The future δώσω is entirely regular, the final o of the stem being lengthened before the σ of the future exactly as in the case (for example) of δηλόω. From δώσω all of the future active and middle is formed, in exactly the same way as the corresponding forms of λύω.

487. The first aorist ἔδωκα is quite regularly formed except that κ stands instead of σ.

488. The perfect active δέδωκα is entirely regular. From δέδωκα all of the perfect active is quite regularly formed.

489. The perfect middle δέδομαι is quite regular except that the final vowel of the stem is not lengthened before the personal endings (see §448). From δέδομαι all of the perfect middle and passive is quite regularly formed.

490. The aorist passive ἐδόθην is quite regular, except that the final vowel of the stem is not lengthened before the tense suffix -θε. From ἐδόθην all of the aorist passive and future passive is quite regularly formed.

The Present System of δίδωμι

491. The sign of the present system of δίδωμι is the reduplication (of a different form from that in the perfect), which is prefixed to the stem.

492. The present active indicative of δίδωμι is as follows:

Sing.		Plur.	
1.	δίδωμι, *I give*	1.	δίδομεν, *we give*
2.	δίδως, *thou givest*	2.	δίδοτε, *ye give*
3.	δίδωσι(ν), *he gives*	3.	διδόασι(ν), *they give*

493. The final vowel of the stem (the stem with the reduplication being διδο-) is lengthened in the singular number, but not in the plural.

494. The personal endings are added directly to the stem, without any variable vowel.

495. These endings are -μι, -ς, -τι (or -σι), -μεν, -τε, -ασι.

496. The present active subjunctive is as follows:

	Sing.		Plur.
1.	διδῶ	1.	διδῶμεν
2.	διδῷς	2.	διδῶτε
3.	διδῷ	3.	διδῶσι(ν)

497. There has been contraction here, as is shown by the accent. The personal endings are the same as in ω verbs.

498. The present active imperative is as follows:

	Sing.		Plur.
2.	δίδου, *give (thou)*	2.	δίδοτε, *give (ye)*
3.	διδότω, *let him give*	3.	διδότωσαν, *let them give*

499. The present active infinitive is διδόναι, *to give*. The irregular accent should be noticed.

500. The present active participle is διδούς, διδοῦσα, διδόν, giving.

501. The genitive singular is διδόντος, διδούσης, διδόντος. The masculine and neuter are declined regularly according to the third declension and the feminine regularly according to the first declension. The dative plural masculine and neuter is διδοῦσι(ν).

502. The accent is irregular in the nominative, not being recessive. Thereafter it follows the general noun rule, except in the genitive plural feminine, διδουσῶν, where the special rule for nouns of the first declension is followed (see §14, §51).

174

503. The imperfect active indicative is as follows:

Sing.		Plur.	
1.	ἐδίδουν, *I was giving*	1.	ἐδίδομεν, *we were giving*
2.	ἐδίδους, *thou wast giving*	2.	ἐδίδοτε, *ye were giving*
3.	ἐδίδου, *he was giving*	3.	ἐδίδοσαν, *they were giving*

504. The characteristic reduplication, δι-, of the present of course appears here, since the imperfect is always a part of the present system. The augment is regular. The final vowel of the stem is lengthened in the singular, as in the present. But in the imperfect it is lengthened to ου instead of to ω. The same secondary endings appear as in the ω conjugation, except that the alternative ending -σαν appears instead of -ν in the third person plural. (See §127).

505. The present and imperfect middle and passive of δίδωμι may be found in §596. Only a few of these forms occur in the New Testament. They can easily be recognized as they occur.

Aorist Active of δίδωμι

506. The aorist active of δίδωμι is peculiar in that it is first aorist in the indicative and second aorist in the other moods.

507. The aorist active indicative is as follows:

Sing.		Plur.	
1.	ἔδωκα, *I gave*	1.	ἐδώκαμεν, *we gave*
2.	ἔδωκας, *thou gavest*	2.	ἐδώκατε, *ye gave*
3.	ἔδωκε(ν), *he gave*	3.	ἔδωκαν, *they gave*

508. It will be observed that the conjugation is exactly like that of ἔλυσα, the first aorist active of λύω. But the tense suffix is κ instead of σ. See §171-§177.

509. The aorist active subjunctive is as follows:

Sing.		Plur.	
1.	δῶ	1.	δῶμεν
2.	δῷς	2.	δῶτε
3.	δῷ	3.	δῶσι

510. The conjugation is exactly like the present active subjunctive. But the second aorist has the mere verb stem, whereas the present prefixes the reduplication δι-.

511. The aorist active imperative is as follows:

Sing.		Plur.	
2.	δός, *give*	2.	δότε, *give (ye)*
3.	δότω, *let him give*	3.	δότωσαν, *let them give*

512. These forms are like the present (without the reduplication), except for δός in the second person singular.

513. The aorist active infinitive is δοῦναι, to give.

514. The aorist active participle is δούς, δοῦσα, δόν, having given. It is declined like the present participle διδούς.

515. The aorist middle of δίδωμι occurs only a very few times in the New Testament. The forms can easily be understood with the aid of a lexicon.

The Second Aorist of γινώσκω

516. γινώσκω, *I know*, is an ω verb. But it has a second aorist active of the μι form. The stem is γνο- which is nearly everywhere lengthened to γνω-.

517. Learn the conjugation in §601.

The Article before μέν and δέ.

518. Before μέν or δέ the article is often used as a pronoun meaning he, she, it, they.

Examples: (1) τοῦτο ἠρώτησαν αὐτόν, ὁ δὲ ἀπεκρίθη αὐτοῖς, *this they asked him. And he answered them.* (2) ἦλθον πρὸς αὐτοὺς αἰτῶν τι παρ' αὐτῶν· οἱ δὲ ἐποίησαν οὐδέν, *I came to them asking something from them. But they did nothing.*

519. It should be observed very carefully that this usage is quite different from all the uses of the article which have been studied heretofore. For example, in the phrase οἱ ἐν τῷ οἴκῳ, *those in the house*, it would be a great mistake to think that the article is used as a pronoun meaning those. On the contrary, the English idiom *those in the house* (in which *those* is not really a demonstrative pronoun at all) is expressed in Greek by saying *the in-the-house people*. In this Greek phrase, οἱ is just as much an ordinary article as in the phrase οἱ ἀγαθοί, *the good people*, ἐν τῷ οἴκῳ being treated as an adjective like ἀγαθός. Or, to take another example, it would be a great mistake to suppose that in the phrase ὁ λύων, *he who looses*, the article is used as a pronoun meaning *he*. On the contrary the article is here just as much an article as in the phrase ὁ ἀγαθός, *the good man*. But before δέ the article can really be used as a pronoun. In ὁ δὲ εἶπεν, *but he said*, there is no adjective or adjective expression for ὁ to go with.

520. The Aorist Participle Denoting the Same Act as the Leading Verb

The aorist participle is sometimes used to denote the same act as the leading verb.

Examples: (1) ἀποκριθεὶς εἶπεν ὁ Ἰησοῦς, *Jesus said by way of answer*, or *Jesus answered and said*. In §233, §254 it was said that the present participle denotes action contemporary with the action of the leading verb and the aorist participle denotes action prior to the action of the leading verb. That rule needed to be impressed firmly upon the mind before the exceptions to it could be considered. But as a matter of fact the rule does not completely represent the facts. Properly speaking the tenses in the participle do not have to do with time, and their fundamental, non-temporal character appears in the usage now under discussion. In ἀποκριθεὶς εἶπεν, the "answering" and the "saying" represent exactly the same act, and the participle simply defines more closely the action denoted by εἶπεν. The phrase does not, however, mean *while he was answering he said*. That would rather be ἀποκρινόμενος εἶπεν. It is recommended that the free translation, *he answered and said*, be adopted invariably for the phrase ἀποκριθεὶς εἶπεν, which is exceedingly common in the Gospels. And it is exceedingly important that this idiom should not be allowed to obscure the fact that in the majority of cases the aorist participle denotes action prior to the time of the leading verb. The student should carefully avoid any confusion between the present and the aorist participle.

177

(2) ὁ δὲ ἀποκριθεὶς εἶπεν, *and he answered and said* (with a slight emphasis on he). Of course ἀποκριθεὶς might here be taken as the substantive participle with ὁ, and the sentence might mean *and the having-answered one said, or and the one who had answered said*. But in a very great many places where these words occur in the gospels, the article is to be taken as a pronoun and the ἀποκριθεὶς is joined only loosely to it, in the manner indicated in the translation above.

521. First Aorist Endings on Second Aorist Stems

Very frequently, in the New Testament, first aorist endings instead of second aorist endings are used on second aorist stems.

Examples: εἶπαν instead of εἶπον (third person plural), εἰπόν instead of εἰπέ (imperative). This usage is much more common in some parts of the aorist than in others. εἶπον in the indicative has almost exclusively first aorist forms. See §186, footnote.

522. Exercises

I 1. παρέδωκα γὰρ ὑμῖν ἐν πρώτοις ὃ καὶ παρέλαβον, ὅτι Χριστὸς ἀπέθανεν ὑπὲρ τῶν ἁμαρτιῶν ἡμῶν κατὰ τὰς γραφάς. 2. μὴ ἔχοντος δὲ αὐτοῦ ἀποδοῦναι ἀπέλυσεν αὐτὸν ὁ κύριος αὐτοῦ. 3. καὶ ἀποκριθεὶς πᾶς ὁ λαὸς εἶπεν Τὸ αἷμα αὐτοῦ ἐφ' ἡμᾶς καὶ ἐπὶ τὰ τέκνα ἡμῶν. 4. θέλω δὲ τούτῳ τῷ ἐσχάτῳ δοῦναι ὡς καὶ σοί. 5. ἐσθιόντων δὲ αὐτῶν λαβὼν ὁ Ἰησοῦς ἄρτον καὶ εὐλογήσας ἔκλασεν[1] καὶ δοὺς τοῖς μαθηταῖς εἶπεν Λάβετε φάγετε, τοῦτό ἐστιν τὸ σῶμά μου. καὶ λαβὼν ποτήριον[2] καὶ εὐχαριστήσας ἔδωκεν αὐτοῖς λέγων Πίετε ἐξ αὐτοῦ πάντες. 6. καὶ εἶπαν λέγοντες πρὸς αὐτόν Εἰπὸν ἡμῖν ἐν ποίᾳ ἐξουσίᾳ ταῦτα ποιεῖς, ἢ τίς ἐστιν ὁ δούς σοι τὴν ἐξουσίαν ταύτην. ἀποκριθεὶς δὲ εἶπεν πρὸς αὐτούς Ἐρωτήσω κἀγὼ[3] λόγον, καὶ εἴπατέ μοι. 7. ὁ γὰρ ἄρτος τοῦ θεοῦ ἐστιν ὁ καταβαίνων ἐκ τοῦ οὐρανοῦ καὶ ζωὴν διδοὺς τῷ κόσμῳ. 8. λέγει αὐτοῖς Ὑμεῖς δὲ τίνα με λέγετε εἶναι; ἀποκριθεὶς δὲ Σίμων Πέτρος εἶπεν Σὺ εἶ ὁ Χριστὸς ὁ υἱὸς τοῦ θεοῦ τοῦ ζῶντος. 9. λέγει αὐτῷ ὁ Ἰησοῦς Πορεύου· ὁ υἱός σου ζῇ. ἐπίστευσεν ὁ ἄνθρωπος τῷ λόγῳ ὃν εἶπεν αὐτῷ ὁ Ἰησοῦς καὶ ἐπορεύετο. 10. ὁρᾶτε μή τις κακὸν

---

[1] Aorist active indicative of κλάω, I break.

[2] ποτήριον, τό, a cup.

[3] κἀγώ stands for καὶ ἐγώ.

ἀντὶ κακοῦ τινι ἀποδῷ. 11. ἦλθεν ἡ ὥρα, ἰδοὺ παραδίδοται ὁ υἱὸς τοῦ ἀνθρώπου εἰς τὰς χεῖρας τῶν ἁμαρτωλῶν. ἐγείρεσθε, ἄγωμεν[1]· ἰδοὺ ὁ παραδιδούς με ἤγγικεν. 12. καὶ ἰδοὺ εἷς προσελθὼν αὐτῷ εἶπεν Διδάσκαλε, τί ἀγαθὸν ποιήσω ἵνα σχῶ ζωὴν αἰώνιον; ὁ δὲ εἶπεν αὐτῷ Τί με ἐρωτᾷς περὶ τοῦ ἀγαθοῦ; εἷς ἐστιν ὁ ἀγαθός· εἰ δὲ θέλεις εἰς τὴν ζωὴν εἰσελθεῖν τήρει τὰς ἐντολάς. 13. καὶ προσελθὼν ὁ πειράζων εἶπεν αὐτῷ Εἰ υἱὸς εἶ τοῦ θεοῦ, εἰπὲ ἵνα οἱ λίθοι οὗτοι ἄρτοι γένωνται. ὁ δὲ ἀποκριθεὶς εἶπεν Γέγραπται Οὐκ ἐπ' ἄρτῳ μόνῳ ζήσεται ὁ ἄνθρωπος. 14. καὶ προσελθόντες οἱ μαθηταὶ εἶπαν αὐτῷ Διὰ τί ἐν παραβολαῖς λαλεῖς αὐτοῖς; ὁ δὲ ἀποκριθεὶς εἶπεν ὅτι[2] Ὑμῖν δέδοται γνῶναι τὰ μυστήρια τῆς βασιλείας τῶν οὐρανῶν, ἐκείνοις δὲ οὐ δέδοται. 15. ἔλεγον αὐτῷ οἱ μαθηταί Ἀπόλυσον αὐτούς, ὁ δὲ ἀποκριθεὶς εἶπεν αὐτοῖς Δότε αὐτοῖς ὑμεῖς φαγεῖν.

II 1. The woman besought the apostle that he might give her something. But he[3] answered her nothing. 2. Those who had killed the women said that they had known the king. But he answered and said that he was not willing to give them what they asked. 3. If we believe on Him who loved us and gave Himself in behalf of us, we shall have eternal life instead of death. 4. While the apostle was giving to the children the things which they had asked, the women were giving gifts to us. 5. The Lord delivered over the gospel to the apostles, and they delivered it over to the Gentiles. 6. What shall we give back to Him who gave Himself in behalf of us? 7. Behold He gives us eternal life. Let us therefore do His will. 8. What shall anyone give instead of his life? 9. Whatever we give to Him will not be enough. 10. Whatever thou wishest that men should give to thee, give thou also to them. 11. Let them give thanks to those who delivered over to them the gospel. 12. They asked the Lord what they should give to Him. And He answered and said to them that to do the will of God is greater than all the gifts. 13. Those women are giving back to the children the things which they

---

[1] ἄγω is sometimes used in the intransitive sense, I go.

[2] ὅτι frequently introduces direct (instead of indirect) discourse. When it introduces direct discourse, it must be left untranslated. In such cases, it takes the place of our quotation marks.

[3] In all such cases, the slight emphasis on the he in English is to be expressed in Greek by the pronominal use of the article before δέ.

have taken from them, lest the king cast them out of the city. 14. When the priests had said these things to those who were in the city, the apostle departed. 15. What is this? Will he give us his flesh? 16. Whatever He asks I will give. But He gave to me eternal life.

Lesson XXXII

Conjugation of τίθημι, ἀφίημι, δείκνυμι, and ἀπόλλυμι. Accusative and Infinitive in Result Clauses. The Subjunctive after ἕως.

523. Vocabulary

ἀνοίγω, (for principal parts of this verb and the other verbs, see the general vocabulary), I open

ἀπόλλυμι or ἀπολλύω, I destroy; middle, I perish

ἀρχή, ἡ, a beginning

ἀφίημι, I let go, I permit, I leave, I forgive (when it means forgive, ἀφίημι takes the acc. of the thing forgiven and the dat. of the person to whom it is forgiven)

δείκνυμι and δεικνύω, I show

εὑρίσκω, I find

ἐπιτίθημι, I lay upon (with acc. of the thing laid and dat. of the person or thing upon which it is laid)

ἕως, adv. with gen., up to, until; conj., while, until

καθώς, adv., just as

καιρός, ὁ, a time, a fixed time, an appointed time

μνημεῖον, τό, a tomb

μόνον, adv., only

πῦρ, πυρός, τό, a fire

σημεῖον, τό, a sign

στόμα, στόματος, τό, a mouth

τίθημι, I place, I put; τίθημι τὴν ψυχήν, I lay down my life

ὑπάγω, I go away

χαίρω, I rejoice (ἐχάρην, 2nd aor. pass., I rejoiced)

χρόνος, ὁ, time (especially a period of time, as distinguished from καιρός, a definite or appointed time)

ὧδε, adv., hither, here

ὥσπερ, adv., just as

ὥστε, conj., so that

524. The principal parts of the μι verb τίθημι, *I place, I put*, are as follows:

τίθημι, θήσω, ἔθηκα, τέθεικα, τέθειμαι, ἐτέθην.

525. The stem is θε-. The present system is reduplicated after the same manner as δίδωμι. The future is regular. The first aorist is regular except that (like δίδωμι) it has κ instead of σ. The perfect active and the perfect middle are regular except that θε- is lengthened to θει-

181

instead of to θη-. The aorist passive is regular except that (1) the final vowel of the stem is not lengthened, and (2) the stem θε- is changed to τε- to avoid having two θ's come in successive syllables.

526. Learn the active voice of the present system of τίθημι in §598.

527. The treatment of the stem and of the endings in the present system is very much the same as in the case of δίδωμι. The declension of the participle τιθείς is like that of λυθείς, the aorist passive participle of λύω.

528. Learn the active voice of the aorist system of τίθημι in §599.

529. Like δίδωμι, τίθημι has a first aorist active in the indicative and a second aorist active in the other moods. The second aorist participle θείς is declined like the present participle τιθείς.

530. The present middle and aorist middle forms of τίθημι can easily be recognized when they occur, if it be remembered that the second aorist has the mere verb stem θε-, whereas the present has the stem τιθε-. Thus if a form ἀνεθέμην be encountered, the student should see that ἀν- is plainly the preposition ἀνα-, ε is the augment, θε is the stem of τίθημι, and -μην is the secondary ending in the first person singular middle. Therefore, the form is second aorist middle indicative, first person singular. On the other hand, ἐτίθεντο belongs to the present system because it has the τι- which is the sign of the present system; it is imperfect, not present, because it has the augment and a secondary ending. It is evidently imperfect middle or passive indicative, third person plural.

The Conjugation of ἀφίημι

531. ἀφίημι, *I let go, I permit, I leave, I forgive,* is a compound verb composed of the preposition ἀπό (ἀφ' before the rough breathing) and the μι verb ἵημι. The stem of ἵημι is ἑ-.

532. The forms can usually be recognized if it be remembered that the ἱ- before the stem ἑ- is the sign of the present system, and that the short forms with ἑ- alone are second aorist. Thus ἀφείς is evidently second aorist participle (εἵς coming from the stem ἑ- as θείς from the stem θε-). In the indicative there is a first aorist active in κ instead of σ,

182

as is the case with δίδωμι and τίθημι. The irregular forms of ἀφίημι can be found in the lexicons and reference grammars.

533. Conjugation of δείκνυμι **and** ἀπόλλυμι.

These two verbs have some μι forms in the present system. The μι forms can be recognized from the fact that they add the personal ending directly to the present stem. The present stem ends in υ. Both δείκνυμι and ἀπόλλυμι are also sometimes conjugated like ω verbs even in the present system. See the vocabulary.

Accusative and Infinitive after ὥστε

534. ὥστε, *so that*, expressing result, is sometimes followed by the accusative and infinitive.

Example: ἐθεράπευσεν αὐτούς· ὥστε τὸν ὄχλον θαυμάσαι . . . . ., *he healed them; so that the crowd marveled* . . . . .

535. The accent of ὥστε apparently violates the general rules of accent. But originally the τε was an enclitic separate from the ὡς. So also ὥσπερ and οὔτε (for the latter see vocabulary in Lesson XXXIII).

536. The Subjunctive with ἕως ἄν

The conjunction ἕως, when it means *until*, takes the subjunctive with ἄν, except when the verb which it introduces refers to an actual occurrence in past time. The ἄν is sometimes omitted. When ἕως means *while*, it takes the indicative. The phrase ἕως οὗ in which ἕως is a preposition and οὗ the genitive singular neuter of the relative pronoun, has the same meaning as ἕως (conjunction) alone.

Examples: (1) μείνατε ἕως ἄν ἔλθω, *remain until I come*. (2) ἔμεινεν ἕως οὗ ἦλθον, *he remained until I came* (actual occurrence in past time).

537. Exercises

Ι 1. διὰ τοῦτό με ὁ πατὴρ ἀγαπᾷ ὅτι ἐγὼ τίθημι τὴν ψυχήν μου, ἵνα πάλιν λάβω αὐτήν. οὐδεὶς ἦρεν αὐτὴν ἀπ᾽ ἐμοῦ, ἀλλ᾽ ἐγὼ τίθημι αὐτὴν ἀπ᾽ ἐμαυτοῦ. ἐξουσίαν ἔχω θεῖναι αὐτήν, καὶ ἐξουσίαν ἔχω πάλιν λαβεῖν αὐτήν· ταύτην τὴν ἐντολὴν ἔλαβον παρὰ τοῦ πατρός μου. 2. αὕτη ἐστὶν ἡ ἐντολὴ ἡ ἐμή, ἵνα ἀγαπᾶτε ἀλλήλους καθὼς ἠγάπησα ὑμᾶς. μείζονα ταύτης ἀγάπην οὐδεὶς ἔχει, ἵνα τις τὴν ψυχὴν αὐτοῦ θῇ ὑπὲρ τῶν φίλων[1] αὐτοῦ. 3. ἀλλὰ ἐλθὼν ἐπίθες τὴν χεῖρά σου ἐπ' αὐτὴν καὶ ζήσεται. 4. ὁ δὲ Ἰησοῦς εἶπεν Ἄφετε τὰ παιδία καὶ μὴ κωλύετε[2] αὐτὰ ἐλθεῖν πρὸς με· τῶν γὰρ τοιούτων[3] ἐστὶν ἡ βασιλεία τῶν οὐρανῶν. καὶ ἐπιθεὶς τὰς χεῖρας αὐτοῖς ἐπορεύθη ἐκεῖθεν[4]. 5. καὶ προσευξάμενοι ἐπέθηκαν αὐτοῖς τὰς χεῖρας. 6. τότε ἐπετίθεσαν τὰς χεῖρας ἐπ' αὐτούς, καὶ ἐλάμβανον πνεῦμα ἅγιον. 7. ἀκούσαντες δὲ ἐβαπτίσθησαν εἰς τὸ ὄνομα τοῦ κυρίου Ἰησοῦ· καὶ ἐπιθέντος αὐτοῖς τοῦ Παύλου[5] χεῖρας ἦλθε τὸ πνεῦμα τὸ ἅγιον ἐπ' αὐτούς. 8. ζωοποιεῖ[6] ὁ υἱὸς τοῦ θεοῦ ὃν θέλει. 9. ὑμεῖς ὃ ἠκούσατε ἀπ' ἀρχῆς[7], ἐν ὑμῖν μενέτω. ἐὰν ἐν ὑμῖν μείνῃ ὃ ἀπ' ἀρχῆς ἠκούσατε, καὶ ὑμεῖς ἐν τῷ υἱῷ καὶ ἐν τῷ πατρὶ μενεῖτε. 10. καὶ ἐγενετο ὡσεὶ[8] νεκρός, ὥστε τοὺς πολλοὺς λέγειν ὅτι ἀπέθανεν. 11. ἴσθι ἐκεῖ ἕως ἂν εἴπω σοι· μέλλει γὰρ Ἡρῴδης[9] ζητεῖν τὸ παιδίον τοῦ ἀπολέσαι αὐτό. 12. Κύριε, σῶσον, ἀπολλύμεθα. 13. καὶ ἀνοίξας τὸ βιβλίον εὗρεν τὸν τόπον. 14. τὰ δὲ ἐκπορευόμενα ἐκ τοῦ στόματος ἐκ τῆς καρδίας ἐξέρχεται. 15. οὐ περὶ τούτων δὲ ἐρωτῶ μόνον, ἀλλὰ καὶ περὶ τῶν πιστευόντων διὰ τοῦ λόγου αὐτῶν εἰς ἐμέ, ἵνα πάντες ἓν ὦσιν, καθὼς σύ, πατήρ[10], ἐν ἐμοὶ κἀγὼ ἐν σοί, ἵνα καὶ αὐτοὶ ἐν ἡμῖν ὦσιν, ἵνα ὁ κόσμος πιστεύῃ ὅτι σύ με ἀπέστειλας. 16. εἶπεν οὖν ὁ Ἰησοῦς Ἔτι χρόνον μικρὸν μεθ' ὑμῶν εἰμι καὶ ὑπάγω πρὸς τὸν πέμψαντά με. 17. ὅτε δὲ ἤγγισεν ὁ καιρὸς τῶν καρπῶν, ἀπέστειλεν τοὺς δούλους αὐτοῦ. 18. αὐτὸς δὲ σωθήσεται, οὕτως δὲ ὡς διὰ πυρός.

II 1. This commandment he laid upon them, that they should lay down their lives in behalf of their brethren. 2. If ye forgive those who

---

[1] φίλος, ὁ, a friend.

[2] κωλύω, I hinder.

[3] τοιοῦτος, τοιαύτη, τοιοῦτο, such. Often used with the article.

[4] ἐκεῖθεν, adv., thence.

[5] Παῦλος, ὁ, Paul.

[6] ζωοποιέω, I make alive, I quicken.

[7] In many such phrases the article is omitted in Greek where it is used in English.

[8] ὡσεί is a strengthened form of ὡς.

[9] Ἡρῴδης, ου, ὁ, Herod.

[10] πατήρ has a vocative form, πάτερ. But even such nouns sometimes use the nominative form in the vocative case.

persecute you, I also will forgive you. 3. When the men had found him who had done this thing they left him and went away. 4. Having put the body into the tomb he went away. 5. We saw those who were laying down their lives in behalf of the children. 6. The women saw where the body was placed. 7. We shall question him until he answers us. 8. We ought to give thanks to Him who has forgiven us our sins. 9. We did not know Him, but He knew us. 10. Give me the body in order that I may place it in a tomb. 11. He showed all things to you, in order that you might place them in your hearts. 12. The apostle answered and said to those who were questioning him that he would not put these gifts into the temple. 13. After we had seen the sign which Jesus had shown to us, we believed on Him.

Lesson XXXIII

Conjugation of ἵστημι and οἶδα. The Optative Mood. Conditions Contrary to Fact. Uses of γίνομαι.

538. Vocabulary

ἀνίστημι, *I cause to rise*, in the present, fut., and 1st aor. act.; intransitive, *I stand up, I arise*, in the 2nd aor. and perf. act., and in the middle.

δοκέω, *I seem, I think*

δύναμαι, dep. (the present system conjugated like the middle of ἵστημι), *I am able*

δύναμις, δυνάμεως, ἡ, *power, a miracle*

ἔβην, 2nd aor. (of the μι form) of βαίνω (conjugated like the 2nd aor. of ἵστημι)

ἕτερος, α, ον, *another* (sometimes, but not always, implies difference of kind, whereas ἄλλος often denotes mere numerical distinction)

ἵστημι, transitive, *I cause to stand*, in the pres., fut. and 1st aor. act.; intransitive, *I stand*, in the perf. (which

has the sense of a present = *I stand*) and in the 2nd aor.

κάθημαι, dep. of the μι form, *I sit* (pres. part. καθήμενος, *sitting*)

οἶδα, 2nd perf. used as pres., *I know*

ὅλος, η, ον, adj., *whole, all*

ὅμοιος, α, ον, adj., *like, similar* (with the dative of that to which anything is similar)

οὔτε, *and not, nor* (οὔτε. . . .οὔτε, *neither.... nor*)

παραγίνομαι, *I become near, I arrive, I come* (παραγίνομαι εἰς τὴν πόλιν, *I arrive in the city*)

φανερόω, *I make manifest, I manifest*

φημί, *I say* (a μι verb with stem φα-. Much less common than λέγω)

ὡς, adv. and conj., *as, when* (some of its other uses have already been studied)

539. The principal parts of the μι verb ἵστημι, I cause to stand, are as follows:

ἵστημι, στήσω, ἔστησα, ἔστηκα, ἔσταμαι, ἐστάθην, 2nd aor. act. ἔστην.

540. The stem is στα-. The present system is reduplicated by the prefixing of ἱ-. The future and first aorist systems are perfectly regular, the στα- of the stem being lengthened to στη- before the σ of the tense suffixes. The perfect active is regular except that the ε- of the reduplication has the rough breathing. The perfect middle and passive retains the στα- of the stem unchanged instead of lengthening its vowel. The aorist passive also retains the στα-, but otherwise is regular.

541. Learn the active voice of the present system of ἵστημι in §600.

542. The treatment of the stem and of the endings in the present system is very much the same as in the case of δίδωμι and τίθημι. The declension of the participle ἱστάς is like that of λύσας, the aorist active participle of λύω, except for the accent.

543. Learn the middle and passive forms of the present system of ἵστημι in §600. It will be noticed that the endings are joined directly to the reduplicated stem ἱστα-, except in the subjunctive mood.

544. ἵστημι differs from δίδωμι and τίθημι in that it has a complete second aorist active as well as a complete first aorist active. The first aorist means *I caused to stand* (transitive), and the second aorist means *I stood* (intransitive).

545. Learn the second aorist active of ἵστημι in §601.

546. It will be observed that the conjugation is very much like that of the aorist passive of λύω. The participle στάς is declined like the present participle ἱστάς.

547. A second aorist middle of ἵστημι does not occur.

548. In addition to the first perfect active participle, ἑστηκώς, ἵστημι has a second perfect participle ἑστώς, ἑστῶσα, ἑστός, gen. ἑστῶτος, etc. Both ἑστηκώς and ἑστώς mean *standing*.

549. Learn the conjugation of οἶδα, *I know* (a second perfect used as a present, the pluperfect, ᾔδειν, being used as an imperfect) in §603.

550. The Optative Mood

In the classical period, the Greek language had another mood, the optative, in addition to those which we have studied. In New Testament Greek, however, most of the classical uses of the optative have practically disappeared. The optative is still retained to express a wish. Thus μὴ γένοιτο (γένοιτο being the second aorist optative, third person singular, of γίνομαι) means *may it not take place, God forbid*. The few other optative forms in the New Testament can be noted when they occur.

551. Conditions Contrary to Fact

Conditions contrary to fact are expressed by the secondary tenses of the indicative in both protasis and apodosis. The protasis is introduced by εἰ, and the apodosis has the particle ἄν, which, however, is sometimes omitted.

Example: κύριε, εἰ ἦς ὧδε, οὐκ ἄν ἀπέθανεν ὁ ἀδελφός μου, *Lord, if thou hadst been here, my brother would not have died.*

Uses of γίνομαι

552. Thus far, in the exercises, it has usually been possible to translate γίνομαι by the English word *become*. But very often, in the New Testament, such a translation is impossible. The English word *become* requires a predicate nominative, but in very many cases γίνομαι has no predicate nominative. In such cases it means *happen, come into being, come to pass, appear, arise, be made*. Sometimes it can be translated by the words *come* or *be*.

Examples: (1) ἐν ἐκείναις ταῖς ἡμέραις ἐγένετο ἱερεύς τις, *in those days there was (appeared in history) a certain priest.* (2) πάντα δι' αὐτοῦ ἐγένετο, *all things came into being (or were made) through him.* (3) εἶδεν τὰ γενόμενα, *he saw the things that had happened.* (4) φωνὴ ἐγένετο ἐκ τῶν οὐρανῶν, *a voice came out of the heavens.* [But it must not be supposed that γίνομαι is a verb of motion.]

553. The usage of καὶ ἐγένετο and ἐγένετο δὲ, meaning *and it came to pass*, calls for special comment. There are three forms of this usage, which may be illustrated as follows[1].

(1) καὶ ἐγένετο αὐτὸν ἐλθεῖν, *and it came to pass that he came*. Here the accusative and infinitive depend on ἐγένετο in a way that is at least after the analogy of ordinary Greek usage.

(2) καὶ ἐγένετο καὶ ἦλθεν, *and it came to pass and he came*. The literal English translation is here intolerable, and the Greek also is not in accordance with the ordinary usage of the Greek language, but is derived from a Hebrew idiom.

(3) καί ἐγένετο ἦλθεν, *and it came to pass he came*. This also is not an ordinary Greek usage, ἦλθεν, being left without a construction. Both (2) and (3), as well as (1) may be translated freely *and it came to pass that he came.*

554. Exercises

I 1. διὰ τοῦτο ὁ κόσμος οὐ γινώσκει ἡμᾶς ὅτι οὐκ ἔγνω αὐτόν. Ἀγαπητοί, νῦν τέκνα θεοῦ ἐσμεν, καὶ οὔπω ἐφανερώθη τί ἐσόμεθα. οἴδαμεν ὅτι ἐὰν φανερωθῇ ὅμοιοι αὐτῷ ἐσόμεθα, ὅτι ὀψόμεθα αὐτὸν καθώς ἐστιν. 2. ἔλεγον οὖν αὐτῷ Ποῦ ἐστιν ὁ πατήρ σου; ἀπεκρίθη Ἰησοῦς Οὔτε ἐμὲ οἴδατε οὔτε τὸν πατέρα μου· εἰ ἐμὲ ἤδειτε, καὶ τὸν πατέρα μου ἂν ἤδειτε. 3. ζητήσετέ με καὶ οὐχ εὑρήσετε, καὶ ὅπού εἰμὶ ἐγὼ ὑμεῖς οὐ δύνασθε ἐλθεῖν. 4. καὶ συνέρχεται πάλιν ὁ ὄχλος, ὥστε μὴ δύνασθαι αὐτοὺς μηδὲ ἄρτον φαγεῖν. 5. ἠκούσατε ὅτι ἐγὼ εἶπον ὑμῖν Ὑπάγω καὶ ἔρχομαι πρὸς ὑμᾶς. εἰ ἠγαπᾶτέ με, ἐχάρητε ἂν ὅτι πορεύομαι πρὸς τὸν πατέρα, ὅτι ὁ πατὴρ μείζων μού ἐστιν. 6. εὗρεν ἄλλους ἑστῶτας καὶ λέγει αὐτοῖς Τί ὧδε ἑστήκατε ὅλην τὴν ἡμέραν; 7. προφήτην ὑμῖν ἀναστήσει κύριος ὁ θεὸς ἐκ τῶν ἀδελφῶν ὑμῶν ὡς ἐμέ· αὐτοῦ ἀκούσεσθε[2] κατὰ πάντα ὅσα ἂν λαλήσῃ ὑμῖν. 8. καὶ ἀναστὰς ὁ ἀρχιερεὺς εἶπεν αὐτῷ Οὐδὲν ἀποκρίνῃ; 9. τότε οὖν εἰσῆλθεν καὶ ὁ ἄλλος μαθητὴς ὁ ἐλθὼν πρῶτος εἰς τὸ μνημεῖον, καὶ εἶδεν καὶ ἐπίστευσεν· οὐδέπω[3] γὰρ ᾔδεισαν τὴν γραφήν, ὅτι δεῖ αὐτὸν ἐκ

---

[1] This method of illustration is taken, in essentials, from J. H. Moulton, Grammar of New Testament Greek, Vol. I, "Prolegomena," 2nd Edition, 1906, p. 16.

[2] The future of ἀκούω is here deponent.

[3] οὐδέπω, not yet.

νεκρῶν ἀναστῆναι. 10. εἰ ἐν Σοδόμοις¹ ἐγενήθησαν αἱ δυνάμεις αἱ γενόμεναι ἐν σοί, ἔμεινεν ἂν μέχρι² τῆς σήμερον³. 11. ἔδωκεν αὐτοῖς δύναμιν καὶ ἐξουσίαν ἐπὶ πάντα τὰ δαιμόνια. 12. ἐγένετο δὲ ἐν τῷ βαπτισθῆναι ἅπαντα⁴ τὸν λαὸν καὶ Ἰησοῦ βαπτισθέντος καὶ προσευχομένου ἀνεῳχθῆναι τὸν οὐρανόν, καὶ καταβῆναι τὸ πνεῦμα τὸ ἅγιον. 13. ἐγένετο δὲ ἐν ταῖς ἡμέραις ἐκείναις ἐξελθεῖν αὐτὸν εἰς τὰ ὄρη προσεύξασθαι. 14. ἐξῆλθον δὲ ἰδεῖν τὸ γεγονός, καὶ ἦλθον πρὸς τὸν Ἰησοῦν, καὶ εὗρον καθήμενον τὸν ἄνθρωπον ἀφ᾽ οὗ τὰ δαιμόνια ἐξῆλθον. 15. καὶ ἐγένετο ἐν τῷ εἶναι αὐτὸν ἐν τόπῳ τινὶ προσευχόμενον, ὡς ἐπαύσατο⁵, εἶπέν τις τῶν μαθητῶν αὐτοῦ πρὸς αὐτὸν Κύριε δίδαξον ἡμᾶς προσεύχεσθαι, καθὼς καὶ Ἰωάνης⁶ ἐδίδαξεν τοὺς μαθητὰς αὐτοῦ. 16. ὁ δὲ ἔφη αὐτῷ Ἀγαπήσεις κύριον τὸν θεόν σου ἐν ὅλῃ τῇ καρδίᾳ σου. 17. δοκεῖτε ὅτι εἰρήνην παρεγενόμην δοῦναι ἐν τῇ γῇ; 18. περὶ τίνος ὁ προφήτης λέγει τοῦτο; περὶ ἑαυτοῦ ἢ περὶ ἑτέρου τινός; 19. αὐτὸς ὑμᾶς βαπτίσει ἐν πνεύματι ἁγίῳ καὶ πυρί.

II 1. He forgave those who had risen up against their king. 2. We know that those who are sitting in the house will not go out until they see the apostle. 3. When Jesus had gone down from the mountain, the disciples saw the man sitting in the house. 4. We saw the apostles standing in the presence of the chief priests. 5. When the women had arrived in the city they saw Jesus doing many miracles. 6. In those days there rose up a certain king who did not know us. 7. Thou hast manifested Thyself to those who are sitting in darkness. 8. When he had seen these things he did not know what he was saying. 9. We are not able to know all these things unless the Lord manifests them to us. 10. We have found the One who is able to take away our sins. 11. We know that no one is able to do what the king does.

---

¹ Σόδομα, ων, τά, plural in singular sense, Sodom.
² μέχρι with gen., until, up to.
³ σήμερον, adv., today, ἡ σήμερον (supply ἡμέρα), today.
⁴ ἅπας, ἅπασα, ἅπαν, all (a strengthened form of πας).
⁵ παύομαι (middle), I cease.
⁶ Ἰωάνης, ου, ὁ, John.

Paradigms

Paradigms

First Declension

555. The declension of ὥρα, ἡ, stem ὡρα-, *an hour*, ἀλήθεια, ἡ, stem ἀληθεια-, *truth*, δόξα, ἡ, stem δόξα-, *glory*, and γραφή, ἡ, stem γραφα-, *a writing, a Scripture*, is as follows:

Sing.

N.V.	ὥρα	ἀλήθεια	δόξα	γραφή
G.	ὥρας	ἀληθείας	δόξης	γραφῆς
D.	ὥρᾳ	ἀληθείᾳ	δόξῃ	γραφῇ
A.	ὥραν	ἀλήθειαν	δόξαν	γραφήν

Plur.

N.V.	ὧραι	ἀλήθειαι	δόξαι	γραφαί
G.	ὡρῶν	ἀληθειῶν	δοξῶν	γραφῶν
D.	ὥραις	ἀληθείαις	δόξαις	γραφαῖς
A.	ὥρας	ἀληθείας	δόξας	γραφάς

556. The declension of προφήτης, ὁ, stem προφητα-, *a prophet*, and μαθητής, ὁ, stem μαθητα-, *a disciple*, is as follows:

Sing.

N.	προφήτης	μαθητής
G.	προφήτου	μαθητοῦ
D.	προφήτῃ	μαθητῇ
A.	προφήτην	μαθητήν
V.	προφῆτα	μαθητά

Plur.

N.V.	προφῆται	μαθηταί
G.	προφητῶν	μαθητῶν
D.	προφήταις	μαθηταῖς
A.	προφήτας	μαθητάς

557. The declension of λόγος, ὁ, stem λογο-, *a word*, ἄνθρωπος, ὁ, stem ἀνθρωπο-, *a man*, υἱός, ὁ, stem υἱο-, *a son*, and δοῦλος, ὁ, stem δουλο-, *a slave*, is as follows:

	Sing.			
N.	λόγος	ἄνθρωπος	υἱός	δοῦλος
G.	λόγου	ἀνθρώπου	υἱοῦ	δούλου
D.	λόγῳ	ἀνθρώπῳ	υἱῷ	δούλῳ
A.	λόγον	ἄνθρωπον	υἱόν	δοῦλον
V.	λόγε	ἄνθρωπε	υἱέ	δοῦλε
	Plur.			
N.V.	λόγοι	ἄνθρωποι	υἱοί	δοῦλοι
G.	λόγων	ἀνθρώπων	υἱῶν	δούλων
D.	λόγοις	ἀνθρώποις	υἱοῖς	δούλοις
A.	λόγους	ἀνθρώπους	υἱούς	δούλους

558. The declension of δῶρον, τό, stem δωρο-, *a gift*, is as follows:

	Sing.		Plur.
N. A. V.	δῶρον	N.	δῶρα
G.	δώρου	G.	δώρων
D.	δώρῳ	D.	δώροις

Third Declension

559. The declension of νύξ, ἡ, stem νυκτ-, *a night*, σάρξ, ἡ, stem σαρκ-, *flesh*, ἄρχων, ὁ, stem ἀρχοντ-, *a ruler*, is as follows:

Sing.

N.	νύξ	σάρξ	ἄρχων
G.	νυκτός	σαρκός	ἄρχοντος
D.	νυκτί	σαρκί	ἄρχοντι
A.	νύκτα	σάρκα	ἄρχοντα
V.	νύξ	σάρξ	ἄρχων

Plur.

N.V.	νύκτες	σάρκες	ἄρχοντες
G.	νυκτῶν	σαρκῶν	ἀρχόντων
D.	νυξί(ν)	σαρχί(ν)	ἄρχουσι(ν)
A.	νύκτας	σάρκας	ἄρχοντας

560. The declension of ἐλπίς, ἡ, stem ἐλπιδ-, *hope*, and χάρις, ἡ, stem χαριτ-, *grace*, is as follows:

Sing.

N.	ἐλπίς	χάρις
G.	ἐλπίδος	χάριτος
D.	ἐλπίδι	χάριτι
A.	ἐλπίδα	χάριν
V.	ἐλπί	χάρις

Plur.

N.V.	ἐλπίδες	χάριτες
G.	ἐλπίδων	χαρίτων
D.	ἐλπίσι(ν)	χάρισι(ν)
A.	ἐλπίδας	χάριτας

561. The declension of ὄνομα, τό, stem ὀνοματ-, *a name,* is as follows:

	Sing.		Plur.
N. A. V.	ὄνομα	N.	ὀνόματα
G.	ὀνόματος	G.	ὀνομάτων
D.	ὀνόματι	D.	ὀνόμασι(ν)

562. The declension of γένος, τό, stem γενεσ-, *a race,* is as follows:

	Sing.		Plur.
N. A. V.	γένος	N.	γένη
G.	γένους	G.	γενῶν
D.	γένει	D.	γένεσι(ν)

563. The declension of πόλις, ἡ, stem πολι-, *a city,* is as follows:

	Sing.		Plur.
N.	πόλις	N.V.	πόλεις
G.	πόλεως	G.	πόλεων
D.	πόλει	D.	πόλεσι(ν)
A.	πόλιν	A.	πόλεις
V.	πόλι		

564. The declension of βασιλεύς, ὁ, stem βασιλευ-, a king, is as follows:

	Sing.		Plur.
N.	βασιλεύς	N.V.	βασιλεῖς
G.	βασιλέως	G.	βασιλέων
D.	βασιλεῖ	D.	βασιλεῦσι(ν)
A.	βασιλέα	A.	βασιλεῖς
V.	βασιλεῦ		

565. The declension of πατήρ, ὁ, stem πατερ-, *a father*, and ἀνήρ, ὁ, stem ἀνερ-, *a man*, is as follows:

		Sing.
N.	πατήρ	ἀνήρ
G.	πατρός	ἀνδρός
D.	πατρί	ἀνδρί
A.	πατέρα	ἄνδρα
V.	πάτερ	ἄνερ
		Plur.
N.V.	πατέρες	ἄνδρες
G.	πατέρων	ἀνδρῶν
D.	πατράσι(ν)	ἀνδράσι(ν)
A.	πατέρας	ἄνδρας

μήτηρ, μητρός, ἡ, *a mother*, is declined like πατήρ.

566. The declension of χείρ, ἡ, stem χειρ-, a *hand*, and γυνή, ἡ, stem γυναικ-, a *woman*, is as follows:

		Sing.
N.	χείρ	γυνή
G.	χειρός	γυναικός
D.	χειρί	γυναικί
A.	χεῖρα	γυναῖκα
V.	χείρ	γύναι
		Plur.
N.V.	χεῖρες	γυναῖκες
G.	χειρῶν	γυναικῶν
D.	χερσί(ν)	γυναιξί(ν)
A.	χεῖρας	γυναῖκας

567. The Article

The declension of the article, ὁ, ἡ, τό, *the,* is as follows:

	Sing.				Plur.		
	Masc.	Fem.	Neut.		Masc.	Fem.	Neut.
N.	ὁ	ἡ	τό	N.	οἱ	αἱ	τά
G.	τοῦ	τῆς	τοῦ	G.	τῶν	τῶν	τῶν
D.	τῷ	τῇ	τῷ	D.	τοῖς	ταῖς	τοῖς
A.	τόν	τήν	τό	A.	τούς	τάς	τά

Adjectives

568. The declension of ἀγαθός, ή, όν, *good,* is as follows:

	Sing.				Plur.		
	M.	F.	N.		M.	F.	N.
N	ἀγαθός	ἀγαθή	ἀγαθόν	NV	ἀγαθοί	ἀγαθαί	ἀγαθά
G	ἀγαθοῦ	ἀγαθῆς	ἀγαθοῦ	G	ἀγαθῶν	ἀγαθῶν	ἀγαθῶν
D	ἀγαθῷ	ἀγαθῇ	ἀγαθῷ	D	ἀγαθοῖς	ἀγαθαῖς	ἀγαθοῖς
A	ἀγαθόν	ἀγαθήν	ἀγαθόν	A	ἀγαθούς	ἀγαθάς	ἀγαθά
V	ἀγαθέ	ἀγαθή	ἀγαθόν				

569. The declension of μικρός, ά, όν, *small,* is as follows:

	Sing.				Plur.		
	M.	F.	N.		M.	F.	N.
N.	μικρός	μικρά	μικρόν	N.V.	μικροί	μικραί	μικρά
G.	μικροῦ	μικρᾶς	μικροῦ	G.	μικρῶν	μικρῶν	μικρῶν
D.	μικρῷ	μικρᾷ	μικρῷ	D.	μικροῖς	μικραῖς	μικροῖς
A.	μικρόν	μικράν	μικρόν	A.	μικρούς	μικράς	μικρά
V.	μικρέ	μικρά	μικρόν				

570. The declension of δίκαιος, α, ον, *righteous*, is as follows:

	Sing.				Plur.		
	M.	F.	N.		M.	F.	N.
N.	δίκαιος	δικαία	δίκαιον	N.V.	δίκαιοι	δίκαιαι	δίκαια
G.	δικαίου	δικαίας	δικαίου	G.	δικαίων	δικαίων	δικαίων
D.	δικαίῳ	δικαίᾳ	δικαίῳ	D.	δικαίοις	δικαίαις	δικαίοις
A.	δίκαιον	δικαίαν	δίκαιον	A.	δικαίους	δικαίας	δίκαια
V.	δίκαιε	δίκαια	δίκαιον				

571. The declension of μείζων, μεῖζον, *greater*, is as follows:

	Sing.			Plur.	
	M.F.	N.		M.F.	N.
N.	μείζων	μεῖζον	N.	μείζονες (μείζους)	μείζονα(μείζω)
G.	μείζονος	μείζονος	G.	μειζόνων	μειζόνων
D.	μείζονι	μείζονι	D.	μείζοσι(ν)	μείζοσι(ν)
A.	μείζονα (μείζω)	μεῖζον	A.	μείζονας (μείζους)	μείζονα

572. The declension of ἀληθής, ές, *true*, is as follows:

	Sing.			Plur.	
	M.F.	N.		M.F.	N.
N.	ἀληθής	ἀληθές	N.V.	ἀληθεῖς	ἀληθῆ
G.	ἀληθοῦς	ἀληθοῦς	G.	ἀληθῶν	ἀληθῶν
D.	ἀληθεῖ	ἀληθεῖ	D.	ἀληθέσι(ν)	ἀληθέσι(ν)
A.	ἀληθῆ	ἀληθές	A.	ἀληθεῖς	ἀληθῆ
V.	ἀληθές	ἀληθές			

573. The declension of πᾶς, πᾶσα, πᾶν, *all*, is as follows:

	Sing.				Plur.		
	M.	F.	N.		M.	F.	N.
N.	πᾶς	πᾶσα	πᾶν	N.V.	πάντες	πᾶσαι	πάντα
G.	παντός	πάσης	παντός	G.	πάντων	πασῶν	πάντων
D.	παντί	πάσῃ	παντί	D.	πᾶσι(ν)	πάσαις	πᾶσι(ν)
A.	πάντα	πᾶσαν	πᾶν	A.	πάντας	πάσας	πάντα

574. The declension of πολύς, πολλή, πολύ, *much*, is as follows:

	Sing.				Plur.	
	M.	F.	N.		M.	F.	N.
N.	πολύς	πολλή	πολύ	N.V.	πολλοί	πολλαί	πολλά
G.	πολλοῦ	πολλῆς	πολλοῦ	G.	πολλῶν	πολλῶν	πολλῶν
D.	πολλῷ	πολλῇ	πολλῷ	D.	πολλοῖς	πολλαῖς	πολλοῖς
A.	πολύν	πολλήν	πολύ	A.	πολλούς	πολλάς	πολλά

575. The declension of μέγας, μεγάλη, μέγα, *great*, is as follows:

	Sing.				Plur.		
	M.	F.	N.		M.	F.	N.
N	μέγας	μεγάλη	μέγα	N	μεγάλοι	μεγάλαι	μεγάλα
G	μεγάλου	μεγάλης	μεγάλου	G	μεγάλων	μεγάλων	μεγάλων
D	μεγάλῳ	μεγάλη	μεγάλῳ	D	μεγάλοις	μεγάλαις	μεγάλοις
A	μέγαν	μεγάλην	μέγα	A	μεγάλους	μεγάλας	μεγάλα
V	μεγάλε	μεγάλη	μέγα	V	μεγάλοι	μεγάλαι	μεγάλα

Participles

576. The declension of λύων, λύουσα, λῦον, *loosing*, the present active participle of λύω, is as follows:

	Sing.				Plur.		
	M.	F.	N.		M.	F.	N.
N	λύων	λύουσα	λῦον	N	λύοντες	λύουσαι	λύοντα
G	λύοντος	λυούσης	λύοντος	G	λυόντων	λυόντων	λυόντων
D	λύοντι	λυούσῃ	λύοντι	D	λύουσι(ν)	λυούσαις	λύουσι(ν)
A	λύοντα	λύουσαν	λῦον	A	λύοντας	λυούσας	λύοντα

577. The declension of λύσας, λύσασα, λῦσαν, *having loosed*, the aorist active participle of λύω, is as follows:

	M.	Sing. F.	N.
N.	λύσας	λύσασα	λῦσαν
G.	λύσαντος	λυσάσης	λύσαντος
D.	λύσαντι	λυσάσῃ	λύσαντι
A.	λύσαντα	λύσασαν	λῦσαν

	M.	Plur. F.	N.
N.	λύσαντες	λύσασαι	λύσαντα
G.	λυσάντων	λυσασῶν	λυσάντων
D.	λύσασι(ν)	λυσάσαις	λύσασι(ν)
A.	λύσαντας	λυσάσας	λύσαντα

578. The declension of λελυκώς, λελυκυῖα, λελυκός, the perfect active participle of λύω, is as follows:

	M.	Sing. F.	N.
N.	λελυκώς	λελυκυῖα	λελυκός
G.	λελυκότος	λελυκυίας	λελυκότος
D.	λελυκότι	λελυκυίᾳ	λελυκότι
A.	λελυκότα	λελυκυῖαν	λελυκός

	M.	Plur. F.	N.
N.	λελυκότες	λελυκυῖαι	λελυκότα
G.	λελυκότων	λελυκυιῶν	λελυκότων
D.	λελυκόσι(ν)	λελυκυίαις	λελυκόσι(ν)
A.	λελυκότας	λελυκυίας	λελυκότα

579. The declension of λυθείς, λυθεῖσα, λυθέν, *having been loosed,*
the aorist passive participle of λύω, is as follows:

	Sing.		
	M.	F.	N.
N.	λυθείς	λυθεῖσα	λυθέν
G.	λυθέντος	λυθείσης	λυθέντος
D.	λυθέντι	λυθείσῃ	λυθέντι
A.	λυθέντα	λυθεῖσαν	λυθέν

	Plur.		
N.	λυθέντες	λυθεῖσαι	λυθέντα
G.	λυθέντων	λυθεισῶν	λυθέντων
D.	λυθεῖσι(ν)	λυθείσαις	λυθεῖσι(ν)
A.	λυθέντας	λυθείσας	λυθέντα

580. The declension of ὤν, οὖσα, ὄν, *being,* the present participle of
εἰμί, is as follows:

	Sing.				Plur.		
	M.	F.	N.		M.	F.	N.
N.	ὤν	οὖσα	ὄν	N.	ὄντες	οὖσαι	ὄντα
G.	ὄντος	οὔσης	ὄντος	G.	ὄντων	οὐσῶν	ὄντων
D.	ὄντι	οὔσῃ	ὄντι	D.	οὖσι(ν)	οὔσαις	οὖσι(ν)
A.	ὄντα	οὖσαν	ὄν	A.	ὄντας	οὔσας	ὄντα

Pronouns

581. The declensions of the personal pronouns, ἐγώ, *I*, σύ, *thou*, and αὐτός, ή, ό, *he, she, it*, are as follows:

		M.	F.	N.
ἐγώ	σύ	αὐτός	αὐτή	αὐτό

Sing.

			M.	F.	N.
N.	ἐγώ	σύ	αὐτός	αὐτή	αὐτό
G.	ἐμοῦ(μου)	σοῦ	αὐτοῦ	αὐτῆς	αὐτοῦ
D.	ἐμοί(μοι)	σοί	αὐτῷ	αὐτῇ	αὐτῷ
A.	ἐμέ(με)	σέ	αὐτόν	αὐτήν	αὐτό

Plur.

			M.	F.	N.
N.	ἡμεῖς	ὑμεῖς	αὐτοί	αὐταί	αὐτά
G.	ἡμῶν	ὑμῶν	αὐτῶν	αὐτῶν	αὐτῶν
D.	ἡμῖν	ὑμῖν	αὐτοῖς	αὐταῖς	αὐτοῖς
A.	ἡμᾶς	ὑμᾶς	αὐτούς	αὐτάς	αὐτά

582. The declension of οὗτος, αὕτη, τοῦτο, *this*, is as follows:

	Sing.				Plur.		
	M.	F.	N.		M.	F.	N.
N.	οὗτος	αὕτη	τοῦτο	N.	οὗτοι	αὗται	ταῦτα
G.	τούτου	ταύτης	τούτου	G.	τούτων	τούτων	τούτων
D.	τούτῳ	ταύτῃ	τούτῳ	D.	τούτοις	ταύταις	τούτοις
A.	τοῦτον	ταύτην	τοῦτο	A.	τούτους	ταύτας	ταῦτα

ἐκεῖνος, η, ο, *that*, has the same endings as αὐτός.

583. The declension of the relative pronoun, ὅς, ἥ, ὅ, *who, which, what*, is as follows:

		Sing.				Plur.	
	M.	F.	N.		M.	F.	N.
N.	ὅς	ἥ	ὅ	N.	οἵ	αἵ	ἅ
G.	οὗ	ἧς	οὗ	G.	ὧν	ὧν	ὧν
D.	ᾧ	ᾗ	ᾧ	D.	οἷς	αἷς	οἷς
A.	ὅν	ἥν	ὅ	A.	οὕς	ἅς	ἅ

584. The declension of the interrogative pronoun, τίς, τί, *who? which? what?*, and the indefinite pronoun, τις, τι, *some one, something*, is as follows:

		τίς, τί		τις, τι	
		Sing.			
	M.F.	N.	M.F.	N.	
N.	τίς	τί	τις	τι	
G.	τίνος	τίνος	τινός	τινός	
D.	τίνι	τίνι	τινί	τινί	
A.	τίνα	τί	τινά	τι	
		Plur			
	M.F.	N.	M.F.	N.	
N.	τίνες	τίνα	τινές	τινά	
G.	τίνων	τίνων	τινῶν	τινῶν	
D.	τίσι(ν)	τίσι(ν)	τισί(ν)	τισί(ν)	
A.	τίνας	τίνα	τινάς	τινά	

585. The declension of the reflexive pronouns, ἐμαυτοῦ, ῆς, *of myself*, and σεαυτοῦ, ῆς, *of thyself*, is as follows:

	Sing.			
	M.	F.	M.	F.
G.	ἐμαυτοῦ	ἐμαυτῆς	σεαυτοῦ	σεαυτῆς
D.	ἐμαυτῷ	ἐμαυτῇ	σεαυτῷ	σεαυτῇ
A.	ἐμαυτόν	ἐμαυτήν	σεαυτόν	σεαυτήν

	Plur			
	M.F.	N.	M.F.	N.
G.	ἑαυτῶν	ἑαυτῶν	ἑαυτῶν	ἑαυτῶν
D.	ἑαυτοῖς	ἑαυταῖς	ἑαυτοῖς	ἑαυταῖς
A.	ἑαυτούς	ἑαυτάς	ἑαυτούς	ἑαυτάς

586. The declension of the reflexive pronoun ἑαυτοῦ, ἧς, οὖ, *of himself, of herself, of itself,* is as follows:

	Sing.			Plur.	
M.	F.	N.	M.	F.	N.
G. ἑαυτοῦ	ἑαυτῆς	ἑαυτοῦ	G. ἑαυτῶν	ἑαυτῶν	ἑαυτῶν
D. ἑαυτῷ	ἑαυτῇ	ἑαυτῷ	D. ἑαυτοῖς	ἑαυταῖς	ἑαυτοῖς
A. ἑαυτόν	ἑαυτήν	ἑαυτό	A. ἑαυτούς	ἑαυτάς	ἑαυτά

Numerals

587. The declension of εἷς, μία, ἕν, *one,* is as follows:

	M.	F.	N.
N.	εἷς	μία	ἕν
G.	ἑνός	μιᾶς	ἑνός
D.	ἑνί	μιᾷ	ἑνί
A.	ἕνα	μίαν	ἕν

588. The declension of τρεῖς, τρία, *three,* is as follows:

	M.F.	N.
N.	τρεῖς	τρία
G.	τριῶν	τριῶν
D.	τρισί(ν)	τρισί(ν)
A.	τρεῖς	τρία

The declension of τέσσαρες, τέσσαρα, *four,* is as follows:

	M.F.	N.
N.	τέσσαρες	τέσσαρα
G.	τεσσάρων	τεσσάρων
D.	τέσσαρσι(ν)	τέσσαρσι(ν)
A.	τέσσαρας	τέσσαρα

589. The Regular Verb

The conjugation of Λύω, I loose, stem λυ-, is as follows:

Principal Parts		Λύω			Λύσω		ἔλυσα		λέλυκα			ἐλύθην	
		Pres.Act.	Imp.Act.	Pres.M.P.	Imp.M.P.	Fut.Act.	Fut.Mid.	Aor.Act.	Aor.Mid.	Perf.Act.	Plup.Act.	Perf.M.P.	Aor.Pass.	Fut.Pass.
Indic.	S. 1.	Λύω	ἔλυον	λύομαι	ἐλυόμην	λύσω	λύσομαι	ἔλυσα	ἐλυσάμην	λέλυκα	(ἐ)λελύκειν	λέλυμαι	ἐλύθην	λυθήσομαι
	2.	λύεις	ἔλυες	λύῃ	ἐλύου	λύσεις	λύσῃ	ἔλυσας	ἐλύσω	λέλυκας	(ἐ)λελύκεις	λέλυσαι	ἐλύθης	λυθήσῃ
	3.	λύει	ἔλυε(ν)	λύεται	ἐλύετο	λύσει	λύσεται	ἔλυσε(ν)	ἐλύσατο	λέλυκε(ν)	(ἐ)λελύκει	λέλυται	ἐλύθη	λυθήσεται
	Pl. 1.	λύομεν	ἐλύομεν	λυόμεθα	ἐλυόμεθα	λύσομεν	λυσόμεθα	ἐλύσαμεν	ἐλυσάμεθα	λελύκαμεν	(ἐ)λελύκειμεν	λελύμεθα	ἐλύθημεν	λυθησόμεθα
	2.	λύετε	ἐλύετε	λύεσθε	ἐλύεσθε	λύσετε	λύσεσθε	ἐλύσατε	ἐλύσασθε	λελύκατε	(ἐ)λελύκειτε	λέλυσθε	ἐλύθητε	λυθήσεσθε
	3.	λύουσι(ν)	ἔλυον	λύονται	ἐλύοντο	λύσουσι(ν)	λύσονται	ἔλυσαν	ἐλύσαντο	λελύκασι(ν) λελύκαν	(ἐ)λελύκεισαν	λέλυνται	ἐλύθησαν	λυθήσονται
Subj.	S. 1.	Λύω		λύωμαι				λύσω	λύσωμαι				λυθῶ	
	2.	λύῃς		λύῃ				λύσῃς	λύσῃ				λυθῇς	
	3.	λύῃ		λύηται				λύσῃ	λύσηται				λυθῇ	
	Pl. 1.	λύωμεν		λυώμεθα				λύσωμεν	λυσώμεθα				λυθῶμεν	
	2.	λύητε		λύησθε				λύσητε	λύσησθε				λυθῆτε	
	3.	λύωσι(ν)		λύωνται				λύσωσι(ν)	λύσωνται				λυθῶσι(ν)	
Imper.	S. 2.	λῦε		λύου				λῦσον	λῦσαι				λύθητι	
	3.	λυέτω		λυέσθω				λυσάτω	λυσάσθω				λυθήτω	
	Pl. 2.	λύετε		λύεσθε				λύσατε	λύσασθε				λύθητε	
	3.	λυέτωσαν		λυέσθωσαν				λυσάτωσαν	λυσάσθωσαν				λυθήτωσαν	
Inf.		λύειν		λύεσθαι		λύσειν	λύσεσθαι	λῦσαι	λύσασθαι	λελυκέναι		λελύσθαι	λυθῆναι	
Part.		λύων		λυόμενος		λύσων	λυσόμενος	λύσας	λυσάμενος	λελυκώς		λελυμένος	λυθείς	
		λύουσα		λυομένη		λύσουσα	λυομένη	λύσασα	λυσαμένη	λελυκυῖα		λελυμένη	λυθεῖσα	
		λῦον		λυόμενον		λῦσον	λυσόμενον	λῦσαν	λυσάμενον	λελυκός		λελυμένον	λυθέν	

590. The present system of τιμάω, *I honor,* is as follows:

		Pres.Act.	Imp.Act.	Pres.M.P.	Imp.M.P. Indic.
Indic.	S.	1. (τιμάω) τιμῶ	(ἐτίμαον) ἐτίμων	(τιμάομαι) τιμῶμαι	(ἐτιμαόμην) ἐτιμώμην
		2. (τιμάεις) τιμᾷς	(ἐτίμαες) ἐτίμας	(τιμάῃ) τιμᾷ	(ἐτιμάου) ἐτιμῶ
		3. (τιμάει) τιμᾷ	(ἐτίμαε) ἐτίμα	(τιμάεται) τιμᾶται	(ἐτιμάετο) ἐτιμᾶτο
	Pl.	1. (τιμάομεν) τιμῶμεν	(ἐτιμάομεν) ἐτιμῶμεν	(τιμαόμεθα) τιμώμεθα	(ἐτιμαόμεθα) ἐτιμώμεθα
		2. (τιμάετε) τιμᾶτε	(ἐτιμάετε) ἐτιμᾶτε	(τιμάεσθε) τιμᾶσθε	(ἐτιμάεσθε) ἐτιμᾶσθε
		3. (τιμάουσι(ν)) τιμῶσι(ν)	(ἐτίμαον) ἐτίμων	(τιμάονται) τιμῶνται	(ἐτιμάοντο) ἐτιμῶντο
Subj.	S.	1. (τιμάω) τιμῶ		(τιμάωμαι) τιμῶμαι	
		2. (τιμάῃς) τιμᾷς		(τιμάῃ) τιμᾷ	
		3. (τιμάῃ) τιμᾷ		(τιμάηται) τιμᾶται	
	Pl.	1. (τιμάωμεν) τιμῶμεν		(τιμαώμεθα) τιμώμεθα	
		2. (τιμάητε) τιμᾶτε		(τιμάησθε) τιμᾶσθε	
		3. (τιμάωσι(ν)) τιμῶσι(ν)		(τιμάωνται) τιμῶνται	
Imper.	S.	2. (τίμαε) τίμα		(τιμάου) τιμῶ	
		3. (τιμαέτω) τιμάτω		(τιμαέσθω) τιμάσθω	
	Pl.	2. (τιμάετε) τιμᾶτε		(τιμάεσθε) τιμᾶσθε	
		3. (τιμαέτωσαν) τιμάτωσαν		(τιμαέσθωσαν) τιμάσθωσαν	
Inf.		(τιμάειν) τιμᾶν		(τιμάεσθαι) τιμᾶσθαι	
Part.		(τιμάων) τιμῶν		(τιμαόμενος) τιμώμενος	
		(τιμάουσα) τιμῶσα		(τιμαομένη) τιμωμένη	
		(τιμάον) τιμῶν		(τιμαόμενον) τιμώμενον	

591.

The present system of φιλέω, *I love*, is as follows:

	Pres.Act.	Imp.Act.	Pres.M.P.	Imp.M.P. Indic.
Indic. S. 1.	ῶ	(ἐφίλεον) ἐφίλουν	(φιλέομαι) φιλοῦμαι	(ἐφιλεόμην) ἐφιλούμην
2.	(φιλέεις) ῖς	(ἐφίλεες) ἐφίλεις	(φιλέῃ) φιλῇ	(ἐφιλέου) ἐφιλοῦ
3.	(φιλέει) φιλεῖ	(ἐφίλεε) ἐφίλει	(φιλέεται) φιλεῖται	(ἐφιλέετο) ἐφιλεῖτο
Pl. 1.	(φιλέομεν) φιλοῦμεν	(ἐφιλέομεν) ἐφιλοῦμεν	(φιλεόμεθα) φιλούμεθα	(ἐ ... όμεθα) ἐφιλούμεθα
2.	(φιλέετε) φιλεῖτε	(ἐφιλέετε) ἐφιλεῖτε	(φιλέεσθε) φιλεῖσθε	(ἐφιλέεσθε) ἐφιλεῖσθε
3.	(φιλέουσι(ν)) φιλοῦσι(ν)	(ἐφίλεον) ἐφίλουν	(φιλέονται) φιλοῦνται	(ἐφιλέοντο) ἐφιλοῦντο
Subj. S. 1.	(φιλέω) φιλῶ		(φιλέωμαι) φιλῶμαι	
2.	(φιλέῃ) φιλῇς		(φιλέῃ) φιλῇ	
3.	(φιλέῃ) φιλῇ		(φιλέηται) φιλῆται	
Pl. 1.	(φιλέωμεν) φιλῶμεν		(φιλεώμεθα) φιλώμεθα	
2.	(φιλέητε) φιλῆτε		(φιλέησθε) φιλῆσθε	
3.	(φιλέωσι(ν)) ῶσι(ν)		(φιλέωνται) φιλῶνται	
Imper. S. 2.	(φίλεε) φίλει		(φιλέου) φιλοῦ	
3.	(φιλεέτω) φιλεέτω		ἐσθω φιλείσθω	
2.	(φιλέετε) φιλεῖτε		(φιλέεσθε) φιλεῖσθε	
3.	(φιλεέτωσαν) φιλείτωσαν		ισθωσαν	
Inf.	(φιλέε) φιλεῖν		(φιλέ) ισθαι	
Part.	(φιλέ) ὤν		(φιλεόμενος)	
	(φιλέουσα) φιλοῦσα		φιλουμένη	
	(φιλ) ῦν		(φιλεόμενον)	

592.

The present system of δηλόω, I make manifest, is as follows:

		Pres.Act.	Imp.Act.	Pres.M.P.	Imp.M.P. Indic.
Indic.	S. 1	δηλῶ (δηλόω)	(ἐδήλοον) ἐδήλουν	δηλοῦμαι (δηλόομαι)	(ἐδηλοόμην) ἐδηλούμην
	2	δηλοῖς (δηλόεις)	(ἐδήλοες) ἐδήλους	δηλοῖ (δηλόῃ)	(ἐδηλόου) ἐδηλοῦ
	3	δηλοῖ (δηλόει)	(ἐδήλοε) ἐδήλου	δηλοῦται (δηλόεται)	(ἐδηλόετο) ἐδηλοῦτο
	Pl. 1	δηλοῦμεν (δηλόομεν)	(ἐδηλόομεν) ἐδηλοῦμεν	δηλούμεθα (δηλοόμεθα)	(ἐδηλοόμεθα) ἐδηλούμεθα
	2	δηλοῦτε (δηλόετε)	(ἐδηλόετε) ἐδηλοῦτε	δηλοῦσθε (δηλόεσθε)	(ἐδηλόεσθε) ἐδηλοῦσθε
	3	δηλοῦσι(ν) (δηλόουσι(ν))	(ἐδήλοον) ἐδήλουν	δηλοῦνται (δηλόονται)	(ἐδηλόοντο) ἐδηλοῦντο
Subj.	S. 1	δηλῶ (δηλόω)		δηλῶμαι (δηλόωμαι)	
	2	δηλοῖς (δηλόῃς)		δηλοῖ (δηλόῃ)	
	3	δηλοῖ (δηλόῃ)		δηλῶται (δηλόηται)	
	Pl. 1	δηλῶμεν (δηλόωμεν)		δηλώμεθα (δηλοώμεθα)	
	2	δηλῶτε (δηλόητε)		δηλῶσθε (δηλόησθε)	
	3	δηλῶσι(ν) (δηλόωσι(ν))		δηλῶνται (δηλόωνται)	
Imper.	S. 2	δήλου (δήλοε)		δηλοῦ (δηλόου)	
	3	δηλούτω (δηλοέτω)		δηλούσθω (δηλοέσθω)	
	Pl. 2	δηλοῦτε (δηλόετε)		δηλοῦσθε (δηλόεσθε)	
	3	(δηλοέτωσαν) δηλούτωσαν		(δηλοέσθωσαν) δηλούσθωσαν	
Inf.		δηλοῦν (δηλόειν)		δηλοῦσθαι (δηλόεσθαι)	
Part.		δηλῶν (δηλόων)		δηλούμενος (δηλοόμενος)	
		δηλοῦσα (δηλόουσα)		δηλουμένη (δηλοομένη)	
		δηλοῦν (δηλόον)		δηλούμενον (δηλοόμενον)	

593. Second Aorist Active and Middle The second aorist active and middle of λείπω, *I leave*, is as follows:

		2nd Aor. Act. Indic.	2nd Aor. Mid. Indic.
Sing.	1.	ἔλιπον	ἐλιπόμην
	2.	ἔλιπες	ἐλίπου
	3.	ἔλιπε(ν)	ἐλίπετο
Plur.	1.	ἐλίπομεν	ἐλιπόμεθα
	2.	ἐλίπετε	ἐλίπεσθε
	3.	ἔλιπον	ἐλίποντο
		Subj.	Subj.
Sing.	1.	λίπω	λίπωμαι
	2.	λίπῃς	λίπῃ
	3.	λίπῃ	λίπηται
Plur.	1.	λίπωμεν	λιπώμεθα
	2.	λίπητε	λίπησθε
	3.	λίπωσι(ν)	λίπωνται
		Imper.	Imper.
Sing.	2.	λίπε	λιποῦ
	3.	λιπέτω	λιπέσθω
Plur.	2.	λίπετε	λίπεσθε
	3.	λιπέτωσαν	λιπέσθωσαν
		Inf.	Inf.
		λιπεῖν	λιπέσθαι
		Part.	Part.
		λιπών, λιποῦσα, λιπόν	λιπόμενος, η, ον

Future and Aorist of Liquid Verbs

594. The future active and middle of κρίνω, *I judge,* is as follows:

595. The first aorist active and middle of κρίνω, *I judge,* is as follows:

Fut. Act.
Indic.

Sing. 1. κρινῶ
2. κρινεῖς
3. κρινεῖ

Plur. 1. κρινοῦμεν
2. κρινεῖτε
3. κρινοῦσι(ν)

Fut. Mid.
Indic.

Sing. 1. κρινοῦμαι
2. κρινῇ
3. κρινεῖται

Plur. 1. κρινούμεθα
2. κρινεῖσθε
3. κρινοῦνται

	1st Aor. Act. Indic.	1st Aor. Mid. Indic.
S. 1.	ἔκρινα	ἐκρινάμην
2.	ἔκρινας	ἐκρίνω
3.	ἔκρινε(ν)	ἐκρίνατο
Pl. 1.	ἐκρίναμεν	ἐκρινάμεθα
2.	ἐκρίνατε	ἐκρίνασθε
3.	ἔκριναν	ἐκρίναντο
	Subj.	**Subj.**
S. 1.	κρίνω	κρίνωμαι
2.	κρίνῃς	κρίνῃ
3.	κρίνῃ	κρίνηται
Pl. 1.	κρίνωμεν	κρινώμεθα
2.	κρίνητε	κρίνησθε
3.	κρίνωσι(ν)	κρίνωνται
	Imper.	**Imper.**
S. 2.	κρῖνον	κρῖναι
3.	κρινάτω	κρινάσωθω
Pl. 2.	κρίνατε	κρίνασθε
3.	κρινάτωσαν	κρινάσθωσαν
	Inf.	**Inf.**
	κρῖναι	κρίνασθαι
	Part.	**Part.**
	κρίνας, κρίνασα, κρῖναν	κρινάμενος, η, ον

Verbs in μι.

596. The present system of δίδωμι, stem δο- *I give*, is as follows:

Pres. Act. Imp. Act. Pres. M. P. Imp. M. P. S

		Pres. Act. Indic.	Imperf.Act. Indic.	Pres. M.P. Indic.	Imperf.M.P. Indic.
Sing.	1.	δίδωμι	ἐδίδουν	δίδομαι	ἐδιδόμην
	2.	δίδως	ἐδίδυυς	δίδοσαι	ἐδίδοσο
	3.	δίδωσι(ν)	ἐδίδου	δίδοται	ἐδίδοτο
Plur.	1.	δίδομεν	ἐδίδομεν	διδόμεθα	ἐδιδόμεθα
	2.	δίδοτε	ἐδίδοτε	δίδοσθε	ἐδίδοσθε
	3.	διδόασι(ν)	ἐδίδοσαν	δίδονται	ἐδίδοντο

		Subj.	Subj.
Sing.	1.	διδῶ	(διδῶμαι
	2.	διδῷς	διδῷ
	3.	διδῷ	διδῶται
Plur.	1.	διδῶμεν	διδώμεθα
	2.	διδῶτε	διδῶσθε
	3.	διδῶσι(ν)	διδῶνται)

		Imper.	Imper.
Sing.	2.	δίδου	(δίδοσο
	3.	διδότω	διδόσθω
Plur.	2.	δίδοτε	δίδοσθε
	3.	διδότωσαν	διδόσθωσαν)

Infin.	Infin.
διδόναι	δίδοσθαι

Part.	Part.
διδούς, διδοῦσα, διδόν	διδόμενος, η, ον

597. The aorist active and middle of δίδωμι, *I give*, is as follows:

		Aor. Act. Indic.	Aor. Mid. Indic.
Sing.	1.	ἔδωκα	ἐδόμην
	2.	ἔδωκας	ἔδου
	3.	ἔδωκε(ν)	ἔδοτο
Plur.	1.	ἐδώκαμεν	ἐδόμεθα
	2.	ἐδώκατε	ἔδοσθε
	3.	ἔδωκαν	ἔδοντο

		Subj.	Subj.
Sing.	1.	δῶ	(δῶμαι)
	2.	δῷς	(δῷ)
	3.	δῷ	(δῶται)
Plur.	1.	δῶμεν	(δώμεθα)
	2.	δῶτε	(δῶσθε)
	3.	δῶσι(ν)	(δῶνται)

		Imper.	Imper.
Sing.	2.	δός	(δοῦ)
	3.	δότω	(δόσθω)
Plur.	2.	δότε	(δόσθε)
	3.	δότωσαν	(δόσθωσαν)

Infin.	Infin.
δοῦναι	(δόσθαι)

Part.	Part.
δούς, δοῦσα, δόν	(δόμενος, η, ον)

212

598. The present system of τίθημι, stem θε-, *I place*, is as follows:

		Pres. Act. Indic.	Imperf.Act. Indic.	Pres. M.P. Indic.	Imperf.M.P. Indic.
Sing.	1.	τίθημι	ἐτίθην	τίθεμαι	ἐτιθέμην
	2.	τίθης	ἐτίθεις	τίθεσαι	ἐτίθεσο
	3.	τίθησι(ν)	ἐτίθει	τίθεται	ἐτίθετο
Plur.	1.	τίθεμεν	ἐτίθεμεν	τιθέμεθα	ἐτιθέμεθα
	2.	τίθετε	ἐτίθετε	τίθεσθε	ἐτίθεσθε
	3.	τιθέασι(ν)	ἐτίθεσαν	τίθενται	ἐτίθεντο

		Subj.	Subj.
Sing.	1.	τιθῶ	(τιθῶμαι
	2.	τιθῇς	τιθῇ
	3.	τιθῇ	τιθῆται
Plur.	1.	τιθῶμεν	τιθώμεθα
	2.	τιθῆτε	τιθῆσθε
	3.	τιθῶσι(ν)	τιθῶνται)

		Imper.	Imper.
Sing.	2.	τίθει	τίθεσο
	3.	τιθέτω	τιθέσθω
Plur.	2.	τίθετε	τίθεσθε
	3.	τιθέτωσαν	τιθέσθωσαν

Infin.	Infin.
τιθέναι	τίθεσθαι

Part.	Part.
τιθείς, τιθεῖσα, τιθέν	τιθέμενος, η, ον

599. The aorist active and middle of τίθημι, *I place,* is as follows:

		Aor. Act. Indic.	Aor. Mid. Indic.
Sing.	1.	ἔθηκα	ἐθέμην
	2.	ἔθηκας	ἔθου
	3.	ἔθηκε(ν)	ἔθετο
Plur.	1.	ἐθήκαμεν	ἐθέμεθα
	2.	ἐθήκατε	ἔθεσθε
	3.	ἔθηκαν	ἔθεντο

		Subj.	Subj.
Sing.	1.	θῶ	θῶμαι
	2.	θῇς	θῇ
	3.	θῇ	θῆται
Plur.	1.	θῶμεν	θώμεθα
	2.	θῆτε	θῆσθε
	3.	θῶσι(ν)	θῶνται

		Imper.	Imper.
Sing.	2.	θές	θοῦ
	3.	θέτω	θέσθω
Plur.	2.	θέτε	θέσθε
	3.	θέτωσαν	θέσθωσαν

	Infin.	Infin.
	θεῖναι	(θέσθαι)

	Part.	Part.
	θείς, θεῖσα, θέν	(θέμενος, η, ον)

600. The present system of ἵστημι, stem στα-, *I cause to stand*, is as follows:

		Pres. Act. Indic.	Imperf.Act. Indic.	Pres. M.P. Indic.	Imperf.M.P. Indic.
Sing.	1.	ἵστημι	ἵστην	ἵσταμαι	ἱστάμην
	2.	ἵστης	ἵστης	ἵστασαι	ἵστασο
	3.	ἵστησι(ν)	ἵστη	ἵσταται	ἵστατο
Plur.	1.	ἵσταμεν	ἵσταμεν	ἱστάμεθα	ἱστάμεθα
	2.	ἵστατε	ἵστατε	ἵστασθε	ἵστασθε
	3.	ἱστᾶσι(ν)	ἵστασαν	ἵστανται	ἵσταντο

		Subj.	Subj.
Sing.	1.	ἱστῶ	(ἱστῶμαι
	2.	ἱστῇς	ἱστῇ
	3.	ἱστῇ	ἱστῆται
Plur.	1.	ἱστῶμεν	ἱστώμεθα
	2.	ἱστῆτε	ἱστῆσθε
	3.	ἱστῶσι(ν)	ἱστῶνται)

		Imper.	Imper.
Sing.	2.	ἵστη	ἵστασο
	3.	ἱστάτω	ἱστάσθω
Plur.	2.	ἵστατε	ἵστασθε
	3.	ἱστάτωσαν	ἱστάσθωσαν

	Infin.	Infin.
	ἱστάναι	ἵστασθαι

	Part.	Part.
	ἱστάς, ἱστᾶσα, ἱστάν	ἱστάμενος, η, ον

601. The second aorist active of ἵστημι, *I cause to stand* (intransitive in second aorist), and of γινώσκω, stem γνο-, *I know*, is as follows:

		Indic.	Indic.
Sing.	1.	ἔστην	ἔγνων
	2.	ἔστης	ἔγνως
	3.	ἔστη	ἔγνω
Plur.	1.	ἔστημεν	ἔγνωμεν
	2.	ἔστητε	ἔγνωτε
	3.	ἔστησαν	ἔγνωσαν

		Subj.	Subj.
Sing.	1.	στῶ	γνῶ
	2.	στῇς	γνῷς
	3.	στῇ	γνῷ (γνοῖ)
Plur.	1.	στῶμεν	γνῶμεν
	2.	στῆτε	γνῶτε
	3.	στῶσι(ν)	γνῶσι(ν)

		Imper.	Imper.
Sing.	2.	στῆθι	γνῶθι
	3.	στήτω	γνώτω
Plur.	2.	στῆτε	γνῶτε
	3.	στήτωσαν	γνώτωσαν

Infin.	Infin.
στῆναι	γνῶναι

Part.	Part.
στάς, στᾶσα, στάν	(γνούς, γνοῦσα, γνόν)

602. The conjugation of εἰμί, *I am,* is as follows:

		Present Indic.	Imperf. Indic.	Future Indic.
Sing.	1.	εἰμί	ἤμην	ἔσομαι
	2.	εἶ	ἦς	ἔσῃ
	3.	ἐστί(ν)	ἦν	ἔσται
Plur.	1.	ἐσμέν	ἦμεν	ἐσόμεθα
	2.	ἐστέ	ἦτε	ἔσεσθε
	3.	εἰσί(ν)	ἦσαν	ἔσονται

		Subj.
Sing.	1.	ὦ
	2.	ἦς
	3.	ᾖ
Plur.	1.	ὦμεν
	2.	ἦτε
	3.	ὦσι(ν)

		Imper.
Sing.	2.	ἴσθι
	3.	ἔστω
Plur.	2.	ἔστε
	3.	ἔστωσαν

Infin.

εἶναι

Part.

ὤν, οὖσα, ὄν

Conjugation of οἶδα

603. The conjugation of οἶδα, *I know*, is as follows:

		Perfect Indic.	Pluperfect Indic.
Sing.	1.	οἶδα	ᾔδειν
	2.	οἶδας	ᾔδεις
	3.	οἶδε(ν)	ᾔδει
Plur.	1.	οἴδαμεν	ᾔδειμεν
	2.	οἴδατε	ᾔδειτε
	3.	οἴδασι(ν)	ᾔδεισαν

		Subj.
Sing.	1.	εἰδῶ
	2.	εἰδῇς
	3.	εἰδῇ
Plur.	1.	εἰδῶμεν
	2.	εἰδῆτε
	3.	εἰδῶσι(ν)

		Imper.
Sing.	2.	ἴσθι
	3.	ἴστω
Plur.	2.	ἴστε
	3.	ἴστωσαν

Infin.

εἰδέναι

Part.

εἰδώς, εἰδυῖα, εἰδός

Vocabularies

I. Greek-English Vocabulary

(The enclosing of a verb form in parentheses indicates that no part of the tense system indicated by that form occurs in the New Testament. The figures refer to sections.)

ἀγαθός, ή, όν, adj., §61, §568, good

ἀγαπάω, ἀγαπήσω, ἠγάπησα, ἠγάπηκα, ἠγάπημαι, ἠγαπήθην, §313, I love

ἀγάπη, ἡ, love

ἄγγελος, ὁ, a messenger, an angel

ἀγιάζω, (ἀγιάσω), ἡγίασα, (ἡγίακα), ἡγίασμαι, ἡγιάσθην, I sanctify, I consecrate, I hallow

ἅγιος, α, ον, adj., holy

ἀγρός, ὁ, a field

ἄγω, ἄξω, ἤγαγον, (ἦχα), ἦγμαι, ἤχθην, I lead

ἀδελφός, ὁ, a brother

αἷμα, αἵματος, τό, blood

αἴρω, ἀρῶ, ἦρα, ἦρκα, ἦρμαι, ἤρθην, I take up, I take away.

αἰτέω, αἰτήσω, ἤτησα, ἤτηκα, (ἤτημαι), ἠτήθην, I ask (in the sense of request), I ask for

αἰών, αἰῶνος, ὁ, an age

αἰώνιος, ον, adj., §481, eternal

ἀκήκοα, 2nd perf. of ἀκούω

ἀκολουθέω, ἀκολουθήσω, ἠκολούθησα, ἠκολούθηκα, I follow (takes the dative)

ἀκούω, ἀκούσω, ἤκουσα, ἀκήκοα, (ἤκουσμαι), ἠκούσθην, I hear (takes the genitive or the accusative)

ἀλήθεια, ἡ, §53, §555, truth

ἀληθής, ές, adj., §360-§362, §572, true

ἀλλά, conj., but (a stronger adversative than δέ)

ἀλλήλων, οις, ους, reciprocal pron., §343, of each other, of one another

ἄλλος, η, ο, other, another

ἁμαρτάνω, ἁμαρτήσω, ἡμάρτησα or ἥμαρτον, ἡμάρτηκα, (ἡμάρτημαι), (ἡμαρτήθην), I sin

ἁμαρτία, ἡ, a sin, sin

ἁμαρτωλός, ὁ, a sinner

ἄν, a particle which cannot be translated separately into English, §400, §536, §551.

ἀναβαίνω, I go up

ἀναβλέπω, I look up, I receive my sight

ἀναλαμβάνω, I take up

ἀνεῳχθῆναι, aor. pass. infin. of ἀνοίγω

ἀνήρ, ἀνδρός, ὁ, §565, a man (as distinguished from women and children)

220

ἄνθρωπος, ὁ, §31-§33, §557, a man (as distinguished from other beings)

ἀνίστημι, I cause to rise; in the intransitive tenses (see under ἵστημι) and in the middle, I stand up, I arise

ἀνοίγω, ἀνοίξω, ἀνέῳξα, or ἤνοιξα or ἠνέῳξα, ἀνέῳγα, ἀνέῳγμαι or ἠνέῳγμαι or ἤνοιγμαι, ἀνεῴχθην or ἠνοίχθην or ἠνεῴχθην, I open

ἀντί, prep. with gen., instead of

ἀπέθανον, 2nd. aor. of ἀποθνήσκω

ἀπέρχομαι, I go away, I depart

ἀπέστειλα, aor. of ἀποστέλλω

ἀπό, prep. with gen., from

ἀποδίδωμι, I give back, I give what is owed or promised, I pay

ἀποθνήσκω, ἀποθανοῦμαι, ἀπέθανον, I die

ἀποκρίνομαι, (ἀποκρινοῦμαι), ἀπεκρινάμην, (ἀποκέκριμαι), ἀπεκρίθην, dep. with passive forms and rarely with middle forms, I answer (takes the dative)

ἀποκτείνω, ἀποκτενῶ, ἀπέκτεινα, aor. pass. ἀπεκτάνθην, I kill

ἀπόλλυμί or ἀπολλύω, ἀπολέσω or ἀπολῶ, ἀπώλεσα, ἀπόλωλα, 2nd aor. mid. ἀπωλόμην, §533, I destroy; middle, I perish

απολύω, I release, I dismiss

ἀποστέλλω, ἀποστελῶ, ἀπέστειλα, ἀπέσταλκα, ἀπέσταλμαι, ἀπεστάλην, I send (with a commission)

ἀπόστολος, ὁ, an apostle

ἄρτος, ὁ, a piece of bread, a loaf, bread

ἀρχή, ἡ, a beginning

ἀρχιερεύς, ἀρχιερέως, ὁ, a chief priest, a high priest

ἄρχω, ἄρξω, ἦρξα, I rule (takes the genitive); middle, §344 (footnote 26), I begin

ἄρχων, ἄρχοντος, ὁ, §211, §559, a ruler

ἀρῶ, fut. of αἴρω

αὐτός, ἡ, ὁ, §96 f., §105 f., §581, pron., himself, herself, itself, same; personal pron., he, she, it

ἀφίημι, ἀφήσω, ἀφῆκα, ἀφεῖκα, ἀφεῖμαι, (ἀφείθην), §531 f. also §604 and §605, I let go, I leave, I permit; I forgive (with the accusative of the sin or debt forgiven and the dative of the person forgiven)

βαίνω, βήσομαι, ἔβην, βέβηκα, §164, §538, I go

(occurs in the New Testament only in composition)

βάλλω, βαλῶ, ἔβαλον, βέβληκα, βέβλημαι, ἐβλήθην, *I throw, I cast, I put*

βαπτίζω, βαπτίσω, ἐβάπτισα, (βεβάπτικα), βεβάπτισμαι, ἐβαπτίσθην, *I baptize*

βασιλεία, ἡ, *a kingdom*

βασιλεύς, βασιλέως, ὁ, §355-§357, §564, *a king*

βήσομαι, fut. of βαίνω

βιβλίον, τό, *a book*

βλέπω, βλέψω, ἔβλεψα, *I see* (βλέπω is the common word for *I see* in the present and imperfect. In the other tenses the principal parts given under ὁράω are commonly used)

Γαλιλαία, ἡ, *Galilee*

γάρ, conj., postpositive, *for*

γέγονα, 2nd perf. of γίνομαι

γενήσομαι, fut. of γίνομαι

γεννάω, γεννήσω, ἐγέννησα, γεγέννηκα, γεγέννημαι, ἐγεννήθην, *I beget*; also of the mother, *I bear*

γένος, γένους, τό, §352-§354, §562, *a race, a kind*

γῆ, ἡ, §403, *earth, a land*

γίνομαι, γενήσομαι, ἐγενόμην, γέγονα, γεγένημαι, ἐγενήθην, §424

(footnote 33), §550, §552 f., *I become, I come into being, I appear in history, I am*; γίνεται, *it comes to pass, it happens*

γινώσκω, γνώσομαι, ἔγνων, ἔγνωκα, ἔγνωσμαι, ἐγνώσθην, §516 f., §601, *I know*

γνώσομαι, fut. of γινώσκω

γράμμα, γράμματος, τό, *a letter*

γραμματεύς, γραμματέως, ὁ, *a scribe*

γραφή, ἡ, §56-§58, §555, *a writing, a Scripture*; αἱ γραφαί, *the Scriptures*

γράφω, γράψω, ἔγραψα, γέγραφα, γέγραμμαι, ἐγράφην, §206, §258, *I write*

γυνή, γυναικός, ἡ, §566, *a woman*

δαιμόνιον, τό, *a demon*

δέ, conj., postpositive, §90 f., *and, but*

δέδοται, from δίδωμι, perfect middle or passive indicative 3rd person sing.

δεῖ, impersonal verb, §292, *it is necessary*

δείκνυμι or δεικνύω, δείξω, ἔδειξα, (δέδειχα), δέδειγμαι, ἐδείχθην, §533, *I show*

δέχομαι, δέξομαι, ἐδεξάμην, δέδεγμαι, ἐδέχθην, *I receive*

δηλόω, δηλώσω, ἐδήλωσα, (δεδήλωκα), (δεδήλωμαι), ἐδηλώθην, §317-§322, §592, I make manifest, I show

διά, prep. with gen., through; with acc., on account of

διδάσκαλος, ὁ, a teacher.

διδάσκω, διδάξω, ἐδίδαξα, (δεδίδαχα), (δεδίδαγμαι), ἐδιδάχθην, I teach

δίδωμι, δώσω, ἔδωκα, δέδωκα, δέδομαι, ἐδόθην, §482-§515, §596 f., I give

διέρχομαι, I go through

δίκαιος, α, ον, adj., §62, §570, righteous

δικαιοσύνη, ἡ, righteousness

διώκω, διώξω, ἐδίωξα, δεδίωκα, δεδίωγμαι, ἐδιώχθην, I pursue, I persecute

δοκέω, (δόξω), ἔδοξα, I think, I seem

δόξα, ἡ, §54 f., §555, glory

δοξάζω, δοξάσω, ἐδόξασα, (δεδόξακα), δεδόξασμαι, ἐδοξάσθην, I glorify

δοῦλος, ὁ, §38, §557, a slave, a servant

δύναμαι, δυνήσομαι, (δεδύνημαι), ἠδυνήθην or ἠδυνάσθην, imperfect ἐδυνάμην or ἠδυνάμην, §538, I am able

δύναμις, δυνάμεως, ἡ, power

δύο, §373, dat. δυσί(ν), two

δῶρον, τό, §41 f., §558, a gift

ἐάν, conditional particle, with subj., §288, if; ἐάν μή, unless, except

ἐάν, particle, sometimes used with the subj. in the same way as ἄν

ἑαυτοῦ, ῆς, οῦ, reflexive pron., §339 f., §586, of himself, of herself, of itself

ἔβαλον, 2nd aor. of βάλλω

ἐβλήθην, aor. pass. of βάλλω

ἐγγίζω, ἐγγιῶ, or ἐγγίσω, ἤγγισα, ἤγγικα, I come near

ἐγγύς, adv., near

ἐγείρω, ἐγερῶ, ἤγειρα, ---, ἐγήγερμαι, ἠγέρθην, I raise up; in passive sometimes as deponent, I rise

ἐγενήθην, aor. pass. (in form) of γίνομαι

ἐγενόμην, 2nd aor. of γίνομαι

ἔγνωκα, perf. of γινώσκω

ἔγνων, 2nd aor. of γινώσκω

ἐγνώσθην, aor. pass. of γινώσκω

ἐγώ, ἐμοῦ or μου, pron., §94, §581, I

ἐδιδάχθην, aor. pass. of διδάσκω

ἔθνος, ἔθνους, τό, a nation; plur., nations, Gentiles

εἰ, particle, §288-§290, if, whether; εἰ μή, unless, except

εἶδον, 2nd aor. of ὁράω

εἰμί, ἔσομαι, §580, §602, I am

εἶπον, 2nd aor. of λέγω
(sometimes regarded as
second aorist of φημί)
εἰρήνη, ἡ, *peace*
εἰς, prep. with acc., *into*
εἷς, μία, ἕν, numeral, §371,
§587, *one*
εἰσέρχομαι, *I go in, I enter*
ἐκ (before vowels ἐξ), prep.
with gen., *out of*
ἐκβάλλω, *I throw out, I cast out*
ἐκεῖ, adv., *there*
ἐκεῖνος, η, ο, pron., §103 f.,
that
ἐκηρύχθην, aor. pass. of
κηρύσσω
ἐκκλησία, ἡ, *a church*
ἐκπορεύομαι, *I go out*
ἔλαβον, 2nd aor. of λαμβάνω
ἐλεέω, ἐλεήσω, ἠλέησα,
(ἠλέηκα), ἠλέημαι,
ἠλεήθην, *I pity, I have mercy
on.*
ἐλεύσομαι, fut. of ἔρχομαι
ἐλήλυθα, 2nd perf. of ἔρχομαι
ἐλήμφθην, aor. pass. of
λαμβάνω
ἐλπίζω, ἐλπιῶ, ἤλπισα,
ἤλπικα, *I hope*
ἐλπίς, ἐλπίδος, ἡ, §211, §560, *a
hope*
ἐμαυτοῦ, ῆς, refl. pron., §337,
§585, *of myself*
ἔμεινα, aor. of μένω
ἐμός, ή, όν, possessive adj.,
§473 f., *my, belonging to me*

ἔμπροσθεν, adv., *in front,
before, in the presence of*
ἐν, prep. with dat., *in*
ἐντολή, ἡ, *a commandment*
ἐνώπιον, adv., *in front of, in the
presence of, before*
ἐξ, form of ἐκ used before
vowels
ἕξ, indeclinable, numeral, *six*
ἐξέρχομαι, *I go out, I come out*
ἔξεστι(ν), impersonal verb,
§292, *it is lawful*
ἐξουσία, ἡ, *authority*
ἔξω, adv., *outside*
ἔξω, fut. of ἔχω ἑόρακα or
ἑώρακα, perf. of ὁράω
ἐπαγγελία, ἡ, *a promise*
ἔπεσον, 2nd aor. of πίπτω
ἐπερωτάω, *I ask a question of, I
question, I interrogate*
ἐπί, prep. with gen., *over, on, at
the time of*; with dat., *on the
basis of, at*; with acc., *on, to,
against*
ἐπιστρέφω, ἐπιστρέψω,
ἐπέστρεψα, (ἐπέστροφα),
ἐπέστραμμαι,
ἐπεστράφην, *I turn to, I
turn, I return*
ἐπιτίθημι, *I place upon, I put
upon, I lay upon* (with acc. of
the thing placed and dat. of
the person or thing upon
which it is placed)
ἔργον, τό, *a work*
ἔρημος, ἡ, *a desert*

ἐρρέθην or ἐρρήθην, aor. pass. of λέγω (or φημί)

ἔρχομαι, ἐλεύσομαι, ἦλθον, ἐλήλυθα, I come, I go

ἐρῶ, fut. of λέγω (sometimes regarded as future of φημί)

ἐρωτάω, ἐρωτήσω, ἠρώτησα, (ἠρώτηκα), (ἠρώτημαι), ἠρωτήθην, I ask (originally of asking a question, but in the New Testament also of asking in the sense of requesting)

ἐσθίω, φάγομαι, ἔφαγον, I eat

ἔσομαι, fut. of εἰμί

ἔσχατος, η, ον, adj., last

ἔσχον, 2nd aor. of ἔχω ἕτερος, α, ον, §538, other, another, different

ἔτι, adv., still, yet

ἑτοιμάζω, ἑτοιμάσω, ἡτοίμασα, ἡτοίμακα, ἡτοίμασμαι, ἡτοιμάσθην, I prepare

ἔτος, ἔτους, τό, a year

ευ- Verbs beginning thus are sometimes augmented to ηυ- and sometimes not

εὐαγγελίζω, (εὐαγγελίσω), εὐηγγέλισα, (εὐηγγέλικα), εὐηγγέλισμαι, εὐηγγελίσθην, in middle often deponent, I preach the gospel, I evangelize (with acc. of the message preached and acc. or dat. of the persons to whom it is preached)

εὐαγγέλιον, τό, a gospel

εὐθέως, adv., immediately, straightway

ευθύς, adv., immediately, straightway

εὐλογέω, εὐλογήσω, εὐλογησα, εὐλόγηκα, εὐλόγημαι, εὐλογήθην, I bless

εὑρίσκω, εὑρήσω, εὗρον, εὕρηκα, (εὕρημαι), εὑρέθην, I find

εὐχαριστέω, εὐχαριστήσω, εὐχαρίστησα, (εὐχαρίστηκα), (εὐχαρίστημαι), εὐχαριστήθην, I give thanks

ἔφαγον, 2nd aor. of ἐσθίω

ἔφη, imperf. act. indic., 3rd pers. sing., of φημί

ἐχθρός, ὁ, an enemy

ἔχω, ἕξω, ἔσχον, ἔσχηκα, imperf. εἶχον, I have

ἑώρακα or ἑόρακα, perf. of ὁράω

ἕως, adv. with gen., up to, until; conj., §536, while, until

ζάω, ζήσω or ζήσομαι, ἔζησα, I live

ζητέω, ζητήσω, ἐζήτησα, I seek

ζωή, ἡ, life ἤ, conj., §462, than, or

ἤγαγον, 2nd aor. of ἄγω

225

ἠγέρθην, aor. pass. of ἐγείρω
ἤδη, adv., *already*
ἤθελον, imperf. of θέλω
ἦλθον, 2nd aor. of ἔρχομαι
ἡμέρα, ἡ, *a day*
ἡμέτερος, α, ον, poss. adj.,
    §473 f., *our, belonging to us*
ἤνεγκα or ἤνεγκον, aor. of
    φέρω
ἠνέχθην, aor. pass. of φέρω
ἦρα, aor. of αἴρω
θάλασσα, ἡ, *a lake, a sea*
θάνατος, ὁ, *death*
θαυμάζω, θαυμάσομαι,
    ἐθαύμασα, (τεθαύμακα),
    aor. pass. ἐθαυμάσθην, *I
    wonder, I marvel, I wonder at*
θέλημα, θελήματος, τό, *a will*
θέλω, θελήσω, ἠθέλησα,
    imperf. ἤθελον, §364, *I
    wish, I am willing*
θεός, ὁ, *God*
θεραπεύω, θεραπεύσω,
    ἐθεράπευσα,
    (τεθεράπευκα),
    τεθεράπευμαι,
    ἐθεραπεύθην, *I heal*
θεωρέω, θεωρήσω,
    ἐθεώρησα, *I behold*
θνήσκω, used only in perf.
    τέθνηκα, *I am dead*, and in
    pluperfect
Ἰάκωβος, ὁ, *James*
ἴδιος, α, ον, adj., *one's own*
ἰδού, particle, *behold! lo!*

ἰδών, ἰδοῦσα, ἰδόν, 2nd aor.
    part. of ὁράω
ἱερεύς, ἱερέως, ὁ, *a priest*
ἱερόν, τό, *a temple* (compare
    ναός)
Ἰησοῦς, -οῦ, ὁ, §310, *Jesus*
ἱκανός, ἡ, όν, *sufficient, able,
    considerable*
ἱμάτιον, τό, *a garment*
ἵνα, conj., §286 f., §477, *in order
    that* (with subj.)
Ἰουδαῖος, ὁ, *a Jew*
ἴσθι 2nd person Imperative of
    εἰμί and 2nd person
    Imperative of οἶδα. See §602
    and §603.
ἵστημι, στήσω, ἔστησα, 2nd
    aor. ἔστην, ἔστηκα,
    (ἔσταμαι), ἐστάθην, §539-
    §548, §600 f., *I cause to stand*
    (in pres., imperf., fut., 1st
    aor., and in passive); *I stand*
    (in 2nd aor. and in perf.)
ἰσχυρότερος, α, ον, adj.,
    stronger (comparative
    degree of ἰσχυρός, ά, όν,
    strong)
Ἰωάνης, ου, ὁ, *John*
κἀγώ = καὶ ἐγώ
καθαρός, ά, όν, adj., *pure,
    clean*
κάθημαι, dep., *I sit*
καθώς, adv., *just as* καί, §146,
    and, even, also;
καί. . . καί, §148, *both . . . and*

καιρός, ὁ, a time, an appointed
time
κακός, ή, όν, adj., bad, evil
καλέω, καλέσω, ἐκάλεσα,
κέκληκα, κέκλημαι,
ἐκλήθην, §323, I call
καλός, ή, όν, adj., good,
beautiful
καλῶς, adv., well
καρδία, ἡ, a heart
καρπός, ὁ, a fruit
κατά, prep. with gen., down,
from, against; with acc.,
according to, throughout,
during
καταβαίνω, I go down
κατέρχομαι, I come down, I go
down
κελεύω, (κελεύσω),
ἐκέλευσα, I command
κηρύσσω, κηρύξω, ἐκήρυξα,
(κεκήρυχα), (κεκήρυγμαι),
ἐκηρύχθην, I proclaim, I
preach
κόσμος, ὁ, a world, the world
κρείσσων, ον, adj., better (used
as comparative degree of
ἀγαθός)
κρίνω, κρινῶ, ἔκρινα,
κέκρικα, κέκριμαι,
ἐκρίθην, §328-§331, §594 f.,
I judge
κρίσις, κρίσεως, ἡ, a judgment
κύριος, ὁ, a lord, the Lord
κώμη, ἡ, a village

λαλέω, λαλήσω, ἐλάλησα,
λάληκα, λελάλημαι,
ἐλαλήθην, I speak
λαμβάνω, λήμψομαι,
ἔλαβον, εἴληφα, εἴλημμαι,
ἐλήμφθην, I take, I receive
λαός, ὁ, a people
λέγω, ἐρῶ, εἶπον, εἴρηκα,
εἴρημαι, ἐρρέθην or
ἐρρήθην, I say
λείπω, λείψω, ἔλιπον,
(λέλοιπα), λέλειμμαι,
ἐλείφθην, §190-§194, §296,
§593, I leave
λήμψομαι, fut. of λαμβάνω
λίθος, ὁ, a stone
λόγος, ὁ, §557, a word
λοιπός, ή, όν, adj., remaining;
οἱ λοιποί, the rest
λύω, λύσω, ἔλυσα, λέλυκα,
λέλυμαι, ἐλύθην, §589, I
loose, I destroy, I break
μαθητής, ὁ, §556, a disciple
μακάριος, α, ον, adj., blessed
μᾶλλον, adv., more, rather
μαρτυρέω, μαρτυρήσω,
ἐμαρτύρησα,
μεμαρτύρηκα,
μεμαρτύρημαι,
ἐμαρτυρήθην, I bear
witness, I witness
μαρτυρία, ἡ, a witnessing, a
witness
μέγας, μεγάλη, μέγα, adj.,
§370, §575, great

μείζων, ον, adj., §459, §461, §571, *greater* (comparative degree of μέγας)

μέλλω, μελλήσω, imperfect ἤμελλον or ἔμελλον, *I am about* (to do something), *I am going* (to do something)

μέν . . . δέ, *on the one hand . . . on the other* (used in contrasts. Often it is better to leave the μέν untranslated and translate the δέ by but)

μένω, μενῶ, ἔμεινα, μεμένηκα, *I remain, I abide*

μετά, prep. with gen., *with*; with acc., *after*

μετανοέω, μετανοήσω, μετενόησα, *I repent*

μή, negative adverb, §256, §478 f., *not* (used with moods other than the indicative)

μή, conj., §475 f., *lest, in order that not* (with the subj.)

μηδέ, *and not, nor, not even*; μηδέ . . . μηδέ, *neither . . . nor*

μηδείς, μηδεμία, μηδέν, §372, *no one, nothing*

μηκέτι, adv., *no longer*

μήποτε, *lest perchance* (with the subj.) μήτηρ, μητρός, ἡ, §565, *a mother*

μικρός, ά, όν, adj., §62, §569, *little, small*

μνημεῖον, τό, *a tomb*

μόνον, adv., *only*

μόνος, η, ον, adj., *alone, only*

μυστήριον, τό, *a mystery*

ναός, ὁ, *a temple* (the temple building itself, as distinguished from ἱερόν, the whole sacred precinct)

νεκρός, ά, όν, adj., *dead*

νόμος, ὁ, *a law, the Law*

νῦν, adv., *now*

νύξ, νυκτός, ἡ, §211, §559, *a night*

ὁ, ἡ, τό, definite article, §63, §567, *the*

ὁδός, ἡ, *a way, a road*

οἶδα, 2nd perf. used as present, §549, §603, *I know*

οἰκία, ἡ, *a house*

οἶκος, ὁ, *a house*

ὀλίγος, η, ον, adj., *few, little*

ὅλος, η, ον, adj., *whole, all*

ὅμοιος, α, ον, adj., *like, similar*

ὄνομα, ὀνόματος, τό, §222, §561, *a name*

ὅπου, adv., *where* (relative)

ὅπως, conj., *in order that* (with subj.) ὁράω, ὄψομαι, εἶδον, ἑώρακα or ἑόρακα, (ὦμμαι), ὤφθην, 2nd aor. part. ἰδών, §186 (footnote 16), §249-§251, *I see* (in the present ὁράω is less common than βλέπω)

ὄρος, ὄρους, τό, *a mountain*

ὅς, ἥ, ὅ, rel. pron., §395-§399, §583, *who, which*

228

ὅσος, ὅση, ὅσον, rel. adj., *as great as, as much as, as many as*

ὅστις, ἥτις, ὅτι, indef. rel. pron., *whoever, whichever, whatever*

ὅταν, *whenever* (with subj.)

ὅτε, adv., *when*

ὅτι, conj., §307f., §522 (footnote 5), *that, because*

οὐ (οὐκ before vowels, οὐχ before the rough breathing), adv., §118, §256, *not*

οὐδέ, conj., *and not, nor, not even*, §147; οὐδέ . . . οὐδέ, *neither . . . nor*

οὐδείς, οὐδεμία, οὐδέν, §372, *no one, nothing*

οὐκ, form of οὐ used before vowels and diphthongs that have smooth breathing.

οὐκέτι, adv., *no longer*

οὖν, conj., postpositive, *accordingly, therefore*

οὔπω, adv., *not yet*

οὐρανός, ὁ, *heaven*

οὖς, ὠτός, τό, *an ear*

οὔτε, conj., §535, *and not;* οὔτε. . . οὔτε, *neither . . . nor*

οὗτος, αὕτη, τοῦτο, demonstrative pron., §102, §104, §582, *this*

οὕτως, adv., *thus, so*

οὐχ, form of οὐ used before vowels and diphthongs that have rough breathing

ὀφείλω, *I owe, I ought*

ὀφθαλμός, ὁ, *an eye*

ὄχλος, ὁ, *a crowd, a multitude*

ὄψομαι, fut. of ὁράω

παίδιον, τό, *a little child*

πάλιν, adv., *again*

παρά, prep. with gen., *from;* with dat., *beside, in the presence of;* with acc., *alongside of*

παραβολή, ἡ, *a parable*

παραγίνομαι, *I become present, I arrive, I come*

παραδίδωμι, *I deliver over, I hand over*

παρακαλέω, *I exhort, I encourage, I beseech, I comfort*

παραλαμβάνω, *I receive, I take along*

πᾶς, πᾶσα, πᾶν, adj., §365-§369, §573, *all, every*

πάσχω, (πείσομαι), ἔπαθον, πέπονθα, *I suffer, I experience*

πατήρ, πατρός, ὁ, §565, *a father*

πείθω, πείσω, ἔπεισα, πέποιθα, πέπεισμαι, ἐπείσθην, *I persuade*

πειράζω, (πειράσω), ἐπείρασα, (πεπείρακα), πεπείρασμαι, ἐπειράσθην, *I tempt, I attempt*

πέμπω, πέμψω, ἔπεμψα, (πέπομφα), (πέπεμμαι), ἐπέμφθην, *I send* πεντακισχίλιοι, αι, α, *five thousand*

πέντε, indeclinable, *five*

περί, prep. with gen., *concerning, about*; with acc., *around*

περιπατέω, περιπατήσω, περιεπάτησα, περιπεπάτηκα, *I walk*

Πέτρος, ὁ, *Peter*

πίνω, πίομαι, ἔπιον, πέπωκα, (πέπομαι), ἐπόθην, *I drink*

πίπτω, πεσοῦμαι, ἔπεσον or ἔπεσα, πέπτωκα, *I fall*

πιστεύω, πιστεύσω, ἐπίστευσα, πεπίστευκα, πεπίστευμαι, ἐπιστεύθην, §184, *I believe* (takes the dat.); πιστεύω εἰς with acc., *I believe in* or *on*

πίστις, πίστεως, ἡ, *faith*

πιστός, ή, όν, adj., *faithful*

πλείων, ον, adj., *more* (comparative degree of πολύς).

πλῆθος, πλήθους, τό, *a multitude*

πλήρης, ες (sometimes indeclinable), adj., *full*

πληρόω, πληρώσω, ἐπλήρωσα, πεπλήρωκα, πεπλήρωμαι, ἐπληρώθην, *I fill, I fulfill*

πλοῖον, τό, *a boat*

πνεῦμα, πνεύματος, τό, *a spirit, the Spirit*

ποιέω, ποιήσω, ἐποίησα, πεποίηκα, πεποίημαι, (ἐποιήθην), *I do, I make*

ποῖος, α, ον, *what sort of?*

πόλις, πόλεως, ἡ, §349-§351, §563, *a city*

πολύς, πολλή, πολύ, adj., §370, §574, *much, great*; in plur., *many*

πονηρός, ά, όν, adj., *evil*

πορεύομαι, πορεύσομαι, ἐπορευσάμην, πεπόρευμαι, ἐπορεύθην, dep., usually with passive forms, *I go*

πότε, interrog. adv., *when?*

ποτέ, particle, enclitic, *at some time;*

μήποτε, *lest perchance.*

ποῦ, interrog. adv., *where?*

πούς, ποδός, ὁ, *a foot*

πρό, prep. with gen., *before*

πρός, prep. with acc., *to*

προσέρχομαι, *I come to, I go to* (with dat.)

προσεύχομαι, προσεύξομαι, προσηυξάμην, *I pray*

προσκυνέω, προσκυνήσω, προσεκύνησα, *I worship* (usually with dat., sometimes with acc.).

προσφέρω, *I bring to* (with acc. of the thing brought and dat. of the person to whom it is brought).

πρόσωπον, τό, *a face, a countenance*

προφήτης, ου, ὁ, §79, §556, *a prophet*

πρῶτος, η, ον, adj., *first*

πῦρ, πυρός, τό, *a fire*

πῶς, interrog. adv., *how?*

ῥηθείς, ῥηθεῖσα, ῥηθέν, aor. pass. part. of λέγω (φημί)

ῥῆμα, ῥήματος, τό, *a word*

σάββατον, τό, (plural σάββατα, σαββάτων, σάββασι(ν), sometimes with singular meaning), *a sabbath*

σάρξ, σαρκός, ἡ, §219, §221, §559, *flesh*

σεαυτοῦ, ῆς, reflexive pron., §338, §585, *of thyself*

σημεῖον, τό, *a sign*

Σίμων, Σίμωνος, ὁ, *Simon*

σκότος, σκότους, τό, *darkness*

σός, ἡ, όν, possessive adj., §473 f., *thy, belonging to thee*

σοφία, ἡ, *wisdom*

σπείρω, (σπερῶ), ἔσπειρα, ---, ἔσπαρμαι, ἐσπάρην, *I sow*

στάδιον, τό, plur., τὰ στάδια or οἱ στάδιοι, *a stadium, a furlong*

σταυρόω, σταυρώσω, ἐσταύρωσα, (ἐσταύρωκα), ἐσταύρωμαι, ἐσταυρώθην, *I crucify*

στόμα, στόματος, τό, *a mouth*

στρατιώτης, ου, ὁ, *a soldier*

σύ, σοῦ, pron., §95, §581, *thou*

σύν, prep. with dat., *with*

συνάγω, *I gather together*

συναγωγή, ἡ, *a synagogue*

συνέρχομαι. *I come together, I go together*

σχῶ, 2nd aor. subj. of ἔχω

σώζω, σώσω, ἔσωσα, σέσωκα, σέσω(σ)μαι, ἐσώθην, *I save*

σῶμα, σώματος, τό, *a body*

σωτηρία, ἡ, *salvation*

τέθνηκα, perf. of θνήσκω

τέκνον, τό, *a child*

τέσσαρες, τέσσαρα, §588, *four*

τηρέω, τηρήσω, ἐτήρησα, τετήρηκα, τετήρημαι, ἐτηρήθην, *I keep*

τίθημι, θήσω, ἔθηκα, τέθεικα, τέθειμαι, ἐτέθην, §524-§530, §598 f., *I place, I put*

τιμάω, τιμήσω, ἐτίμησα, (τετίμηκα), τετίμημαι, (ἐτιμήθην), §317-§321, §590, *I value, I honor*

τίς, τί, interrog. pron., §385-§387, §390 f., §584, *who? which? what?*

τις, τι, indef. pron., §388-§390, §584, *someone, something, a certain one, a certain thing, anyone, anything*

τόπος, ὁ, *a place*

τότε, adv., *then*

τρεῖς, τρία, §588, *three*

τυφλός, ὁ, *a blind man*

ὕδωρ, ὕδατος, τό, *water*

υἱός, ὁ, §39 f., §557, *a son*

ὑμέτερος, α, ον, possessive adj., §473 f., *your, belonging to you*

ὑπάγω, *I go away, I depart*

ὑπέρ, prep. with gen., *in behalf of*; with acc., *above*

ὑπό, prep. with gen., *by* (of the agent); with acc., *under*

ὑποστρέφω, ὑποστρέψω, ὑπέστρεψα, *I return*

φανερόω, φανερώσω, ἐφανέρωσα, (πεφανέρωκα), πεφανέρωμαι, ἐφανερώθην, *I make manifest, I manifest*

Φαρισαῖος, ὁ, *a Pharisee*

φέρω, οἴσω, ἤνεγκα, or ἤνεγκον, ἐνήνοχα, (ἐνήνεγμαι), ἠνέχθην, *I bear, I carry, I bring*

φημί, ἐρῶ, εἶπον, εἴρηκα, εἴρημαι, ἐρρέθην or ἐρρήθην, *I say* (the principal parts may also be regarded as belonging to λέγω, which is far commoner in the present than is φημί)

φιλέω, (φιλήσω), ἐφίλησα, πεφίληκα, (πεφίλημαι), (ἐφιλήθην), §317-§321, §591, *I love*

φοβέομαι, aor. ἐφοβήθην, dep. with pass. forms, *I fear*

φυλακή, ἡ, *a guard, a prison*

φωνή, ἡ, *a voice, a sound*

φῶς, φωτός, τό, *a light*

χαίρω, χαρήσομαι, 2nd aor. pass. ἐχάρην, *I rejoice*

χαρά, ἡ, joy χάρις, χάριτος, ἡ, §347 f., §560, *grace*

χείρ, χειρός, ἡ, §566, *a hand*

Χριστός, ὁ, *Messiah, Christ*

χρόνος, ὁ, *a period of time, time*

χώρα, ἡ, *a country*

χωρίς, adv. with gen., *apart from*

ψυχή, ἡ, *a life, a soul*

ὧδε, adv., *hither, here*

ὤν, οὖσα, ὄν, pres. part. of εἰμί

ὥρα, ἡ, §48-§51, §555, *an hour*

ὡς, adv. and conj., *as* (with numerals, *about*)

ὥσπερ, §535, *just as*

ὥστε, §534 f., *so that* (often followed by accus. and infin.)

ὤφθην, aor. pass of ὁράω

English-Greek Vocabulary

A certain one, τις; a certain
 thing, neuter of τις.
Abide, μένω.
Able, ἱκανός.
Able, am, δύναμαι.
About, περί with gen.
About (with numerals), ὡς.
Above, ὑπέρ with acc.
According to, κατά with acc.
Accordingly, οὖν.
After, μετά with acc.
Again, πάλιν.
Against, ἐπί with acc., κατά
 with gen.
Age, αἰών. All, πᾶς, ὅλος.
Alongside of, παρά with acc.
Already, ἤδη.
Also, καί.
Am, εἰμί, γίνομαι.
Am able, δύναμαι.
Am about (to do something),
 μέλλω.
Am going (to do something),
 μέλλω.
Am willing, θέλω.
And, καί, δέ.
And not, οὐδέ, οὔτε, μηδέ.
Angel, ἄγγελος.
Another, ἄλλος, ἕτερος.
Answer, ἀποκρίνομαι.
Anyone, τις.
Anything, neut. of τις.
Apart from, χωρίς.
Apostle, ἀπόστολος.
Appear in history, γίνομαι.
Around, περί with acc.

Arrive, παραγίνομαι. As, ὡς.
As great as, as much as, as
 many as, ὅσος.
Ask (a question), ἐρωτάω.
Ask (request), αἰτέω, ἐρωτάω.
Ask a question of, ἐπερωτάω.
At, ἐπί with dat.
At some time, ποτέ.
At the time of, ἐπί with gen.
Authority, ἐξουσία.
Bad, κακός.
Baptize, βαπτίζω.
Be, εἰμί.
Bear, φέρω; of a mother,
 γεννάω.
Bear witness, μαρτυρέω.
Beautiful, καλός.
Because, ὅτι.
Become, γίνομαι.
Become present,
 παραγίνομαι.
Before, πρό with gen.
Beget, γεννάω.
Begin, middle of ἄρχω.
Beginning, ἀρχή.
Behold (verb), θεωρέω.
Behold! (particle), ἰδού.
Believe, πιστεύω.
Beseech, παρακαλέω.
Beside, παρά with dat.
Better, κρείσσων.
Bless, εὐλογέω.
Blessed, μακάριος.
Blind man, τυφλός.
Blood, αἷμα.
Boat, πλοῖων.

Body, σῶμα.
Book, βιβλίον.
Both . . . and, καί . . . καί.
Bread, ἄρτος.
Break, λύω.
Bring, φέρω.
Bring to, προσφέρω.
Brother, ἀδελφός.
But, ἀλλά, δέ.
By (of the agent), ὑπό with gen.
By means of, expressed by the simple dat.
By the side of, παρά with dat.
Call, καλέω.
Carry, φέρω.
Cast, βάλλω.
Cast out, ἐκβάλλω.
Cause to rise, ἀνίστημι (in the transitive tenses).
Cause to stand, ἵστημι (in the transitive tenses).
Chief priest, ἀρχιερεύς.
Child, τέκνον; little child, παιδίον.
Christ, Χριστός.
Church, ἐκκλησία.
City, πόλις.
Clean, καθαρός.
Come, ἔρχομαι.
Come down, κατέρχομαι.
Come into being, γίνομαι.
Come near, ἐγγίζω.
Come out, ἐξέρχομαι.
Come to, προσέρχομαι.
Come to pass, γίνομαι.
Come together, συνέρχομαι.

Comfort, παρακαλέω.
Command, κελεύω.
Commandment, ἐντολή.
Concerning, περί with gen.
Consecrate, ἁγιάζω.
Considerable, ἱκανός.
Countenance, πρόσωπον.
Country, χώρα.
Crowd, ὄχλος.
Crucify, σταυρόω.
Darkness, σκότος.
Day, ἡμέρα.
Dead, νεκρός.
Dead, am, perfect of θνήσκω.
Death, θάνατος.
Deliver over, παραδίδωμι.
Demon, δαιμόνιον.
Depart, ὑπάγω, ἀπέρχομαι.
Desert, ἔρημος.
Destroy, ἀπόλλυμι, λύω.
Die, ἀποθνήσκω.
Disciple, μαθητής.
Dismiss, ἀπολύω.
Do, ποιέω.
Down from, κατά with gen.
Drink, πίνω.
During, κατά with acc.
Each other, ἀλλήλων.
Ear, οὖς.
Earth, γῆ.
Eat, ἐσθίω.
Encourage, παρακαλέω.
Enemy, ἐχθρός.
Enter, εἰσέρχομαι.
Eternal, αἰώνιος.
Evangelize, εὐαγγελίζω.
Even, καί.

Evil, πονηρός, κακός.
Except, εἰ μή, ἐὰν μή.
Exhort, παρακαλέω.
Experience, πάσχω.
Eye, ὀφθαλμός.
Face, πρόσωπον.
Faith, πίστις.
Faithful, πιστός.
Fall, πίπτω.
Father, πατήρ.
Fear, φοβέομαι.
Few, plural of ὀλίγος.
Field, ἀγρός.
Fill, πληρόω.
Find, εὑρίσκω.
Fire, πῦρ.
First, πρῶτος.
Five, πέντε.
Five thousand,
    πεντακισχίλιοι.
Flesh, σάρξ.
Follow, ἀκολουθέω.
Foot, πούς.
For (prep.), use dat.
For (conj.), γάρ.
Forever, εἰς τὸν αἰῶνα.
Forgive, ἀφίημι.
Four, τέσσαρες.
From, ἀπό with gen., παρά
    with gen.
Fulfill, πληρόω.
Full, πλήρης.
Furlong, στάδιον.
Galilee, Γαλιλαία.
Garment, ἱμάτιον.
Gather together, συνάγω.
Gentiles, plur. of ἔθνος.

Gift, δῶρον.
Give, δίδωμι.
Give thanks, εὐχαριστέω.
Give what is owed or
    promised, ἀποδίδωμι.
Glorify, δοξάζω.
Glory, δόξα.
Go, πορεύομαι, ἔρχομαι,
    βαίνω.
Go away, ὑπάγω, ἀπέρχομαι.
Go down, καταβαίνω,
    κατέρχομαι.
Go in, εἰσέρχομαι.
Go out, ἐκπορεύομαι,
    ἐξέρχομαι.
Go through, διέρχομαι.
Go to, προσέρχομαι.
Go together, συνέρχομαι.
Go up, ἀναβαίνω.
God, θεός.
Good, ἀγαθός, καλός.
Gospel, εὐαγγέλιον; preach
    the gospel, εὐαγγελίζω.
Grace, χάρις.
Great, μέγας, πολύς.
Greater, μείζων.
Guard, φυλακή.
Hallow, ἁγιάζω.
Hand, χείρ.
Hand over, παραδίδωμι.
Have, ἔχω.
Have mercy upon, ἐλεέω.
He, αὐτός.
Heal, θεραπεύω.
Hear, ἀκούω.
Heart, καρδία.
Heaven, οὐρανός.

Herself (intensive), feminine of
   αὐτός.
Herself (reflexive), feminine of
   ἑαυτοῦ.
High priest, ἀρχιερεύς.
Himself (intensive), αὐτός.
Himself (reflexive), ἑαυτοῦ.
Holy, ἅγιος.
Honor (verb), τιμάω.
Hope (noun), ἐλπίς.
Hope (verb), ἐλπίζω.
Hour, ὥρα.
House, οἶκος, οἰκία.
How?, πῶς.
I, ἐγώ.
If, εἰ, ἐάν.
Immediately, εὐθέως, εὐθύς.
In, ἐν with dat.
In behalf of, ὑπέρ with gen.
In front of, ἐνώπιον.
In order that, ἵνα, ὅπως.
In order that not, ἵνα μή, μή.
In the presence of, παρά with
   dat., ἐνώπιον, ἔμπροσθεν.
Instead of, ἀντί with gen.
Interrogate, ἐπερωτάω.
Into, εἰς with acc.
It, neuter of αὐτός (also often
   other genders).
It is lawful, ἔξεστι(ν).
Itself (intensive), neuter of
   αὐτός (also often other
   genders).
Itself (reflexive), neuter of
   ἑαυτοῦ (also often other
   genders).
James, Ἰάκωβος.

Jesus, Ἰησοῦς.
Jew, Ἰουδαῖος.
Joy, χαρά.
Judge, κρίνω.
Judgment, κρίσις.
Just as, καθώς, ὥσπερ.
Keep, τηρέω.
Kill, ἀποκτείνω.
Kind, γένος.
King, βασιλεύς.
Kingdom, βασιλεία.
Know, γινώσκω, οἶδα.
Lake, θάλασσα.
Land, γῆ.
Last, ἔσχατος.
Law, νόμος.
Lawful, it is, ἔξεστι(ν).
Lay down (one's life), τίθημι.
Lay upon, ἐπιτίθημι.
Lead, ἄγω.
Leave, ἀφίημι, λείπω.
Lest, μή.
Lest perchance, μήποτε.
Let go, ἀφίημι.
Letter, γράμμα.
Life, ζωή, ψυχή
Light, φῶς.
Like, ὅμοιος.
Little, μικρός, ὀλίγος.
Little child, παιδίον.
Live, ζάω.
Lo!, ἰδού.
Loaf, ἄρτος.
Look up, ἀναβλέπω.
Loose, λύω.
Lord, κύριος.
Love (noun), ἀγάπη.

Love (verb), ἀγαπάω, φιλέω.
Make, ποιέω.
Make manifest, φανερόω,
    δηλόω.
Man, ἄνθρωπος, ἀνήρ.
Manifest (verb), φανερόω,
    δηλόω.
Manifest, make, φανερόω,
    δηλόω.
Many, πολύς (in plural).
Marvel, θαυμάζω.
Mercy, have—upon, ἐλεέω.
Messenger, ἄγγελος.
Messiah, Χριστός.
Miracle, δύναμις.
Mountain, ὄρος.
More (adj.), πλείων.
More (adv.), μᾶλλον.
Mother, μήτηρ.
Mouth, στόμα.
Much, πολύς.
Multitude, πλῆθος, ὄχλος.
My, ἐμός.
Myself (reflexive), ἐμαυτοῦ.
Mystery, μυστήριον.
Name, ὄνομα.
Nation, ἔθνος.
Near (adv.), ἐγγύς.
Near, come, ἐγγίζω.
Necessary, it is, δεῖ.
Neither .... nor, οὐδέ .... οὐδέ,
    μηδέ .... μηδέ, οὔτε .... οὔτε.
Night, νύξ.
No longer, οὐκέτι, μηκέτι.
No one, nothing, οὐδείς,
    μηδείς.
Not, οὐ, μή.

Not even, οὐδέ, μηδέ.
Not yet, οὔπω.
Now, νῦν.
On, ἐπί with gen.
On account of, διά with acc.
On the basis of, ἐπί with dat.
On the one hand .... on the
    other, μέν .... δέ.
One, εἷς.
One another, ἀλλήλων.
One's own, ἴδιος.
Only (adj.), μόνος.
Only (adv.), μόνον.
Open, ἀνοίγω.
Or, ἤ.
Other, ἄλλος, ἕτερος.
Ought, ὀφείλω.
Our, ἡμέτερος.
Out of, ἐκ with gen.
Outside, ἔξω.
Over, ἐπί with gen.
Owe, ὀφείλω.
Own, one's, ἴδιος.
Parable, παραβολή.
Pay (verb), ἀποδίδωμι.
Peace, εἰρήνη.
People, λαός.
Perish, middle of ἀπόλλυμι.
Permit, ἀφίημι.
Persecute, διώκω.
Persuade, πείθω.
Pharisee, Φαρισαῖος.
Piece of bread, ἄρτος.
Pity, ἐλεέω.
Place (noun), τόπος.
Place (verb), τίθημι.
Power, δύναμις.

237

Pray, προσεύχομαι.
Preach, κηρύσσω; preach the
gospel, εὐαγγελίζω.
Prepare, ἑτοιμάζω.
Presence, see In the presence
of.
Priest, ἱερεύς.
Prison, φυλακή.
Proclaim, κηρύσσω.
Promise, ἐπαγγελία.
Prophet, προφήτης.
Pure, καθαρός.
Pursue, διώκω.
Put, τίθημι, βάλλω.
Put upon, ἐπιτίθημι.
Question (verb), ἐπερωτάω.
Race, γένος.
Raise up, ἐγείρω.
Rather, μᾶλλον.
Receive, δέχομαι,
    παραλαμβάνω, λαμβάνω.
Receive one's sight,
    ἀναβλέπω.
Rejoice, χαίρω.
Release, ἀπολύω.
Remain, μένω.
Remaining, λοιπός.
Repent, μετανοέω.
Rest, the, see under λοιπός.
Return, ὑποστρέφω.
Righteous, δίκαιος.
Righteousness, δικαιοσύνη.
Rise, ἀνίστημι (in the
    intransitive tenses and in
    the middle), passive of
    ἐγείρω.
Road, ὁδός.

Rule, ἄρχω.
Ruler, ἄρχών.
Sabbath, σάββατον.
Saint, ἅγιος.
Salvation, σωτηρία.
Same, αὐτός.
Sanctify, ἁγιάζω.
Save, σώζω.
Say, λέγω, φημί.
Scribe, γραμματεύς.
Scripture, γραφή.
Sea, θάλασσα.
See, βλέπω, ὁράω.
Seek, ζητέω.
Seem, δοκέω.
Send, πέμπω, ἀποστέλλω.
Servant, δοῦλος.
She, feminine of αὐτός.
Show, δείκνυμι, δηλόω.
Sign, σημεῖον.
Similar, ὅμοιος.
Simon, Σιμών.
Sin (noun), ἁμαρτία.
Sin (verb), ἁμαρτάνω.
Sinner, ἁμαρτωλός.
Sit, κάθημαι.
Slave, δοῦλος.
Small, μικρός.
So, οὕτως.
So that, ὥστε.
Soldier, στρατιώτης.
Some one, τις.
Something, neuter of τις.
Son, υἱός.
Soul, ψυχή.
Sow, σπείρω.
Speak, λαλέω.

Spirit, πνεῦμα.
Stadium, στάδιον.
Stand, ἵστημι (in the intransitive tenses).
Still, ἔτι.
Stone, λίθος.
Straightway, εὐθέως, εὐθύς.
Stronger, ἰσχυρότερος.
Suffer, πάσχω.
Sufficient, ἱκανός.
Synagogue, συναγωγή.
Take, λαμβάνω.
Take along, παραλαμβάνω.
Take away, αἴρω.
Take up, αἴρω, ἀναλαμβάνω.
Teach, διδάσκω.
Teacher, διδάσκαλος.
Temple, ἱερόν (the whole sacred precinct), ναός (the temple building itself).
Tempt, πειράζω.
Than, ἤ.
Thanks, give, εὐχαριστέω.
That (conj.), ὅτι.
That (demonstrative), ἐκεῖνος.
The, ὁ.
Then, τότε.
There, ἐκεῖ.
Therefore, οὖν.
Think, δοκέω.
This, οὗτος.
Thou, σύ.
Three, τρεῖς.
Through, διά with gen.
Throughout, κατά with acc.
Throw, βάλλω.
Throw out, ἐκβάλλω.

Thus, οὕτως.
Thy, σός.
Thyself (reflexive), σεαυτοῦ.
Time, καιρός (appointed time), χρόνος (period of time).
To, πρός with acc., ἐπί with acc.; indirect object, dat. without prep.
Together, gather, συνάγω.
Tomb, μνημεῖον.
True, ἀληθής.
Truth, ἀλήθεια.
Turn to, turn, ἐπιστρέφω.
Two, δύο. Under, ὑπό with acc.
Unless, εἰ μή, ἐάν μή.
Until, ἕως.
Unto, πρός with acc.
Up to, ἕως with gen.
Value, τιμάω.
Village, κώμη.
Voice, φωνή.
Walk, περιπατέω.
Water, ὕδωρ.
Way, ὁδός.
Well, καλῶς.
What?, neuter of τίς.
What sort of?, ποῖος.
Whatever, neuter of ὅστις.
When (relative), ὅτε.
When?, πότε.
Whenever, ὅταν.
Where (relative), ὅπου.
Where?, ποῦ.
Which (relative), ὅς.
Which?, τίς.

Whichever, ὅστις.
While, ἕως.
Who (relative), ὅς.
Who?, τίς.
Whoever, ὅστις.
Whole, ὅλος.
Why, τί.
Wicked, πονηρός.
Will, θέλημα.
Willing, am, θέλω.
Wisdom, σοφία.
Wish, θέλω.
With, μετά with gen., σύν
    with dat.

Witness (verb), μαρτυρέω.
Witness (noun), μαρτυρία.
Woman, γυνή.
Wonder, wonder at,
    θαυμάζω.
Word, λόγος, ῥῆμα.
World, κόσμος.
Work, ἔργον.
Worship, προσκυνέω.
Write, γράφω.
Writing, γραφή.
Year, ἔτος.
Yet, ἔτι.
Your, ὑμέτερος.

Index

INDEX

Abstract nouns, with the article, §76 (footnote 2).

Accent: pronunciation, §9; general rules, §11; rule of verb accent, §13; rule of noun accent, §14; accent in gen. and dat. of 1st and 2nd decl., §40, §58; in gen. plur. of 1st decl. nouns, §51; in enclitics and words coming before enclitics, §92f.; in compound verbs, §132; in ἔστι(ν), §134; in monosyllables of 3rd decl., §221; in gen. plur. fem, of participles, §228; in aor. pass. part., §263; in contract syllables, §316 (iii); in gen. sing, and plur. of nouns in -ις, -εως, §350; in 2nd aor. imper., §419; in perf. act. infin., §427; in perf. middle and pass. infin. and part., §443f.; in pres. infin. of δίδωμι, §499; in pres. part. of δίδωμι, §502; in ὥστε etc., §535.

Accusative case: for direct object, §34; after prepositions expressing motion toward, §82; as subj. of infin., §304, §306, §534; acc. of extent of space and time, §382; of specification, §470.

Active voice: conjugation, see under *Verbs*; use, §17.

Adjectives: declension summarized, §568-§575; declension of adjs. in -ος, -η(α), -ov, §61f.; of adjs. in -ης, -ες, §360-§362; of irregular adjs., §365-§370; of μείζων, etc., §459-§461; of adjs. of two terminations, §481; attributive and predicate uses of adjs., §68-§74, §381; substantive use, §75; comparison, §456-§461; possessive adjs., §473f.

Adverbs, §463-§465.

Aeolic dialects, p. 1.

Agreement: of verb with subj., §29, §145; of adj. with noun, §66; of pronoun with antecedent, §97 (3), §397, §399, §454 (footnote 2).

Alexander the Great, p. 1.

Alphabet, §1f.

Antepenult, definition, §10.

Aorist tense: formation and conjugation, see under *Verbs*; distinction between first and second aor., §167; use of aor. tense in indic., §122, §168-§170; in participles, §254, §520; in subj., §283; in infin., §299; in imperative, §420.

Apostolic Fathers, p. 3.

Aramaic language, p. 3.

Demonstrative pronouns:
declension, §102f.; use,
§104, §106.

Demosthenes, p. 1.

Deponent verbs, §116, §144,
§207f.; verbs deponent in
some tenses but not in
others, §164; fut. of ἀκούω,
§554 (footnote 1).

Dialects, p. 1.

Diphthongs, §4.

Direct discourse, sometimes
introduced by ὅτι, §522
(footnote 5).

Doric dialects, p. 1.

Double negative, §402
(footnote).

Elision, §97 (footnote 1); §120
(footnote 1 in Greek
exercise).

Enclitics, §92f., §98.

Exercises, remarks on, p. viii.

Exhorting, etc., construction
after words denoting, §477.

Extent of space and time,
expressed by acc., §382.

Fearing, construction after
words denoting, §475.

Feminine nouns in -ος of 2nd
decl., §60.

First Aorist: formation and
conjugation, see under
Verbs; 1st aor. endings on
2nd aor. stems, §186
(footnote 1), §424 (footnote
1), §521.

First Declension: summarized,
§555-§556; nouns in -α and -
η, §47-§58; nouns in -ης,
§79.

Future conditions, §288-§290.

Future tense: conjugation, see
under Verbs.

Gender, §28; of 2nd-decl. nouns
in -ος, §28, §60; of 1st-decl.
nouns in -α and -η, §47, in -
ης, §78; of 3rd-decl. nouns,
§218-§220; of 3rd-decl.
nouns in -μα, §222, in -ις, -
εως, §351, in -ος, -ους, §354,
in -ευς, -εως, §357.

Genitive case: expressing
possession, etc., §35; with
prepositions expressing
separation, §82; with ὑπό
expressing agent, §114f.;
with ἀκούω and ἄρχω,
§108; translation of gen. into
English, §120 (footnote 1 in
English exercise); gen.
absolute, §266; gen. after the
article, §378f., §381; gen. in
the predicate after εἰμί, §402
(footnote 1); of comparison,
§462; with adverbs of place,
§466; gen. of time, §467;
gen. of articular infin.
expressing purpose, §468.

Ginn and Company, §314
(footnote 1).

Grimm-Thayer, p. viii.

Hebrew language, p. 3.

Hebrews, Epistle to the, p. 5.

middle, §253; perf. act., §433f., §578; perf. middle and pass., §444; aor. pass., §259-§263, §579; pres. part. of εἰμί, §580—use: in general, §232, §239; tense, §233, §254, §264, §520; attributive use, §234, §255; substantive use, §235, §237f., §255; various uses summarized, §236, §265; use of aor. part., §254f., §264, §520; part. in genitive absolute, §266; use of perf. pass. part., §452 (3).

Paul, Epistles of, p. 5.

Penult, definition, §10.

Perfect tense: formation and conjugation, see under Verbs; use, §451f.

Person, expressed by endings of verbs, §19.

Personal endings: in the primary tenses, act., §20, middle, §111; in the secondary tenses, active, §127, §173, §199, middle, §139, §180; in the pres. act., §20; in the pres. middle and pass., §111; in the imperf. act., §127f.; in the imperf. middle and pass., §139-§142; in the pres. system, §151; in the fut. act. and middle, §152; in the 1st aor. act., §173-§177; in the 1st aor. middle, §180-§182; in

the 2nd aor. act. and middle, §192; in the aor. pass., §199; in the fut. pass., §200; in the subjunctive mood, §269; in the perf. act., §431; in the perf. middle and pass., §447.

Personal pronouns: declension, §94-§96, §581; use, §97, §106, §474.

Philip of Macedon, p. 1.

Plato, p. 1.

Pluperfect tense, §450, §589.

Plutarch, p. 3.

Position; of the negative, §118; of καί, §146.

Possessive adjectives, §473f.

Postpositives, §91.

Predicate use and position of adjectives, §68f., §71-§74, §381.

Prepositions, §80-§88; prefixed to verbs, §117.

Prepositional phrases: used attributively, §376, §380f.; used substantively, §377, §380f.

Present General conditions, §288 (footnote 1).

Present tense: formation and conjugation, see under Verbs; use, §21, §113; pres. infin. with ἄρχομαι, §344 (footnote 1).

Primary tenses, §20 (with footnote), §111, §152, §431.

Made in the USA
Monee, IL
25 July 2024

cb9bf719-a3a0-4d36-a015-a3a585a08f73R01